The Meritocracy Myth

The Meritocracy Myth

Third Edition

Stephen J. McNamee and Robert K. Miller Jr.

ROWMAN & LITTLEFIELD PUBLISHERS, INC.
Lanham • Boulder • New York • Toronto • Plymouth, UK

Published by Rowman & Littlefield Publishers, Inc.
A wholly owned subsidary of The Rowman & Littlefield Publishing Group, Inc.
4501 Forbes Boulevard, Suite 200, Lanham, Maryland 20706
www.rowman.com

10 Thornbury Road, Plymouth PL6 7PP, United Kingdom

British Library Cataloguing in Publication Information Available

Library of Congress Cataloging-in-Publication Data

McNamee, Stephen J., 1950–
The meritocracy myth / Stephen J. McNamee and Robert K. Miller Jr. — Third Edition.
pages cm
Includes bibliographical references and index.
ISBN 978-1-4422-1981-6 (cloth : alk. paper) — ISBN 978-1-4422-1982-3 (pbk. : alk. paper) —
ISBN 978-1-4422-1983-0 (electronic)
1. Social mobility—United States. 2. Equality—United States. 3. Social capital (Sociology)—United States. I. Miller, Robert K., 1948– II. Title.
√ HN90.S65M35 2014
305.5'13—dc23
2013011708

Printed in the United States of America

Contents

Acknowledgments   vii

1   The American Dream: Origins and Prospects   1

2   On Being Made of the Right Stuff: The Case for Merit   23

3   The Silver Spoon: Inheritance and the Staggered Start   49

4   It's Not What You Know But . . .: Social and Cultural Capital   77

5   Making the Grade: Education and Mobility   101

6   Being in the Right Place at the Right Time: The Luck Factor   125

7   I Did It My Way: The Decline of Self-Employment and the Ascent of Corporations   153

8   An Unlevel Playing Field: Racism, Sexism, and Other Isms   179

9   Growing Inequality in the Twenty-First Century   215

Notes   243

Index   245

About the Authors   255

Acknowledgments

Several people facilitated the completion of this third edition. We thank the editors at Rowman & Littlefield, especially Sarah Stanton, Kathryn Knigge, and Jehanne Schweitzer for their support and assistance in shepherding this edition along. We also acknowledge the intellectual debt we owe to our teachers and mentors. For Stephen McNamee, these include John Murray, Norbert Wiley, Reeve Vanneman, and William Form, and for Robert Miller, they include William Yancey, Leo Rigsby, Richard Juliani, and Bruce Mayhew. We also thank our own students who over the course of our careers have deepened our understanding of the processes of inequality. We especially express our appreciation to Stephen McNamee's graduate research assistant, Hillary Geen, who helped us with the updates and revisions for this edition and to Abby Reiter, who assisted us with the previous edition.

In addition, we are grateful to anonymous reviewers who provided useful suggestions for revision for this edition and to Jeffrey Rosenfeld and Susan McEachern for their helpful comments on earlier versions of the manuscript. We are grateful for the institutional support provided by the University of North Carolina–Wilmington. To our colleagues in the Department of Sociology and Criminology, we extend our appreciation for their encouragement and support.

Stephen McNamee thanks his wife, Christine, for her understanding, patience, and advice in completing this edition. Robert Miller acknowledges with fond memory his late wife, Mary Susan, for her support in all of his professional endeavors. Finally, we thank our adult children, Gregory McNamee, Dr. Catherine McNamee, and Lt. Emory Miller for accepting our legacy of love as the greatest bequest we can provide.

Chapter One

The American Dream

Origins and Prospects

The reason they call it the American Dream is because you have to be asleep to believe it.
—George Carlin, *Brain Droppings*

In the image of the American Dream, America is the land of opportunity. Presumably, if you work hard enough and are talented enough, you can overcome any obstacle and achieve success. No matter where you start out in life, the sky is ostensibly the limit. According to the promise implied by the American Dream, you can go as far as your talents and abilities can take you.

Although most Americans enthusiastically endorse this image in abstract terms (Longoria 2009; *New York Times* 2005; Cullen 2004; Hanson and Zogby 2010; Pew Research Center 2011), their lived experiences often tell them that factors other than individual merit play a role in getting ahead: it takes money to make money (inheritance); it's not what you know but whom you know (connections); what matters is being in the right place at the right time (luck); the playing field isn't level (discrimination); and he or she married into money (marriage).

Americans are ambivalent about economic inequality and often simultaneously hold contradictory beliefs about how income and wealth should be distributed (Longoria 2009). While many Americans, for instance, proudly proclaim the virtues of "getting out of the system what you put into it" (meritocracy), they also steadfastly defend the right of individuals to dispose of their property when they die "as they personally see fit" (inheritance). These beliefs, however, pose a fundamental contradiction between freedom of choice at the individual level and equality of opportunity at the societal

1

level. Simply put, to the extent that income and wealth are distributed on the basis of inheritance, they are not distributed on the basis of merit.

While "merit" is a characteristic of individuals, "meritocracy" is a characteristic of societies as a whole. Meritocracy refers to a social system as a whole in which individuals get ahead and earn rewards in direct proportion to their individual efforts and abilities. The term *meritocracy*, coined by British sociologist Michael Young in his satirical novel *The Rise of the Meritocracy, 1870–2033: An Essay on Education and Equality* (1961), is closely linked with the idea of the American Dream. Although Young envisioned a fictional and futuristic society operating as a meritocracy, the opportunity to achieve the American Dream implies a society that in fact already operates on those principles.

The term *American Dream* was first popularized by historian James Truslow Adams in his 1931 best-selling book, *The Epic of America*. Adams defined it as "that dream of a land in which life should be better and richer and fuller for every man, with opportunity for each according to his ability or achievement" (1931, 404). In a general way, people understand the idea of the American Dream as the fulfillment of the promise of meritocracy. The American Dream is fundamentally rooted in the historical experience of the United States as a nation of immigrants. Unlike European societies dominated by hereditary aristocracies, the ideal in America was that its citizens were "free" to achieve on their own merits. The American Dream was the hope of fulfillment of individual freedom and the chance to succeed in the New World. As Thomas Jefferson (1813) put it, America would replace the European aristocracy of birth with a new American "natural aristocracy of talent and virtue."

In *Facing Up to the American Dream* (1995), Jennifer Hochschild identifies four tenets of the American Dream: (1) who—everyone regardless of origin or station, (2) what—reasonable anticipation or the hopefulness of success, (3) how—through actions under one's individual control, and (4) why—because of the association of true success with virtue in various ways; that is, "virtue leads to success, success makes a person virtuous, success indicates virtue, or apparent success is not real success unless one is also virtuous" (Hochschild 1995, 23).

These meritocratic tenets are deeply ingrained in the American consciousness. Survey research repeatedly confirms that most Americans enthusiastically subscribe to them. For instance, about two-thirds of Americans agree with the statement, "People are rewarded for intelligence and skill," ranking highest among a comparative study of twenty-seven countries, whereas only about one-fifth of Americans believe that "coming from a wealthy family is essential or very important to getting ahead" (Isaacs 2008, 1). In 2011, 91 percent of adults surveyed agreed that hard work is either "very important" or "one of the most important" factors that determine if a person succeeds economically (Lasky 2011). The endorsement of meritocracy, however, is not evenly distributed among Americans. Reflecting the reality of their life experiences, nonwhites and the less privileged are more likely to identify "family background," "whom you know," and "discrimination" as relevant factors in where people end up in the system (Isaacs 2008, 1). Nevertheless, the overall pattern is clear: most Americans believe that meritocracy is not only the way the system *should* work but the way it *does* work. Together, the tenets of the American Dream make up an ideology of inequality. Ideologies provide socially acceptable explanations for the kind and extent of inequality within society. Ideologies are ultimately based on persuasion as a form of social power. Persuasion entails not just making claims but getting society's members to go along as well. It is not enough for some simply to have more than others. For a system of inequality to be stable over the long run, those who have more must convince those who have less that the distribution of who gets what is fair, just, proper, or the natural order of things. The greater the level of inequality, the more compelling and persuasive these explanations must appear to be.

The type of justification or ideology varies depending on the type of inequality. In feudal societies, for instance, the principle of "birthright" and the idea of "the divine right of kings" were used to justify the power and privilege of the nobility over commoners and peasants. In slave societies, slave owners used ideas like "the spoils of victory" or "innate superiority" to justify the ownership of other human beings. In traditional Indian caste societies, inequality was justified by a Hindu belief in reincarnation; that is, one's place in this life was based on one's performance in past lives. In some forms of early Calvinist belief, success was taken as a sign of God's approval. Currently in the United States inequality is "legitimized," or "explained," predominately by an ideology of meritocracy. America is seen as the land of opportunity where people get out of the system what they put into it. Ostensibly, the most talented, hardest working, and most virtuous get ahead. The lazy, shiftless, and inept fall behind. In this formulation, you may not be held responsible for where you start out in life, but you are responsible for where you end up because the system is "fair" and provides ample opportunity to get ahead.

An important aspect of ideologies of inequality is that they do not have to be objectively "true" to persuade those who have less to accept less. Racism, for instance, is predicated on the false assumption of racial superiority. Racism involves a double falsehood: that there are biologically distinct categories within the human population (a view that modern biology soundly rejects) and that these "races" are hierarchically ranked. Americans, including people of color, were long persuaded to accept these myths, and it took centuries of struggle to begin to counter them. Likewise, women long accepted a definition of themselves as inherently inferior to men. The women's movement challenged these definitions, and they too are now largely rejected.

Racism and sexism rest ultimately on biological assumptions of superiority and inferiority that can be demonstrated empirically to be false. From the point of view of those in power, however, an ideal ideology is one that cannot be proven either true or false, such as reincarnation or the divine right of kings. Notwithstanding, as long as people *believe* an ideology to be "true," then it is true for them in its consequences (Thomas and Thomas 1928, 572). People do not act on the world as it is but as they perceive it to be and as they make sense of it. For ideologies of inequality to "legitimize" particular social arrangements, it is not necessary that the ideology be objectively true or even falsifiable; what matters is that people accept and act on it.

Acceptance of meritocracy in America, then, is predicated not on what "is" but on the belief that the system of inequality is "fair" and it "works." According to the ideology of meritocracy, inequality is seen to be fair because everyone presumably has an equal (or at least an adequate) chance to succeed, and success is determined by individual merit. The system supposedly works because it is seen as providing an individual incentive to achieve what is good for society as a whole; that is, those who are most talented, the hardest working, and the most virtuous get and should get the most rewards.

INDIVIDUALISM AND THE ORIGINS OF THE AMERICAN DREAM

The American Dream has as its core an emphasis on the individual. According to the ideology of the American Dream, we are "masters of our own fate." We "go our own way" and "do our own thing." For Americans, "it all comes down to the individual." The American emphasis on individualism is not a historical accident but is firmly rooted in the religious, political, economic, and cultural experience of America as a nation of immigrants.

Religious Origins

One key source of American individualism is the religious backgrounds of the European colonists in America, who were mostly members of numerous Protestant religious sects. These sects were part of the many splinter groups that formed in the aftermath of the Protestant Reformation, which began in Europe in the sixteenth century. The English colonists who claimed America on behalf of the British Crown established the rules of the game. Subsequent immigrant populations had to adopt those rules or risk isolation or exclusion. In this way, the cultural ideals of the initial group of white Anglo-Saxon Protestant (WASP) colonists became the dominant cultural force in America.

Among the early WASP settlers was a group of religious dissidents who landed in 1620 in Massachusetts at a place they called Plymouth after the town in England from which their flagship, the *Mayflower*, had sailed. These religious dissidents had split from the Church of England, which had earlier split from Catholicism. They came to these shores to flee religious persecution at the hands of the official Anglican hierarchy. These "separatists" practiced an extreme form of religious piety, referred to as Puritanism. These Puritans of Plymouth became the vanguard of American cultural values and the wellspring for what became the American upper class.

The constellation of cultural values that became known as the "Protestant ethic" found its greatest expression among the various Puritan sects that formed the dominant religious backgrounds of the early American colonists. German sociologist Max Weber analyzed the principles of the Protestant ethic in his classic work *The Protestant Ethic and the Spirit of Capitalism* (1904–1905). The core of Weber's argument is that the twin ethics of hard work and self-denial were associated with the early development of capitalism. Hard work generated productivity, while self-denial encouraged investment through savings. Capitalism, particularly early capitalism, needed both a highly motivated labor force and investment "capital."

As part of the break with Catholicism, Protestantism emphasized an individual rather than communal relationship with God. Puritans in particular eschewed Catholicism's communalism and the elaborate ritual system associated with it. Instead, the emphasis was on a direct relationship with God through individual prayer and reading of the Bible. The Protestant Reformation also shifted the traditional Catholic view of work as "punishment" for "original sin" to the idea of work as a sacred calling, a mission from God to subdue nature and gain control over it. People should become instruments of God's will on earth and were called upon to transform the world and remake it in God's image, which Weber called "world mastery."

The greatest expression of this ethic was in the Puritan sect of Calvinism. The Calvinists believed in predestination, which meant that people did not earn salvation but were "elected" to it by God. This belief created among the followers what Weber called "salvation anxiety," which led individuals to attempt to ascertain whether they were among the elect. Individuals came to believe that worldly success could be taken as a sign of God's grace. So, driven by salvation anxiety, people worked very hard to become successful so that they could demonstrate to themselves and others that they were among the elect.

These Puritan values of individual "industry, frugality, and prudence" were reflected in early American moralistic novels (Wiess 1969) and were integrated into the core of an emerging national culture (Cullen 2003). The best known of these was a popular series of 107 "rags-to-riches" novels by Horatio Alger (1832–1899), the son of a Unitarian minister and a Harvard graduate, who for a short time also served in the ministry. Puritan themes were reinforced as well in a series of widely used early American primary school readers, written by William McGuffey, who was also a minister turned writer.

While perhaps useful for stimulating the early development of capital, the diligence/asceticism twin ethic was not as useful for sustaining its continued expansion. The problem is that the twin ethic contains within it an internal economic contradiction. With everyone working hard to succeed, it does not take long to produce more than enough goods to meet minimum standards of living. The asceticism part of the ethic, while good for savings, depresses the demand for goods. This hard work/no play combination eventually results in an imbalance between supply and demand. For supply and demand to be reasonably balanced, something has to give. People need either to produce less or to consume more.

Americans came to consume more, motivated in part by the growth of media, which promoted consumerism on a massive scale. This was most evident especially in the period of prosperity following World War I, commonly known as the Roaring Twenties. The inhibitions, frugality, and austerity associated with the ascetic "no play" part of the Puritan ethic waned. Consumption was redefined, not as an evil of self-indulgence but as a just reward for hard work. The "hard work" part of the ethic was retained but transformed. Americans no longer worked hard simply for the glory of God but increasingly for self-enhancement. In this way, the *Protestant* ethic has lost most of its religious underpinnings and survives now in American culture simply as the "work ethic," the moral underpinnings of which have severely eroded (Wuthnow 1996). Secularized vestiges of the Puritan tradition persist in the American values of self-reliance, independence, and responsibility.

Political Origins

Politically, the American emphasis on individualism first found its expression in revolution. Shedding the grip of an aristocratic monarchy, the American colonists embarked on the bold experiment of democracy. In 1776, the Declaration of Independence proclaimed the sovereignty of a new nation and the inalienable right of its citizens to "life, liberty, and the pursuit of happiness." These were God-given rights that the state could not abridge. The spirit of *individual* freedom contained in this document became the blueprint for how the political system of the new nation would operate. The details of the new political blueprint were later incorporated into the Articles of Confederation, adopted in 1781, and expanded with the ratification of the U.S. Constitution in 1788. In the spirit of the previous documents, the Constitution outlined a contract between the citizen and the state, emphasizing (especially in the Bill of Rights) the limits of state power over individual freedoms.

The early European settlers who reached the shores of the New World were not a cross section of the populations they left behind. Those who left were no doubt different from those who remained. Some fled a lack of economic opportunity, while others fled various forms of political or religious persecution and, in some cases, prosecution. The New World offered an opportunity for freedom and a chance to start over. For others, the lure was adventure. Others saw themselves in service to the Crown, expanding the British Empire. Still others came to America involuntarily as indentured servants or were brought as slaves.

The colonists under British rule gradually became more and more resentful of the political and economic constraints imposed by the Crown. More than a century after the first permanent settlements, the colonists revolted. With the success of the American Revolution, a new government was established. The revolutionaries who laid out the plan for the new government had risked everything to gain political and economic freedom, and they were determined not to re-create the same tyranny they had fought so bitterly to defeat. The new government would have no monarch and no unilateral system of control. In the aftermath of battles with the Crown, the framers of the new government were leery of centralized systems of political control. A constitutional system of checks and balances was formed to diffuse power and to hold those who wielded power accountable, and a compromise plan—the federal system—was worked out to balance the need for national unity with the desire for localized control. Democracy, American style, was born. "Freedom" was a key ingredient in this formulation, although it had different meanings for different individuals: freedom of religion for some, freedom to acquire wealth for others, freedom from tyranny for yet others.

Alexis de Tocqueville, in his much-celebrated *Democracy in America* ([1835] 1967), praised America for the early success of its radical experiment in democracy. Key to that success, according to de Tocqueville, was the American emphasis on individualism and equality. By individualism, de Tocqueville meant "a mature and calm feeling, which disposes each member of the community to sever himself from the mass of his fellow creatures" ([1835] 1967, 118). He was careful to distinguish individualism from egotism: "Egotism is a vice as old as the world, which does not belong to one form of society more than another; individualism is of democratic origin, and it threatens to spread in the same ration as the equality of conditions" ([1835] 1967, 118–19). By "equality," de Tocqueville meant the absence of aristocracy, which he also linked to individualism:

> Aristocracy has made a chain of all the members of the community, from the
> peasant to the king: democracy breaks that chain, and severs every link to it.

As social conditions become more equal, the number of persons increases who, although they are neither rich enough nor powerful enough to exercise any great influence over their fellow creatures, have nevertheless acquired or retained sufficient education and fortune to satisfy their own wants. *They owe nothing to any man, they expect nothing from any man; they acquire the habit of always considering themselves as standing alone, and they are apt to imagine that their whole destiny is in their own hands.* ([1835] 1967, 120; emphasis added)

In short, de Tocqueville maintained that in America individuals are free to achieve, not by virtue of hereditary title but by their own individual effort and merit. Thus, the emerging ideal of the American Dream incorporated two meanings of freedom: both political freedom from tyranny and economic freedom to achieve on one's own merits.

Economic Origins

Freedom from political tyranny, however, is not the same as "market freedom," although the two are often mistakenly viewed as inextricable. Free markets mean that prices, profits, and wages are determined by the "free" operation of market forces—the outcome of innumerable matches of supply and demand for goods and services unregulated by governments. In free-market societies, "the invisible hand of the market" operates: the sole determinant of investment—the sale and purchase of land, labor, and business—is individual calculation of costs and benefits intended to maximize profits. But free markets themselves do not guarantee democracy, civil liberties, or political freedom.

In one of the great coincidences of American history, America's economic blueprint for a free-market economy was laid out in the same year, 1776, as its political blueprint for a democratic government. In that pivotal year, the Scottish economist Adam Smith published *An Inquiry into the Nature and Causes of the Wealth of Nations* ([1776] 1976), which became adopted in the United States as the informal bible of American free-market capitalism. It emphasized rational *self*-interest, *individual* competition, *private* ownership, and *laissez-faire* principles. At the time of the publication of Smith's book, roughly three-fourths of the new nation's labor force were, in fact, self-employed, comprising mostly small farmers, merchants, and artisans. A large number of mostly small producers encouraged market competition. Government regulation of business was minimal. Indeed, the economic blueprint seemed to fit.

In feudal economies, everyone essentially works in an aristocracy. Peasants did not own land and had little opportunity to move up in the system. With the decline of feudalism and the rise of market economies, free markets emerged. Individuals could own their *own* land, be their *own* bosses, and move up on the basis of their *own* efforts. In America, the absence of a feudal past, the abundance of land, and periodic regional as well as local labor shortages enhanced these opportunities, thus grounding these notions in the formative stages of the development of America's national value system.

It is important to point out, however, that the democratic free-market blueprint in America never applied equally to everyone. From the very beginning, indentured servants, slaves, non-WASPs, women, and others were systematically excluded from both the protections of the Constitution and the opportunities of free-market capitalism. Despite these exclusions, the dominant cultural image of individual rights and the free market prevailed.

Cultural Origins

The "can do" rugged individualism associated with the American Dream was further reinforced by the formative experience of the American western frontier. The "pioneer spirit" of striking out on one's own and staking a claim was captured in American author Horace Greeley's clarion call to "Go West, young man." The absence of formal government on the frontier, including effective law enforcement, also undoubtedly contributed to feelings of independence and self-reliance. Historian Frederick Jackson Turner, in his classic book *The Frontier in American History* (1947), argued that the frontier was central to the development of American individualism. Turner further linked the rugged individualism of the pioneer with the ideals of democracy: "Quite as deeply fixed in the pioneer's mind as the ideal of individuals was the ideal of democracy. He had a passionate hatred for aristocracy, monopoly and special privilege; he believed in simplicity, economy and the rule of the people" (1947, 37).

Contemporary historians have sharply criticized Turner's largely nostalgic, romantic, and simplistic view of the frontier. They correctly point out that Turner paid little attention to Indians, slaves, or Hispanics; that he had little to say about governmental aid to expansion, much less its selective character; and that his portrayal of the frontier was concentrated on the humid Middle West, to the neglect of the arid West (Limerick 1995). But it is precisely this idealized image of the American frontier that has filtered into the American consciousness, reinforced by countless novels, TV westerns, and Hollywood feature films. The frontier is portrayed as a rough and dangerous place but one with abundant opportunity. Those who were able and willing could tame the wilderness, overcome any obstacle, and realize the American Dream.

MERIT AND NONMERIT EXPLANATIONS FOR INEQUALITY

The American ethos of rugged individualism extends to culturally dominant explanations of behavior, attitudes, and life circumstances. That is, Americans strongly tend to look first to the characteristics of individuals to explain what happens to them. At the same time, there is an uneasy awareness that we are not entirely in control of our own fates. We are also all part of a social order not of our making or choosing that nevertheless profoundly affects us.

This tension between internal (merit) and external (nonmerit) factors in accounting for what happens to us is reflected in rival theoretical explanations for inequality in the social sciences. In sociology, these positions are represented by the functional and conflict theories of inequality. According to the functional theory, all societies make provisions and social arrangements for acquiring and distributing resources necessary for the mutual survival of its members. As a result of these collective efforts, there are tasks that must be done in society as a whole, and individuals must be available to do them. According to this theory, some tasks are more important than others, and some individuals are more competent than others to do them. In order to ensure that the most competent individuals fill the most important and demanding tasks in society, an incentive system of unequal rewards evolves. This unequal system of rewards is seen as necessary to entice the most capable individuals to take on the burden of, and responsibility for, performing these demanding tasks and to develop the skills necessary to do so. Those who perform these most demanding and exclusive tasks both deserve and receive the most rewards. Or, to summarize the theory in more colloquial terms, those who put the most into the system get the most out of it.

Conflict theories of inequality take very different views. According to these theories, the essential cause of inequality is conflict over surplus. Surplus refers to whatever is left over in the society as a whole after its members' minimum survival needs are met. Conflict over surplus produces winners and losers. Ever since societies have produced surplus, some have managed to get more of it than others. Winners may initially get more of the surplus because they are the shrewdest or most enterprising or because they are the most devious, the most unscrupulous, or the most ruthless. Once "winners" accumulate more surplus than others by whatever means, they can expend a portion of the accumulated surplus both to protect their existing surplus and to acquire additional surplus. In addition, winners develop ideologies—narratives of justification regarding their *right* to own. Finally, accumulated surplus is transferred intergenerationally through the process of inheritance, thereby tending to perpetuate existing inequalities across generations. To summarize conflict theories in more colloquial terms, "them that has, gets."

These sociological perspectives and other versions of them in other disciplines have been debated at length (cf. Kerbo 2012, 83–148; McNamee and Miller 1998). It is not our purpose here to fully explicate these theories but instead to put the current discussion into theoretical context. Functional theories imply a system of meritocracy in which individuals get ahead based on their individual talents and abilities. Conflict theories, on the other hand, imply a system of inheritance in which people's life chances are largely determined by their starting point within an existing *structure* of inequality. Functional theorists focus on individual characteristics such as talent, ability, and hard work as the primary determinants of inequality. Conflict theorists focus on nonmerit factors such as inheritance, discrimination, and variation in opportunities as the primary determinants of inequality.

Merit and nonmerit factors are not mutually exclusive explanations for individual economic outcomes. We argue that such outcomes have both individual and structural causes. Indeed, a major challenge of social science research is to sort out how these factors interact in ways that fully account for the kind and extent of inequality that does exist and with what consequences. We contend that the dominant ideology of meritocracy has historically tended to overestimate the effects of merit on economic outcomes and to underestimate the effects of nonmerit factors.

DOWNSIZING THE AMERICAN DREAM

In important ways, the prospects for achieving the American Dream have expanded over time. Specifically, since the nation's founding, a number of groups, including minorities and especially women, have been afforded greater political, economic, and social opportunities. Progress on the expansion of opportunities to groups formerly discriminated against or excluded, however, has been slow and uneven. While there is ongoing discrimination and the effects of past discrimination continue into the present, the overall expansion of greater opportunity to a wider segment of American society is undeniable. From its humble beginnings as a British colony, America has emerged as the wealthiest and most powerful nation in the world. For most of its history and for many, but not all, of its citizens, succeeding generations have enjoyed higher standards of living and expanded opportunities.

Recently, however, the prospects for attaining the American Dream have clearly been diminishing. The American Dream implies not just a general hopefulness for the future and a formula for success but also a sense of what the fulfillment of the dream would mean. Although specifics vary, several outcomes are generally associated with the fulfillment of the American Dream, home ownership, improved life chances for children (especially defined now as sending children to college), opportunities to get rich, and a secure and comfortable retirement. The prospects for fulfillment of the American Dream have dimmed in recent years, and Americans appear to be responding by becoming more pessimistic about the future (Gilbert 2006; Ornstein 2007; Perrucci and Wysong 2007; Pew Research Center 2010).

Home Ownership

In a U.S. Census study appropriately entitled *Tracking the American Dream* (1994), F. John Devaney examined housing trends in the fifty-year period between 1940 and 1990. In terms of fulfillment of the dream, the results are mixed. Between 1890 and 1940, rates of home ownership remained at slightly less than one-half of the American population. In the post–World War II period, stimulated by postwar prosperity and veterans loans as part of the GI Bill, rates of ownership increased dramatically, from 44 percent in 1940 to 62 percent in 1960. Subsidized by government highway funds that linked surrounding communities with central cities, this was also a period of rapid expansion of American suburbs. For many, the ranch house in the suburbs with the two-car garage and meticulously maintained lawn symbolized the fulfillment of the dream. Commuters in these bedroom communities, who worked in the urban areas and had access to their cultural amenities, felt shielded from the problems of central cities. For them, it was the best of both worlds. Economic success, resulting in white flight to the suburbs in the postwar period, however, exacerbated the problems of central cities and, in many cases, increased rates of segregation and racial tension. The tax base of urban areas eroded along with public services, including schools, police and fire protection, and urban sanitation. The fulfillment of the dream for some was for others a nightmare of inner-city crime, drugs, unemployment, poverty, and despair.

Since 1960, home-ownership rates have increased more slowly, from 61.9 percent in 1960, to 63.9 percent in 1985, to 66.8 percent in 1999 (U.S. Census Bureau 2000), to 68.2 percent in 2007 (U.S. Census Bureau 2007). Currently the rate is 66.1 percent (U.S. Census Bureau 2012). A substantially higher proportion of "home ownership" involves mortgages rather than outright ownership. In other words, mortgaged "home owners" don't really "own" their homes until they pay off their mortgages, and almost one-third (30.9 percent) of mortgage holders now owe more on their homes than they are worth in today's depressed housing market (Humphries 2012). In 1890, 72 percent of American home owners owned their own homes outright. By 1990, the corresponding figure had dropped to only 35 percent (Devaney 1994), then shrank again to only 29.3 percent by 2012 (Hopkins 2013). In short, more Americans live in "owner-occupied housing," but a higher portion of them have gone into debt to do so. Mortgage debt reached crisis proportions in 2008, precipitating a general financial meltdown, record numbers of foreclosures and bankruptcies, as well as a series of bank failures leading to a massive $700 billion federal bailout. The uptick in home-ownership rates, as it turned out, was largely an illusion fueled by the housing bubble that produced unrealistic and unsustainable debt levels.

Better Opportunities for the Next Generation

Another aspect of the American Dream is the idea that each new generation will have a higher standard of living and better opportunities than the previous one. Results vary depending on how and when the question was posed, but in general, recent data suggest that most Americans feel that the next generation will be worse off than the current one. According to a recent national survey conducted by the Pew Research Center (2010), in response to the question, "When your children are at the age you are now . . . ," 45 percent of adults responded that the standard of living would be better for their children, with 26 percent responding that their children's standard of living would be worse. These responses demonstrate a drop in the confidence of the standard of living for children in the future. In 2002 when asked the same question, 61 percent of adults felt that the standard of living would be better for their children, and only 10 percent felt it would be worse.

A clearer picture emerges in terms of providing a college education for children. An increasing proportion of Americans have been achieving this aspect of the American Dream. In 1900, only 4 percent of Americans eighteen to twenty-one years old were college students. By 2011, 42 percent of Americans eighteen to twenty-four years old were college students (U.S. Census Bureau 2012). In 1940, 4.6 percent of the population aged twenty-five and older had completed four years or more of college. This figure rose to 30.4 percent by 2011 (U.S. Census Bureau 2012). Although more Americans are entering college, the costs of college education have been increasing at a rate far greater than increases in either family income or the general cost of living. For the 2010–2011 academic year, the average annual costs for tuition, fees, room, and board was $13,564 at a public four-year college and $36,252 at a private not-for-profit four-year college (U.S. Department of Education 2012). States have drastically reduced funds for state-sponsored higher education, and as a result a greater burden for increasing college expenses has shifted to students and their families. Parents and students are increasingly unable to afford these growing costs. As a result, more students themselves are working, taking longer to graduate, being forced to accept student loans at higher interest rates, and in general taking on heavy debt loads to finance their own educations (Dickert-Colin and Rubenstein 2007; Price 2004; Martin and Lehren 2012).

With so many Americans receiving college degrees, however, the overall return on the investment has declined. To put it simply, the labor force is being flooded with new college graduates. The economy is producing fewer college-level jobs than there are new college graduates. The result has been an increase in both underemployment (e.g., college graduates waiting tables) and credential inflation (employers requiring higher levels of education for positions without a corresponding increase in the demands of the positions themselves). Under these conditions, many students perceive that getting a college education will not help them so much as the lack of a college education will hurt them. In what appears to be spiraling credential inflation, increasing numbers of students are responding to the education "arms race" by pursing graduate and professional degrees, not so much because they have an intrinsic interest in various fields of study, but to get a jump on the competition.

Chance to Get Rich

Having at least a chance to get rich holds great appeal for most Americans. The appeal is keenly felt, as evidenced by the excitement generated by state lotteries offering jackpots that soar into the millions and by the popularity of such TV game shows as *Who Wants to Be a Millionaire?* and *Deal or No Deal*. During the dot-com boom of the 1990s, the Internet became the equivalent of a modern "gold rush" as entrepreneurs anxiously sought to stake their dot-com website claims, until the bubble burst in 2000, much like the catastrophic collapse of the housing bubble. Despite these market failures, many Americans cling to the prospect of striking it rich at least sometime in the future. Survey data from a 2005 *New York Times* national poll show that 80 percent of Americans believe that it is possible to "start out poor in this country, work hard, and become rich." Alas, as we will show, the mere *possibility* of getting rich is not the same as the *likelihood* of getting rich.

Self-employment, which we will examine in greater detail in chapter 7, is relevant here because most meteoric rises in personal wealth come not from wages or salaries but through entrepreneurial activity—starting and owning businesses. With the decline of family farms and businesses and the ascendance of corporations in the twentieth century, however, rates of self-employment plummeted. New business starts are notoriously risky. For most Americans, these factors have decreased rather than increased the likelihood of "rags-to-riches" scenarios.

Secure and Comfortable Retirement

A secure and comfortable retirement is, in many ways, the closing chapter of the American Dream. In modern America, a comfortable retirement is achieved through a combination of savings, investments, pensions, and Social Security. In earlier times, people rarely "retired." Those who lived on farms, for instance, relied on adult children to provide for them if they survived and were no longer able to work. Through much of the earlier history of the United States, life expectancy was relatively low, savings were limited, pensions were rare, and Social Security was nonexistent. With the rise of industrial America and union-negotiated contracts, pensions became more common. In 1933, as part of Franklin D. Roosevelt's New Deal initiatives, the federally sponsored Social Security system was established. Until the mid-1970s, poverty rates for those over sixty-five were substantially higher than for other age groups. Many retirees were faced with small and fixed incomes and the erosion of purchasing power as prices increased. The longer they lived, the poorer they became. In 1965, however, Congress passed Medicare, which provided guaranteed access to health care for Americans over sixty-five. This greatly reduced the individual costs of health care for this population. In addition, in the mid-1970s, Social Security payments were automatically adjusted to the Consumer Price Index, eliminating a major source of "fixed incomes" for the elderly. These benefits, combined with post–World War II economic prosperity, greatly improved the economic condition of elderly Americans, who now have a rate of poverty significantly below the national average.

Nevertheless, the future of secure retirements is in serious jeopardy. The Social Security fund is in trouble. Unless taxes are raised or benefits or eligibility reduced, the Social Security system will eventually become insolvent. As the large postwar baby-boomer cohort becomes eligible for benefits, current projections are that after 2020, the treasury will use trust fund assets in excess of interest earnings until the trust fund reserves are exhausted in 2033 (Board of Trustees, U.S. Social Security Administration 2012). There are other ominous developments. Savings rates for Americans are declining sharply, from 9.4 percent of disposable personal income in 1970 to only 4.4 percent by 2012 (U.S. Department of Commerce 2012). The proportion of Americans receiving employer-sponsored pensions is also declining, from 50.6 percent of all workers in 1979 to 42.8 percent of all workers by 2010 (Mishel et al. 2012, 175). Moreover, an increasing proportion of pensions are "defined-contribution" benefits tied to mutual funds and other stocks programs rather than "defined benefits" paid as guarantees to workers. As a result, pensions are not as secure as in the past because of potential downturns in the market and the possibility of businesses going bankrupt prior to workers' retirements. As a result of these developments, workers are delaying retirement and increasingly working beyond traditional retirement age.

The population as a whole is "graying" as life expectancy continues to increase and birthrates continue to decline. The costs of health care continue to increase at a rate much higher than the general increase in the cost of living. These facts are significant because the greatest proportion of health-care expenditure is for the elderly. It is not at all clear that the health needs of an increasingly older population can be met in the coming years.

In some ways, then, the dream has been downsized in recent years. Whatever the likelihood of attaining the American Dream in the future, however, one thing is certain—it will be more attainable for those closer to the top of the system than the bottom.

PLAN OF THE BOOK

In chapter 2, "On Being Made of the Right Stuff," we identify key individual factors usually associated with the meritocratic formula for success: innate talent, hard work, proper attitude, and playing by the rules. We then examine the relationship between these individual traits and where people end up in the system. While it helps to have talent, work hard, and have the right attitude (or at least the right "fit" between specific attitudes or orientations and specific occupations), evidence indicates that the effects of these factors on economic outcomes individually and in combination are modest at best and far less than most presume. We suggest that playing by the rules may actually reduce rather than enhance prospects for economic success.

If getting ahead were simply a matter of being made of the right stuff, we would have a relatively short and simple story to tell. However, there is much more to it than this, and we devote the remainder of this book to telling that story. In fact, the most important determinant of where people end up in the economic pecking order of society is where they started in the first place. Inheritance and the "staggered start" are nonmerit factors discussed in chapter 3, "The Silver Spoon." Instead of a race to get ahead that begins anew with each generation, the race, if it can be called that, is more aptly described as a relay race in which children inherit different starting points from parents. The advantages of being born wealthy are cumulative and substantial. Inheritance, broadly defined as one's initial starting point in life based on parental position, includes having a high childhood standard of living, friends and relatives in high places, cultural advantages, infusions of parental capital while parents are still alive, insulation against failure, better health and greater life expectancy, and inheritance of bulk estates when parents die. Growing up in a privileged family entails greater opportunities to acquire and develop individual competence as well as having that competence recognized and rewarded. The chapter ends with a discussion of America's ownership class—the top 1 percent of the American population that owns about a third of all the available net worth (assets minus liabilities). We argue that this class is set apart from other Americans not only by the sheer amount of wealth it holds but by an exclusive, distinctive, self-isolating, and self-perpetuating way of life that greatly limits opportunities for merit-based mobility into it.

In chapter 4, "It's Not What You Know But . . . ," we discuss two important nonmerit factors that, while part of the American folklore of social placement, are nevertheless typically underestimated in their effects: whom you know (social capital) and fitting in (cultural capital). Social capital refers to social resources: individual and family connections in the larger community, at school, and at work that mediate access to opportunity. Cultural capital refers to a set of cultural resources—bodies of often esoteric and specialized information and knowledge, including style, bearing, manner, and self-presentation skills—that are needed to travel and be fully accepted in high-powered social circles. As with the ownership of wealth, the possession of social and cultural resources is not necessarily evidence of individual merit. Wealth can be converted into social and cultural capital, providing distinct nonmerit advantages to the children of the rich and powerful. Finally, we discuss the related phenomenon of social climbing, which refers to conscious efforts by individuals to gain membership in a group (usually higher in status) through the use of suspect techniques to expropriate the social and cultural capital of more privileged groups.

In chapter 5, "Making the Grade," we examine the complex relationship between education and the American Dream by evaluating competing arguments concerning the relationship between education and social mobility. We begin by presenting the conventional view that education serves as a mechanism that identifies and selects intelligent, talented, and motivated individuals, regardless of class background, and provides educational training in direct proportion to individual merit. The amounts and kinds of education achieved are taken as indicators of merit and are used as criteria of eligibility for occupations and the material rewards attached to them. An alternate view of the role that education plays denies that education operates to promote equality of opportunity or that it serves as an avenue of social mobility. In this alternate view, the American educational system is stratified into several unequal and largely separate parts. Education is tracked by social class and reproduces the class system. In short, schools both reflect and re-create existing inequalities in society. We conclude that education is both a merit and nonmerit factor. That is, students "earn" educational credentials (merit), but access to education and especially quality education is unequally distributed by family background and social class (nonmerit).

In chapter 6, "Being in the Right Place at the Right Time," we discuss factors in addition to individual characteristics and beyond the immediate control of individuals that significantly affect occupational attainment and life chances. We first examine the relationship between the supply of people available to fill jobs and the demand for the kinds of jobs that need to be filled. The demand for workers is based on the number and kinds of jobs that the economy generates, and these differ from place to place and change over time. In their preoccupation with the supply side—worker skills, experience, and other individual characteristics—defenders of the American Dream often ignore the demand side. While individuals do have some control over how skilled they are, they do not have control over what kinds of jobs are available, how many jobs are available, or how many others are seeking those jobs. We show that changes in American industrial and occupational structures over time have occurred quite independently of the capacities of discrete individuals. We show that being in the right place at the right time also matters for acquiring great wealth. Striking it rich—whether it be through inheritance, entrepreneurial ventures, investments, or even hitting the lottery—necessarily involves at least some degree of just plain dumb luck.

Americans embrace the ideal of the "self-made person" who starts with little or nothing and grows a successful business. In chapter 7, "I Did It My Way," we discuss notions of entrepreneurship and its central place in the American Dream. Our evaluation of this claim leads us to examine the rise of the giant corporations, the concomitant decline in self-employment, the numerous barriers to self-employment, and their implications for entrepreneurial activity. The growing concentration, collective assets, and associated economies of scale of the corporate giants tend to undercut competition from small companies and discourage new entrants. Americans cling to the historical legacy and language of free enterprise and the entrepreneurial spirit even though it no longer accurately describes the circumstances of the vast majority of the labor force that now works for somebody else.

In chapter 8, "An Unlevel Playing Field," we discuss discrimination and its implications for the American Dream. Simply put, discrimination is the antithesis of merit. Where there is discrimination, there is no meritocracy, because discriminatory allocations of opportunity and rewards discount or ignore merit and instead replace it with nonmerit criteria. Discrimination allows some (who are not necessarily meritorious) to get ahead at others' expense. What is more, discrimination creates a terrible irony: the very discrimination that invalidates the American Dream for many Americans creates conditions that seem to validate it for others, enabling them to embrace it so fervently. By excluding entire categories of people from equal access to opportunity, discrimination has reduced competition and increased the chances to get ahead of others, who often mistakenly conclude that their success is based exclusively on their own individual "merit." Although discrimination against racial minorities and women is most visible and damaging, at least in terms of costs and numbers affected, other forms of discrimination also interfere with the pursuit of the American Dream. Additional forms of discrimination, including heterosexism, ageism, discrimination against the disabled, religious bigotry, reactive southern regionalism, and "lookism" (preference for the attractive) claim fewer victims. Nevertheless, it would be difficult to convince the victims of these forms of discrimination that their effects are any less real. What is more, these forms of discrimination often become components of cumulative disadvantage, which have been referred to as "multiple jeopardy," or the effects of intersectionalities. We conclude that discrimination trumps merit; the more forms of discrimination that are operative, the more effective the trump.

In the concluding chapter, "Growing Inequality in the Twenty-First Century," we outline the implications of globalization and deindustrialization, the long wage recession, and increasing economic inequality since the 1970s for the sustainability of the notions of meritocracy and the American Dream in the twenty-first century. We examine strategies that individual Americans have developed to cope with the problems created by these changes. Individual coping strategies, however, will not make the system more equal, more meritocratic, or more fair. Changes of this magnitude would require reductions in socially structured inequality, especially inequalities of wealth and power. Structural changes of this magnitude, however, are politically difficult to implement because they appear to violate the underlying individualism of the American Dream and because they threaten the interests of the powerful and privileged. Assuming that there could be the political will to reduce inequality and make the system more meritocratic, we discuss various ways this might be accomplished. In the meantime, the meritocracy myth is sustained even in the face of pervasive discrimination, vast and growing inequalities in wealth and income, and frequently unfair and unjust social institutions. We conclude that although true equality of opportunity is probably not possible, the *myth* of meritocracy in America is itself harmful because its legitimation of inequalities of power and privilege rests on claims that are demonstrably false.

REFERENCES

Adams, James Truslow. 1931. *The Epic of America*. New York: Blue Ribbon Books.

Board of Trustees, U.S. Social Security Administration. 2012. *A Summary of the 2012 Annual Reports*. http://www.ssa.gov/oact/trsum/index.html (accessed August 26, 2012).

Carlin, George. 1997. *Brain Droppings*. New York: Hyperion.

Cullen, Jim. 2003. *The American Dream: A Short History of an Idea That Shaped a Nation*. New York: Oxford University Press.

de Tocqueville, Alexis. [1835] 1967. *Democracy in America*. New York: Schocken Books.

Devaney, F. John. 1994. *Tracking the American Dream: 50 Years of Housing History from the Census Bureau: 1940–1990*. Washington, DC: U.S. Census Bureau.

Dickert-Colin, Stacy, and Ross Rubenstein, eds. 2007. *Economic Inequality and Higher Education: Access, Persistence, and Success*. New York: Sage.

Gilbert, Nathaniel. 2006. *Democracide: America on the Road to Fascism and Bankruptcy*. Bloomington, IN: Author House.

Hanson, Sandra L., and John Zogby. 2010. "The Polls—Trends: Attitudes about the American Dream." *Public Opinion Quarterly* 74, no. 3: 570–84.

Hochschild, Jennifer. 1995. *Facing Up to the American Dream: Race, Class and the Soul of the Nation*. Princeton, NJ: Princeton University Press.

Hopkins, Cory. 2013. "More Homeowners Are Mortgage-Free Than Underwater." Zillow Inc. http://www.zillow.com/blog/2013-01-10/more-homeowners-are-mortgage-free-than-underwater (accessed January 14, 2013).

Humphries, Stan. 2012. "Getting to Know Underwater Homeowners." Zillow Real Estate Research, Zillow Inc. www.zillow.com/blog/research/2012/08/22/getting-to-know-underwater-homeowners (accessed August 24, 2012).

Isaacs, Julia. 2008. "International Comparisons of Economic Mobility." Economic Mobility Project, Brookings Institution and Pew Charitable Trusts. http://www.economicmobility.org/reports_and_research/mobility_in_america?id=0005 (accessed April 7, 2009).

Jefferson, Thomas. [1813] 1959. "Letter to John Adams on Aristocracy," October 28, 1813. In *The Adams-Jefferson Letters: The Complete Correspondence between Thomas Jefferson and Abigail and John Adams*, ed. Lester J. Cappon, 388. Chapel Hill: University of North Carolina Press for the Institute of Early American History and Culture, Williamsburg, Virginia.

Kerbo, Harold R. 2012. *Social Stratification and Inequality: Class Conflict in Historical, Comparative, and Global Perspective*. 8th ed. New York: McGraw-Hill.

Lasky, Samantha. 2011. "Economic Mobility and the American Dream: Where Do We Stand in the Wake of the Great Recession?" Economic Mobility Project, Pew Charitable Trusts. http://www.pewstates.org/research/analysis/economic-mobility-and-the-american-dream-where-do-we-stand-in-the-wake-of-the-great-recession-85899378421 (accessed August 25, 2012).

Limerick, Patricia Nelson. 1995. "Turnerians All: The Dream of a Helpful History in an Intelligible World." *American Historical Review* 100, no. 3: 697–717.

Longoria, Richard T. 2009. *Meritocracy and Americans' Views on Distributive Justice*. Lanham, MD: Lexington Books.

Martin, Andrew, and Andrew W. Lehren. 2012. "A Generation Hobbled by the Soaring Cost of College." *New York Times* online, May 12, 2012. http://www.nytimes.com/2012/05/13/business/student-loans-weighing-down-a-generation-with-heavy-debt.html?_r=2&pagewanted=all (accessed August 26, 2012).

McNamee, Stephen J., and Robert K. Miller Jr. 1998. "Inheritance and Stratification." In *Inheritance and Wealth in America*, ed. Robert K. Miller Jr. and Stephen J. McNamee, 193–213. New York: Plenum Press.

Mishel, Lawrence, Josh Bivens, Elise Gould, and Heidi Shierholz. 2012. *The State of Working America*. 12th ed. A forthcoming Economic Policy Institute book. Ithaca, NY: Cornell University Press.

New York Times. 2005. "Appendix: New York Times Poll on Class." In *Class Matters*, ed. *New York Times*, 244–76. New York: Times Books.

Ornstein, Allan. 2007. *Class Counts: Education, Inequality, and the Shrinking Middle Class*. Lanham, MD: Rowman & Littlefield.

Perrucci, Robert, and Earl Wysong. 2007. *The New Class Society: Goodbye American Dream?* 3rd ed. Lanham, MD: Rowman & Littlefield.

Pew Research Center. 2010. *A Balance Sheet at 30 Months: How the Great Recession Has Changed Life in America*. A Social & Demographic Trends Project, June 30. http://www.pewsocialtrends.org/files/2010/11/759-recession.pdf (accessed August 26, 2012).

———. 2011. *Beyond Red vs. Blue: The Political Typology*. Pew Research Center for the People & the Press, May 4. http://www.people-press.org/files/legacy-pdf/Beyond-Red-vs-Blue-The-Political-Typology.pdf (accessed August 23, 2012).

Price, Derek V. 2004. *Borrowing Inequality: Race, Class, and Student Loans*. Boulder, CO: Lynne Rienner.

Smith, Adam. [1776] 1976. *An Inquiry into the Nature and Causes of the Wealth of Nations*. Ed. R. H. Campbell and A. S. Skinner. Oxford: Clarendon Press.

Thomas, William I., and Dorothy Swaine Thomas. 1928. *The Child in America: Behavior Problems and Programs*. New York: Knopf.

Turner, Frederick Jackson. 1947. *The Frontier in American History*. New York: Henry Holt.

U.S. Census Bureau. 2000. *Statistical Abstract of the United States.* Washington, DC: U.S. Government Printing Office, table 1213.

———. 2007. *Current Population Survey, Housing Vacancies and Home Ownership.* Washington, DC: U.S. Government Printing Office, tables 5 and 14.

———. 2012. *School Enrollment 2007–2011: American Community Survey 5-Year Estimates.* 2007–2011 American Community Survey. Washington, DC: U.S. Government Printing Office.

U.S. Department of Commerce. 2012. "Personal Income and Outlays, June 2012. Revised Estimates: 2009 through May 2012." Bureau of Economic Analysis. http://bea.gov/newsreleases/national/pi/pinewsrelease.htm (accessed August 27, 2012).

U.S. Department of Education. 2007. *Digest of Education Statistics: 2007.* Washington, DC: National Center for Education Statistics, table 192.

———. 2012. "Postsecondary Education: Undergraduate Prices." In *Digest of Education Statistics: 2012.* Washington, DC: National Center for Education Statistics. http://nces.ed.gov/programs/digest/d11 (accessed August 25, 2012).

Weber, Max. [1904–1905] 2002. *The Protestant Ethic and the Spirit of Capitalism.* Trans. Stephen Kahlberg. Los Angeles: Roxbury Publishing.

Wiess, Richard. 1969. *The American Myth of Success: From Horatio Alger to Norman Vincent Peale.* New York: Basic Books.

Wuthnow, Robert. 1996. *Poor Richard's Principle: Recovering the American Dream through the Moral Dimensions of Work, Business, and Money.* Princeton, NJ: Princeton University Press.

Young, Michael. 1961. *The Rise of the Meritocracy, 1870–2033: An Essay on Education and Equality.* Baltimore: Penguin.

Chapter Two

On Being Made of the Right Stuff

The Case for Merit

The rich feel full of merit.
—Mason Cooley, U.S. aphorist

In 1959, seven astronauts were chosen for NASA's Mercury space program. These seven men, selected from an initial pool of thousands of military pilots,[1] were considered the best and the brightest, the strongest and the bravest. In short, they were made of the "right stuff."[2] Getting ahead in America is widely seen in these terms. The popular perception in America is that those who are made of the right stuff are the cream of the crop that rises to the top.

Although there are variations on the theme of meritocracy, we have identified four key ingredients in the American formula for being made of the right stuff: talent, the right attitude, hard work, and moral character. We will review each of these in terms of its impact on getting ahead.

INNATE TALENTS AND ABILITIES

Most people know intuitively that the question, If you're so smart, then why aren't you rich? is not really a question at all but a rhetorical comment implying that there is much more to monetary success than intelligence, whatever that means and however it might be measured.

The use of the results of IQ tests to "prove" the innate superiority or inferiority of culturally distinct peoples has a long and controversial history. In the early part of the twentieth century, "scientific racism" developed in the social sciences, particularly in anthropology. During World War I, the U.S.

Army used the newly developed IQ tests to sort candidates for induction. Interestingly, the results showed that potential inductees sorted themselves fairly neatly into four relatively discrete groups: northern whites, northern blacks, southern whites, and southern blacks. Was this evidence that northern blacks were "smarter" or of a "different race" than southern blacks? Of course, no one dared draw such conclusions. A few years later, the generally low IQ scores of southern, eastern, and central European immigrants were used by the Dillingham Commission to recommend severe limitation of immigration from these areas and resulted in the passage in the early 1920s of what have become known as the Immigration Quota Acts (Schaefer 2005; Parillo 2005). Those tested, of course, were mostly illiterate peasants who were at an extreme disadvantage taking IQ tests designed for English-speaking people. Subsequent test results of these immigrants' children showed that they were not "idiots" at all: the means and distributions were "normal."

The intelligence controversy was reignited with the 1994 publication of Richard Herrnstein and Charles Murray's *The Bell Curve: Intelligence and Class Structure in American Life*. Herrnstein and Murray assert that intelligence is largely genetically inherited and that it largely determines socioeconomic success. Herrnstein and Murray point out that the distribution of intelligence in the general population takes the form of a symmetrical bell curve, or what statisticians refer to as a normal distribution. In normal distributions, the most common score is the average, with most cases bunched closely around it. Variation around the middle is symmetrical in either direction (below and above the average), with most cases close to the average and the number of cases dropping off rapidly the farther away from the average, becoming rare at either end of the distribution. The shape of this curve resembles a bell, hence the name. Many occurrences in nature are "normally" distributed in this manner. Herrnstein and Murray argue that intelligence is another indication of this more general tendency in nature. [3]

Herrnstein and Murray further argue that barriers to upward mobility on the basis of natural talent have largely been eliminated and that a new "cognitive elite" is emerging in America. They contend that as colleges and universities have opened opportunities to a broader economic spectrum of students, educational attainment is increasingly based on academic performance and less on the inheritance of wealth and privilege. Moreover, with new technological demands, there is an increasing premium in society on intellectual prowess. In short, *The Bell Curve* contends that intellectual capability is increasingly replacing socioeconomic background as the new axis of economic inequality in society.

Even at face value, this argument does not fit the facts. If intelligence is shaped like a bell curve, and if it is mostly behind economic outcomes, then why are income and wealth distributions not also bell curve shaped? Indeed, income and especially wealth are very highly skewed, with small percentages of the population getting most of what there is to get (see chapter 3). It takes no talent or intelligence, for instance, to inherent the family fortune. In short, the burden is great on those who claim that such dissimilarly shaped curves (intelligence and economic outcomes) can be strongly related in cause-and-effect terms.

Not surprisingly, the publication of *The Bell Curve* was met with a barrage of criticism (cf. Fischer et al. 1996), especially related to the finding of a fifteen-point average difference in IQ scores for whites and blacks. The upshot of the many criticisms of *The Bell Curve*, however, is that in terms of social and economic outcomes, Herrnstein and Murray greatly overestimated the influence of innate intelligence (nature) and greatly underestimated the influence of environmental factors (nurture). Subsequent reanalysis (Bowles, Gintis, and Groves 2005) confirmed that once measurement errors from previous studies are corrected, the effects of IQ on earnings were "negligible," whereas the effects of wealth, race, and schooling remained "important to the inheritance of economic status."

One of the central aspects of these debates concerns the meaning of innate, or "raw," intelligence itself. Is intelligence a single capacity, or does it have multiple dimensions? Some researchers suggest that there is a general intelligence factor (sometimes called the g factor) that is highly related to separate dimensions of intelligence. Other experts, however, dispute the idea that the complexities of human intelligence can be validly reduced or captured by a single number. Beyond the issue of whether generalized raw intellectual capacity can be measured precisely, other dimensions of what most people would consider "smart" could vary independently. One might distinguish, for instance, "street smarts," "people smarts," or "book smarts" from raw intellectual capacity alone. Individuals with these various kinds of "smarts," who may or may not score high on standardized IQ tests, would nevertheless be perceived by others as clever, shrewd, or knowledgeable in ways that may have economic advantage.

Besides raw intellectual capacity, other presumably innate talents and abilities are also popularly perceived as part of the merit formula. These include, but are not limited to, athletic and artistic abilities. These traits are often associated with meteoric social mobility. The view that such talent can propel someone from rags to riches is not entirely without foundation. When people think of who is really rich in America, professional athletes and artists (e.g., actors, singers, writers), who command huge salaries for their services, often come to mind first. Although star entertainers and athletes such as Simon Cowell, Oprah Winfrey, Floyd "Money" Mayweather, and Tom Cruise earn huge annual incomes for their services ($90 million, $165 million, $85 million, and $75 million, respectively) (*Forbes* 2012b), the really big money in America comes not from working for a living but from owning income-producing property. Among the one hundred highest-paid celebrities in America who are athletes or entertainers (as opposed to owners, directors, and producers), only one, Oprah Winfrey, is among the wealthiest four hundred Americans, making the cut at number 151 (*Forbes* 2012b). It is instructive that Winfrey also owns her own production company, Harpo. The other two nonperforming "entertainers" included in the list of the wealthiest four hundred Americans, George Lucas (number 120) and Steven Spielberg (number 125), also own their own production companies (*Forbes* 2012a).

Although typically among the wealthiest of all Americans, athletes and actors, however, are celebrities who are well known to the general public. Some, such as Oprah Winfrey, come from modest social origins. The phenomenal success of these celebrities tends to reinforce the public perception that in America, you can go as far as your talents and abilities can take you.

One could argue that these "elites" are truly talented and have extraordinary physical qualities not available to the average person (e.g., size, speed, agility, hand-eye coordination). Raw talent alone, however, is not enough. Talent has to be cultivated through recruitment and opportunities for training. Potential talent can go unnoticed, particularly in the absence of opportunities to develop and exhibit it. Training may be expensive and not easily available to people of modest means, particularly in such sports as golf, tennis, swimming, and figure skating.

Sociologist William Chambliss (1989), who studied the world of champion Olympic swimmers, suggests that the concept of inherent talent in and of itself is essentially useless because inherent talent as cause cannot be separated from its effects. That is, talent cannot be used to distinguish success and failure because one does not "know" it is there until success occurs. Chambliss argues that the thresholds for natural ability needed for athletic success (minimum physical strength, coordination, heart/lung capacity, and the like) are remarkably low. Many of the key factors to success in the swimming world are unrelated to raw talent—living in warm climates, having wealthy and supportive parents, and the availability of expert coaching. Where milliseconds often separate "winners" and "losers," Chambliss points out that what distinguishes champions from mere contenders is not inherent physical superiority but more mundane considerations such as technique and training.

Historically, the conspicuous lack of people of color in these individual middle- and upper-middle-class sports is telling. Team sports such as baseball, basketball, and football have generally been more accessible (at least recently), and this is reflected in the racial and socioeconomic makeup of the athletes in these professional sports. Overall, there is a strong relationship between type of sport and the race and class of origin of the professionals within it, which strongly suggests that differential recruitment and opportunity are at work rather than athletic prowess alone. In this regard, it is also noteworthy that athletics as a means of upward social mobility, regardless of talent level, is more available to males than females since there are more paid professional opportunities in men's sports. Even in sports in which both men and women compete, until quite recently prize money has been much greater for men.

The notion of raw artistic talent as a means of upward social mobility is even more suspect. Although "talented" Hollywood actors make millions, it is not clear that the potential pool of "talent" is small. It is unknown how many potential Meryl Streeps or Tom Hanks are out there, but chances are great that there are more of them than there are potential Serena Williams or Kobe Bryants. While there may be millions in the general population who could become movie stars (if "discovered," with the "right" breaks, the "right" acting coaches, the "right" roles, the "right" looks, and so forth), there is probably a much smaller potential pool of individuals who can dunk a basketball from the foul line. This is indicated, for instance, by the high number of crossovers from sports to acting (or broadcasting) but not the other way around. Besides acting, the full extent of the potential pool of "innate" talent in the other performing arts (music, painting, sculpture, and writing) is also equally unknown. As with other extraordinary "gifts," these too have to be nurtured even to be noticed, much less developed to an elite level.

The presumed link between raw talent and celebrity athletes and artists reinforces the meritocracy myth. The presumption is that if *some* celebrities with these talents came from humble origins, then *anyone* who had those potential talents could do the same. However, it does not follow that if *only* those with talent rise to the level of celebrity athlete or artist, then *all* those with talent will become celebrity athletes or artists. Indeed, the actual probabilities of social ascent through athletics or the arts are extremely remote.

The National Basketball Association draft illustrates this principle in the case of athletics. The National College Athletic Association (NCAA), using data from its 1982–2011 Participation Statistics Report, has estimated the probabilities of high school athletes competing beyond the high school level. Of male high school seniors playing interscholastic basketball, around one in thirty, or approximately 3.3 percent, will go on to play men's basketball at an NCAA member institution. Of NCAA male senior basketball players, one in seventy-five, or approximately 1.3 percent, will realize his hoop dreams and get drafted by a National Basketball Association team. Thus, approximately only three in ten thousand, or approximately 0.03 percent, of high school senior boys playing interscholastic basketball will eventually be drafted by an NBA team (NCAA 2012). The NCAA has calculated similar long-shot odds for reaching the professional level in football, baseball, ice hockey, and soccer. The important finding is that many outstanding players with superb skills cultivated and honed by many hours of practice will not realize their professional aspirations. The illusion of potential success in glamour areas such as sports and entertainment ends up being a mobility trap for many youthful aspirants who end up investing time and effort in the long-shot pursuit of fame and fortune at the expense of more realistic avenues of social mobility (Wiley 1967). Such mobility traps may be especially damaging to African Americans (Hoberman 1997). As sport sociologist Jay Coakley notes,

> My best guess is that fewer than 6000 African Americans, or about 1 in 6660, are making a very good living as professional athletes. Data from the U.S. Department of Labor indicates that in 2007, 20,746 African American men and women were classified as "athletes, coaches, umpires, and related workers." In the same year, 499,728 African Americans were physicians and surgeons, 49,049 lawyers, and 70,616 college and university teachers. Therefore, there were twenty-eight times more African Americans working in these three prestigious professions than African American athletes in top-level professional sports; and eight times more African American doctors, lawyers, and college teachers have greater *lifetime* earnings than most athletes whose playing careers, on average, last *less* than five years and whose salaries outside top pro leagues rarely exceed $50,000 a year. . . . An African American male college student today has a ten times better chance of becoming a doctor, lawyer or college teacher than being employed in sports and will make 50 to 100 percent more per year in these non-sport professions. (Coakley 2009, 341)

When it comes to sorting out the potential effects of innate talent of all sorts, the central issue here is not whether being smart, clever, or shrewd, or possessing extraordinary physical prowess, helps at least some people get ahead. It clearly does. The issue is how much difference it makes, and for how many. This is a complex issue, and it is difficult to know precisely what mix of innate endowments and environmental influences has an effect on life outcomes. Most social scientists and neuroscientists now conclude that trying to isolate the effects of "nature" from "nurture" in predicting the probabilities of life outcomes is a wild goose chase; rather than one or the other, what matters is a combination of both and how those factors interact in complex ways. It is clear, however, that innate capacity alone accounts for nothing. Our innate biological capacity as human beings is similar to the "hardware" of a computer. A computer can have tremendous capacity for processing and analyzing information as indicated by the amount of memory available and the processing speed. Nurture or learning is similar to "software" or programming in computers. Computing capacity alone does nothing without either the input of information to process or programming that tells the computer what to do with that information.

In short, in the meritocratic formula for success, it is clear that innate capacity alone accounts for nothing. Our contention is that so-called innate talents and abilities do not just spontaneously produce life outcomes. Minimum biological capacity for success in most human endeavors is probably modest. Beyond minimum thresholds (e.g., smart enough, coordinated enough, and so on), additional increments of capacity probably have negligible economic return for most people. Moreover, there is undoubtedly substantially more inherent potential capacity among individuals in any society than is ever identified, cultivated, or realized.

HAVING THE RIGHT ATTITUDE

Beyond cognitive skills such as intelligence, various attitudes and behavioral traits are often presumed to be associated with economic success. In more familiar terms, these attitudes and traits are summarized by the phrase "having the right attitude." Having the right attitude is associated with qualities like ambition, energy, motivation, and trustworthiness. It may also involve subtler traits like good judgment, sense of personal responsibility, willingness to defer gratification, persistence in the face of adversity, willingness to take risks, getting along with others, assertiveness, independence, and the like. Conversely, a lack of proper attitudes, as evidenced by laziness, shiftlessness, indolence, deficient self-discipline, unreliability, disruptiveness, and so on, is associated with the failure to achieve.

It would seem that these represent two sides of the same coin. However, which side is emphasized makes a big difference in estimating the effects of attitudes and values on life outcomes. Most of the research linking attitudes with mobility has focused not so much on how the "right" attitudes help one get ahead but on how the "wrong" attitudes keep one from getting ahead. This implies that, in effect, one could have the "right" attitudes but not get ahead anyway. Having the "wrong" attitudes, however, would prevent one from getting ahead and may even be responsible for one's falling further behind.

One of the early attempts to link attitudes to prospects for attainment is the "culture-of-poverty" theory. This theory was developed initially in the 1960s by anthropologist Oscar Lewis (1959, 1966), who conducted ethnographic studies of Mexican families living in poverty. This general perspective was later applied mainly to African Americans in the United States (Banfield 1970). For proponents of culture-of-poverty theory, the cause of poverty in these settings is not rooted in inherent individual biological deficiencies but in the "culture" of the poor. The "subculture" of poverty in the groups Lewis studied were said to be fatalistic, hedonistic, and impulsive. There was a high incidence of early initiation into sexual activity, consensual unions, and familial disruption. Lewis interpreted this subculture of poverty as pathological and self-perpetuating. Poor people hang around with other poor people as these values are reinforced in interaction within the group. Children are socialized into antiwork, antischool, antimarriage, antiauthority values passed on from one generation to the next in what becomes a "vicious cycle of poverty."

One of the central issues in the culture-of-poverty debate is whether poverty creates deviant attitudes or whether deviant attitudes create poverty. For Lewis, it is both. Lack of opportunity creates conditions that favor the development of these values, which—while adaptive to a life of poverty—are maladaptive to prospects for upward mobility. Lewis argued that the poor become so ingrained with a lifestyle of poverty that they reject opportunities to move ahead even when opportunities to do so become available. To this extent, poverty is a freely chosen lifestyle. However, the "blame" is not on individuals but on the group to which individuals belong, and the group itself is seen as resistant to change.

Culture-of-poverty theory has been sharply criticized on several grounds. It rests on the twin assumptions that (1) the poor have attitudes or values different from the nonpoor, and (2) these attitudes or values are responsible for the condition of poverty itself. Critics (Coward, Feagin, and Williams 1974; Della Fave 1974; Gould 1999; Rodman 1963; Valentine 1968) have attacked both of these key assumptions. According to critics of the theory, the poor do not have values significantly different from those of the nonpoor. Rather, the poor, like everyone else, adjust their perceptions of reality to accommodate the reality of their situation, resulting in what Hyman Rodman refers to as "the lower class value stretch." It is one thing, for instance, to say that the poor have a "present time orientation" because they are hedonistic thrill seekers who live for the moment. However, it is another thing altogether to say that, regardless of one's personal value system, one is forced to focus on the present if one is not sure where one's next meal might come from. The middle and upper classes have the luxury of being able to plan ahead and defer gratification (for instance, going to college instead of accepting a low-paid service job) precisely because their present is secure. Similarly, the poor may have modest ambitions not because they are unmotivated but because they make a realistic assessment of limited life chances. In this formulation, exhibited behaviors and perceptions associated with a "culture of poverty" reflect the *effects* of poverty, not the causes.

The idea of a situational view of poverty is consistent with the psychologist Abraham Maslow's well-known "hierarchy-of-needs" theory. According to Maslow (1970), humans have a hierarchical order of needs that begins at the fundamental levels of food, clothing, and shelter and advances to "higher-order" needs for independence and "self-actualization." Maslow points out that one cannot attend to higher-order needs if the lower-order needs are not satisfied. In other words, poverty keeps people stuck at lower-order needs, regardless of their desire for higher-order fulfillment.

In addition to a presumption of a "culture of poverty," some conservative commentators have recently suggested at the other end of the continuum that there is something akin to a "culture of wealth," although it is not expressed using that term. One prominent example is Thomas Stanley's *The Millionaire Mind* (2000). A former marketing professor, Stanley sent questionnaires to a sample of self-made millionaires. His sample obviously did not represent millionaires per se, because it excluded those who had inherited their fortunes. The five most frequently selected factors among the self-made millionaires surveyed were, in order of importance, (1) being honest with all people, (2) being well disciplined, (3) getting along with people, (4) having a supportive spouse, and (5) working harder than most people. These factors, as well as the others on the list, make up what Stanley refers to as the "millionaire mind." One might reasonably wonder how "having a supportive spouse" is a mental characteristic. Nevertheless, as the title of the book implies, the message is that being a millionaire is a matter of having the right attitudes. The book, however, is riddled with methodological flaws and inconsistencies. First, there is no control group; that is, there is no statistical comparison between millionaires and nonmillionaires, so we don't know how unique the mind-set of the so-called self-made millionaire respondents really is. Many people, for instance, may report that they are honest, but saying one is honest may be no more prevalent among millionaires than among anyone else. Second, we don't even know how well this sample of self-made millionaire respondents represents self-made millionaires in general. The response rate for the survey among the targeted group of wealthy households was only 20 percent—low by social science standards. Finally, the perception of factors related to success was provided after the fact. Therefore, we don't know if these attitudes really caused wealth or whether wealthy people retrospectively simply attributed their success to attitudes their culture tells them are its source.

A more recent book, *The New Elite: Inside the Minds of the Truly Wealthy* (2009) by wealth consultants Jim Taylor, Doug Harrison, and Stephen Kraus, similarly suggests that there is a "mind-set" of wealth. They surveyed individuals in the upper 10 percent, upper 5 percent, and upper half of 1 percent of wealth holders (regardless of the source of wealth). They suggest that a "new elite" of corporate and venture capitalists has replaced the agrarian and industrial elites of the past. They contend that the new elite are more often self-made and meritorious. In response to what are the keys to their success in business, respondents self-identified in order of highest frequency, "hard work," "perseverance/dedication," and "integrity/treating people well." Once again, however, we have no idea from this study whether the wealthy have these orientations in any greater preponderance than the nonwealthy or if these traits are responsible for success or are post hoc accounts of success consistent with wider cultural ideals.

Along similar lines, Charles Murray, coauthor of *The Bell Curve*, has written a new book, *Coming Apart: The State of White America, 1960–2010*

(2012). Consciously staying away from the controversial race implications of *The Bell Curve*, Murray in this new book depicts a growing gap between a "new upper class" and a "new lower class" among white Americans. He suggests that the growing economic inequality between these groups can be accounted for by a combination of differences in intellectual capacity and "virtues." The new upper class is part of the "cognitive elite" previously identified in *The Bell Curve* who are increasingly being sorted out by "the college sorting machine." With an increasing "market value for brain," the less capable and less competent lower class falls behind both in terms of first academic and then economic achievement. These patterns are reinforced by acute differences in culture between the two groups. Both groups, he argues, are declining in the "founding virtues" that made America great and constitute the basis for "American exceptionalism," but the decline is much faster for the new lower class than the new upper class.

Similar to other flattering portrayals of the "new elite" discussed above, Murray identifies four "founding virtues" which he claims are in greater preponderance among the new upper class: industriousness, honesty, marriage, and religiosity. What is again conflated, however, is cause and effect. Are these "virtues" a cause or an effect of wealth? For instance, Murray measures "industriousness" by such indicators as hours worked, rates of employment, and rates of disability, which can obviously be a consequence of economic circumstance rather than a cause of it. Likewise, Murray measures "honesty" by rates of arrests and incarceration, which are widely known to be higher for the poor than the rich, not because the rich are more "honest" but because the types of criminality engaged in by the lower class are much more likely to result in arrest and incarceration than the types of criminality engaged in by the upper class. Likewise, marriage rates are higher for the wealthy than for the poor, not because the poor do not value marriage but because economic deprivations make the prospects of finding suitable marriage partners slimmer for the poor than the affluent. On religiosity, Murray finds more convergence between the new upper class and the new lower class on indicators such as belief in God and attendance at religious services, as well as toward greater degrees of secularization and less religiosity, but, again, those trends are more pronounced for the new lower class than the new upper class.

All of these portrayals of "the new elite" have in common an ideology of economic success that historian Richard Huber (1971) refers to as the "mind-power ethic." According to this ethic, success is a case of mind over matter. Presumably, success can be acquired through sheer willpower. The mind-power ethic is a major theme running throughout American success self-help books of the twentieth century (Dunkleman 2000). Fueled by a tradition of Protestant individualism, which was later secularized, and reflected in a fascination with psychology, the mind-power ethic peaked with the publication of Norman Vincent Peale's *The Power of Positive Thinking* (1952) and his success formula of "prayerize, picturize, and actualize." This ethic speaks especially to the notion that determination and persistence in the face of whatever obstacles may exist are the true secret of success. In this formulation, individuals are not responsible for where they start out in life, but they are responsible for where they end up. In other words, according to these formulations, wealth or poverty is ultimately a matter of "attitude" broadly defined.

Beyond the culture-of-poverty theories and, more recently, culture-of-wealth theories, there has been surprisingly little systematic research into the effects of noncognitive attitudes and behavioral traits on who gets ahead in America. The results of what research has been done are mixed at best (see Farkas 2003 for a systematic review). The lack of research findings in this area is at least partly due to the difficulty in clearly separating out the effects of all the possible "causes" of who gets ahead (and conversely who falls behind). With respect to attitudes and values, the question becomes *which* attitudes and *which* values?

Attitudes are related to other attitudes, and nuances of meaning among them tend to blend together, so pinpointing a particular combination of "right" attitudes for success becomes difficult. Some research, for instance, suggests that what might matter for getting ahead is not a particular attitude or set of attitudes so much as a *match* of attitudes or orientations in particular arenas of endeavor (Jencks et al. 1979). For instance, the kind of "mind-set" that might make for a successful accountant might be very different than the kind of "mind-set" that might make for a successful artist.

Moreover, do these attitudes, values, and orientations produce *independent* effects on life outcomes, or are they merely related to other possible causal factors? And finally, how are attitudes related to behavior? Humans have a habit of saying one thing (expressed attitudes) but doing something else (exhibited behavior). Also, is the direction of influence clear? That is, do attitudes influence behavior, or does behavior influence attitudes?

It is not clear, then, what specific attitudes are individually determinative of economic success as opposed to being merely associated with or a consequence of it. It is also not clear which particular attitudes are associated with success in particular tasks, occupations, or professions. Furthermore, it is not clear how to measure these attitudes or to distinguish their effects from other related factors such as family background. Much of what passes as the right attitude, for instance, is likely to be at least partially the result of differential access to preferred forms of cultural capital (see chapter 4). Such intangibles as comportment, demeanor, and presentation of self to others (interpreted by others as "attitude") may be more of a reflection of upbringing than uniquely personal or individual attitudes. These traits may be seen as desirable by people in positions of authority even if such traits may not actually affect job performance.

WORKING HARD OR HARDLY WORKING

In the formula for getting ahead, hard work ranks very prominently in most Americans' minds (Lasky 2011; Pew Research Center 2011; Longoria 2009; *New York Times* 2005). In fact, hard work consistently scores among the top three factors necessary for success, usually alternating between the first and second ranks with education and knowing the right people as its closest competitors. It is difficult to disentangle the effects of attitudes such as motivation, industriousness, ambition, and so on from actual hard work. Attitudes alone, however, are likely not as important as actual behavior.

Americans nod their heads knowingly and approvingly whenever the importance of hard work is mentioned in association with the likelihood of success. But what does working hard really mean? Does it refer to the number of hours of worked? Does it refer to the level of exertion expended in the conduct of work? How are these factors related to concrete measures of economic success, that is, wealth and income? As Barbara Ehrenreich (2001) discovered when she spent a year doing menial jobs in America in a participant observation study, often the hardest-working Americans are those who get paid the least. It is the waitress with sore feet at the end of the day after several miles of trudging around between the kitchen and dining area, taking orders, pouring drinks, and carrying dishes and heavy trays of food. It is the lowest-paid member of the construction crew with aching muscles and a sore back after a day of toting heavy loads of lumber and other construction materials on the work site. It is the secretary with carpal tunnel syndrome who works her fingers to the bone typing departmental reports. It is the janitor who moonlights as a house painter and works over sixty hours a week because neither job pays enough to make ends meet. Individuals such as these represent the backbone of the American *working* class. Additional "hard" work of this kind, however, is unlikely to result in any significant wealth or upward social mobility.

Conversely, those with high-paying jobs may not be working any "harder" than those with less-well-paying jobs in the same employing organizations. In most jobs in America, compensation is more directly related to levels of responsibility and authority than it is to number of hours worked or intensity of effort exerted (Kalleberg 2011). Further, those who have the most may actually expend the least amount of effort. The really big money in America, as shown in the following chapter, does not come from working for a living at all but from ownership of property—especially the kind of property that produces additional wealth, such as stocks and bonds, real estate, business assets, and so on. Indeed, those who live off *unearned* income from investments may not need to work at all. If one is wealthy enough, it is possible to hire small armies of accountants, lawyers, and brokers to manage one's holdings and still be among the wealthiest of all Americans.

Still, one wonders how one would actually *know* how hard people work. If we consider the obvious measure of hours worked, the data show that Americans work more than workers in most other developed countries. Among thirty-five developed countries in 2011, the United States ranked twelfth in average annual hours worked per worker at 1,787 hours, or about 34 hours per week (OECD 2012). But do more hours worked translate into greater occupational or economic success? In *Outliers: The Story of Success* (2008), Malcolm Gladwell refers to the "10,000 hour rule," citing studies that show that it takes a minimum of about ten thousand hours of practice to develop world-class expertise in most areas of human endeavor. Gladwell was making the point that talent alone does not spontaneously produce results, as we have also previously indicated. It is a combination of capacity, opportunity, and application that creates very successful people. That is, any capacity that individuals have must not only be initially identified and provided an opportunity to flourish, but also honed through hours of application and practice to reach elite levels. That does not mean, however, that ten thousand hours of application in doing different things produces equivalent results. Most people spend considerably more than ten thousand hours in the work that they do in a lifetime, but they are not all equally successful. Spending ten thousand hours working as a waitress or mastering the yo-yo is unlikely to have as much economic benefit, for instance, as ten thousand hours working as a neurosurgeon.

Since there is a biological limit on how much any one person can "work" and Americans appear in general to work hard, there is simply not enough variation in hours worked to account for the substantial and growing extent of income and wealth inequality. As we have shown, when respondents are asked to state the reason(s) for their success, they almost always answer, "hard work," or some variant. We suggest that an individualist culture provides an individualist answer. Who would actually say, "I don't work hard," or "Hard work has nothing to do with my success"? People claim that they deserve their success because they work hard. Yet deservedness is not equivalent to hard work; and, as has been repeatedly shown, many people who work hard are not especially economically successful, and many who are economically "successful" do not work especially hard (or at all). Clearly, hard work alone is neither a necessary nor a sufficient condition for receiving the most compensation for whatever it is that people do. Hard work matters, but in terms of compensation, what people do matters much more than how "hard" they do it. When people cite hard work as a factor in getting ahead, they really mean hard work in combination with other factors, especially opportunity and acquired skills, both of which are more related to social background than individual capacities.

MORAL CHARACTER

In addition to persistence in the face of adversity, another frequent theme in the American cultural folklore of meritocracy is that being made of the right stuff includes moral character and integrity. But what is "integrity," and in a culture in which integrity is presumably highly valued, who would admit to having little or none? For example, moral fiber and character have been a constant theme in American self-help success books (Dunkleman 2000; Starker 2002; McGee 2005). The early advice manuals, in particular, echoed the twin pillars of the Protestant ethic: diligence and asceticism. In addition to working hard, the "truly" successful person had honor and dignity. People should pursue wealth not for the purposes of self-gratification or personal indulgence but for the glory of God and to help others. In this formulation, success is taken as evidence of God's grace; successful people saw themselves as moral people. There was always some tension, however, between materialism and idealism in the pursuit of wealth.

While honesty and integrity are certainly worthy goals in their own right, in the final analysis, do they help or hinder in the making of money? There is little direct evidence suggesting that these virtues help or hinder the prospects for social mobility. On the one hand, we have numerous testimonials of wealthy individuals who claim such virtues. One of the few studies on the effect of integrity on success comes from *Who Gets Ahead* (Jencks et al. 1979, 154). Among the many noncognitive factors that they examined was integrity, as measured by teachers' accounts of students' personalities longitudinally related to later mobility. They reported that, controlling for other factors, integrity produced a small *inverse* but statistically significant effect. That is, everything else being equal, integrity was associated with less upward mobility.

In the absence of other direct evidence, we suspect that the overall effect of integrity is to suppress rather than enhance upward mobility. We suspect that not cheating, not stealing, and not choosing to get ahead at the expense of others restricts prospects for social mobility and the accumulation of wealth. Wealth can be achieved by honest or dishonest means. The logic of this argument is that those who limit themselves to strictly honest means to get ahead have fewer opportunities to do so than those who do not limit themselves in this way. Direct evidence for the wealth-enhancing character of ruthless and unethical behavior comes from the history of industrial capitalism. Many of the wealthy industrialists of the last century earned notorious reputations as "robber barons" for their relentless and cutthroat pursuit of wealth and power. The indirect evidence for the wealth-enhancing character of unethical behavior comes from the extent of white-collar crime in America. Assuming that the amount of exposed white-collar crime represents only the tip of the iceberg of unscrupulousness, we would surmise, by extension, that making money in America is often accomplished through less than impeccably honest or ethical means.

It is difficult to estimate the full extent of white-collar crime in America. This type of crime has become more sophisticated and includes a variety of financial crimes such as corporate fraud, securities and commodities fraud, health-care fraud, financial institution fraud, mortgage fraud, insurance fraud, mass-marketing fraud, and money laundering (Federal Bureau of Investigation 2012). Because much of this type of crime is hidden in financial complexities and goes undetected, it is difficult to determine its exact cost. Nevertheless, the total cost to society of these kinds of financial crime is clearly staggering. The National White Collar Crime Center estimates the total annual cost of crimes of this type in the United States to be between $300 billion and $660 billion (Kane and Wall 2006). It is more difficult to detect white-collar crime since enforcement efforts of the criminal-justice system are directed toward crimes committed by the poor rather than the rich (Messner and Rosenfeld 2007; Reiman and Leighton 2013), and people are often unaware that they have been victimized. When white-collar crimes are exposed, the sums procured in their commission are often shocking—often totaling in the millions and sometimes even in the billions of dollars. The Ponzi scheme stock fraud perpetrated by Bernard Madoff (an ironic surname for a white-collar criminal) totaling $65 billion is one particularly noteworthy example. Other examples include the notorious and illegal stock manipulations of Ivan Boesky (deal stocks), Michael Milken (junk bonds), and Charles Keating (the savings-and-loan scandal); corporate wrongdoing, including ethics scandals at Enron, WorldCom, Arthur Andersen, Adelphia, Global Crossing, Tyco, and many others; and suspected misconduct in the vast mutual funds and mortgage industries that led to the near collapse of credit markets and the debilitating Great Recession that followed.

Suffice it to say, at least some of the wealth of financiers, executives, and professionals has been gained through often illegal or less than ethical means. This is in addition to untold wealth realized from more conventional organized crime, including drug trafficking, prostitution, pornography, racketeering, gambling, and the like, which itself is estimated to account for approximately 7 percent of the American gross domestic product (Center for Economic Studies 2011; Grammy 2011). In an ideal world, the virtuous succeed and the corrupt fail. But in the real world, too often it seems that this is not the case. As we have suggested, it has become almost commonplace to note how frequently various forms of unethical and immoral behavior are acknowledged to have contributed to profits and success.

A NOTE ON HUMAN CAPITAL

Human capital factors are often included in the "merit" formula for success. Human capital refers to whatever *acquired* skills, knowledge, or experience workers possess that they can exchange for income in open markets. Clearly, having acquired capacity is not the same as being inherently made of the right stuff, because opportunities to acquire skills and experience are independent of the inherent capacity to do things. In human capital theory, wage laborers can "invest" in themselves through the accumulation of education and training, thus increasing their skills and presumably their productive capacities. But, as with investments in other forms of economic capital, investments in human capital require resources and entail an element of risk. Capacities to do things represent the "supply" side of the labor market; the specific capacities employers actually need represent the "demand" side of the labor market. The biggest returns on human capital investments are those in which the capacities acquired are both scarce and in high demand. It is possible, however, to invest in the "wrong" capacities. This can occur, for instance, when individuals are trained for jobs that become obsolete, sometimes even before the training period is complete. Or too many individuals may invest in acquiring the same skills, glutting the market and reducing return on investment. In both cases, one can be very meritorious but also very unemployed. Although we explore the supply effects of human capital in greater detail in chapter 5 and the demand side of the equation in greater detail in chapter 6, the point here is that this type of merit alone does not guarantee success.

THE MYTH OF THE MOST QUALIFIED

Defenders of meritocracy (and critics of affirmative action) often proclaim that the issue of who should get what is simple and straightforward: just hire the *most* qualified person for the job. However, even ignoring the fact that the big money in America comes from economic investments and not from jobs for which people are hired, this is not as simple and straightforward as many presume.

If merit were the sole cause of achievement, for instance, one would wonder why the vast amount of meritocratic talent is found in white males, who clearly dominate leadership positions in key institutions in society. Even setting discrimination and differential access to opportunity aside, how, in fact, would one recognize the *most* qualified applicant for every position in America?

Let us take a somewhat extended example from our own profession. Combined, the authors of this book have over sixty years of experience in higher education. In addition to our own experience in the academic labor market, we have each been on scores of faculty hiring committees in our own department, and in his former role as an associate dean, the senior author has also conducted scores of "courtesy interviews" of job candidates for other departments. For most of our careers, we have been employed in a rapidly growing institution, and as a result we have hired numerous new faculty in our department. For a substantial part of that time, our department combined four disciplines—sociology, anthropology, criminal justice, and social work—so our experience goes beyond one discipline alone.

We need to make two caveats. Hiring in academia is somewhat unusual compared to other sectors of the economy in that it is, for the most part, highly collegial; that is, the decision to hire is a collective one, typically made jointly by the existing members of the faculty in a given department, subject to approval at higher levels. This joint decision-making process reduces the chance of capriciously hiring any one person based on the singular decision of the "boss." Another unique quality of academic hiring is that faculty positions involve national searches; that is, job openings are advertised nationally, casting the widest possible net. All of this is intended to increase the chances of hiring the best person for the job.

Although the intent is to hire the best person for the job, as anyone who has ever participated in the process knows, the problem comes in figuring out what is "best" and who that "best" person might be. The first qualification for the job is to have a PhD from an academically accredited institution in the discipline in which the faculty member will teach and do research. So far, so good. For a typical faculty position in our department, we might receive around one hundred applications. Among these, 95 percent or more of the applicants will have a PhD in the appropriate field. That is, only 5 percent of the applicants can quickly be eliminated as unqualified on that basis. It should be noted, however, that automatically eliminating those without the PhD might itself be a "merit" mistake since every academic field of study has at least a few cases of famous scholars who were giants in their fields of study but never earned a PhD.[4]

After screening candidates for meeting the minimum paper qualifications, the hiring committee then carefully reviews the remaining applications, which consist of a letter of application, an academic resume called a "vita," and three letters of recommendation. Together, these materials represent a "paper presentation of self" of the applicant to the committee.

After serving on a few of these committees, one realizes very quickly that some applicants are better at paper presentation of self than others. That is, holding experience, ability, and qualifications constant, some individuals are simply better than others at presenting their case on paper. Presentation of a case on paper and actual ability to do a job are two different things. More on this later. Based on these paper presentations of self, the hiring committee will develop a short list of maybe ten individuals for closer review. The short list is generated based on all reasonable indicators of merit: teaching record and experience, research record and potential, and "goodness of fit" with the needs of the department. With respect to the latter quality, it should be noted that we often have applicants who are truly outstanding but do not fit the advertised position; that is, they may appear to be the *most* talented or meritorious people in their respective pools overall, but they do not have areas of specialization for the position as advertised (e.g., an applicant is a great demographer, but we are really looking for a gerontologist). Further, as with most academic hires at most universities, we are most often looking to fill entry-level positions at the assistant professor level. This means that we will not usually consider the candidate who is literally the "best" in our pool if such a candidate is, for instance, a senior full professor with a proven track record because such a candidate would be too expensive for the institution to hire. In this sense, we are not looking for the *most* meritorious professor we can find; we are looking for the most meritorious *new* assistant professor we can afford in a specific area we need to fill.

In developing the short list, there are typically differences of opinion among members of the search committee. We try to reach a consensus, but perfect agreement rarely occurs. Majority sentiment prevails, but lack of consensus is itself an indicator of the difficulty of determining what "best" represents. We make a collective best guess as to who the ten best applicants in the pool might be. In developing an initial short list, the committee may well have overlooked the candidate who was, in fact, the best in the pool in terms of how that person ultimately could have done the job. Such a person, for instance, ultimately might have been the best for the job but presented her- or himself poorly on paper. We will never know. One could argue that how one presents oneself on paper is an indicator of merit. However, we also know that some candidates, especially more recently minted PhDs, are better coached than others, and paper presentation of self is often more a reflection of the good advice of senior mentors than of candidate skills. We now have ten or so short-listed candidates but still only one position. The next step is to select three from among the top ten for on-campus interviews.

Perhaps we would do a better job of screening for raw talent if we interviewed more candidates. But resources are limited, both the money kind that is required to pay for on-campus interviews and the time kind related to faculty who must also do all the other things faculty are supposed to do. Often, the short-listed candidates seem indistinguishable in terms of merit. All appear excellent, and looking for distinctions can become an exercise in splitting hairs. Frequently, there is another twist to the hiring drama. A dilemma that frequently unfolds is related to the amount of experience a candidate has. Since we most often hire at the assistant professor level, this means that most of the applicants are new or relatively new PhDs. Relatively new

PhDs present a comparison problem. If candidates are already assistant professors at other institutions, they have more teaching experience and typically more extensive research track records than brand-new PhDs—but that does not necessarily make them "better" or more "meritorious." It is strictly a judgment call for a committee to decide whether potential exceeds track record in comparing new and almost-new PhDs—a source of more than one fierce debate in hiring committees we have been on.

Another potential hiring dilemma concerns "internal" candidates—candidates who are already associated with, or employed by, the university in some other capacity such as part-time instructor or temporary lecturer. In some cases, the internal candidate may be applying for a particular permanent position that they currently occupy on a temporary basis. If strictly merit criteria apply, then internal candidates should be evaluated in the same manner as all other candidates without any preferential consideration. In practice, however, internal candidates often have a distinct advantage apart from strictly merit considerations. They are known by the hiring agents, and often friendships and emotional ties have already been formed. The internal candidate may be "qualified" and "doing a good job" but not necessarily the *most* qualified among all candidates who have applied, some of whom may be not just "good" but "outstanding." Social accountability also comes into play here. It is much easier to send a stranger a letter of rejection than to tell someone in the office next door that he or she did not get the job (and is thus out of his or her current job). The emotional burden of all this may weigh heavily on the decision-making process. To the extent that is the case, strictly merit considerations are compromised.

It is common knowledge in higher education that in some cases internal faculty candidates are essentially "wired in." That is, the application process is only a formality needed to satisfy human resource department requirements for public advertisement. One way institutions can "game" the system in this way is to write a job ad for a position that matches the particular internal candidate that the institution has in mind to such a degree of specificity of background, skills, experience, and specialties that only that particular internal candidate would likely match the advertised position. Qualified external candidates may apply in good faith, not realizing that a decision has essentially already been rendered.

The issue of "trailing partners" presents another potential hiring dilemma. With the postponement of age of first marriage, increasing higher-educational attainment for women, and growing proportion of women in the professoriate, there is an increasing prospect of academic couples simultaneously seeking positions at the same university. The problem is compounded if the couples are in the same discipline and have the same areas of specialty. Typically, only one position is available in an academic department at any one time. It is also unlikely that each partner will be identically "meritorious" in all respects and that both will emerge from a strictly meritocratic review process as more meritorious than all other applicants combined. At the same time, universities are increasingly sensitive to this very human dilemma and are anxious to develop "family-friendly hiring practices."

One way some universities have responded to this potential dilemma is to allow couples to "share" a single position. Another way is for universities to try to find or create a suitable position for a partner. In short, there may be very human, legitimate, and practical reasons to make accommodations under these circumstances (for instance, you lose the most qualified candidate you want unless you can find suitable employment for a partner who may also be as qualified but for whom you have no existing position). At the same time, it should be recognized that such accommodations represent hiring decisions on criteria other than strictly merit considerations alone.

Finally, in an ironic twist, some candidates may be less aggressively pursued if they are viewed as "overly qualified." Here, the hiring agents may predict that a particularly outstanding applicant will likely receive more lucrative or attractive job offers elsewhere. The hiring committee might anticipate that it could not possibly match offers from other high-profile institutions likely interested in such candidates, and thus deem pursuing them to be a waste of time and other resources, which would risk losing more viable candidates for the position under consideration. Sometimes this emerges as a sentiment (or post hoc justification) in which the hiring officials speculate that the "overly qualified" person would end up "not being happy here."

Still other potentially nonmerit factors may come into play in the hiring drama. Do we know any of the people who are writing letters of recommendation for the candidates? Here the social network among the professoriate comes into play. New PhDs are typically not well known, but their professors and references might be. We may give more weight to candidates who are students of professors we know personally or who have "big names" writing for them. Everything else being equal or indistinguishable, the familiarity or prestige of the references might become a factor, as might the prestige of the institution where the candidates were trained. Here, some candidates may benefit from a "halo" effect of the glow of the institution from which they received their training, even though this in itself does not necessarily measure the merit of an individual.

Some of the most heated debates in hiring, however, have more to do with the faculty on the hiring committees than the candidates themselves. Hiring can become a political battle over which faction or coalition will prevail. Factions might develop over methodological, theoretical, or substantive differences within the hiring committee. Everything else being equal (and sometimes even when it is not), faculty members will try to hire someone like themselves. Individual faculty may also be interested in promoting the power of their own faction or in hiring someone who might be a personal asset to them, even if that person is not the most "meritorious" in the pool.

When the dust of these debates clears, normally three candidates are brought to campus for an extended interview, usually lasting two or three full days each. During this time, candidates have one-on-one interviews with faculty and administrators and typically teach a class and give a research presentation. There are also a number of opportunities for informal interaction at dinners, receptions, and community tours. We have been amazed over the years at how frequently the top three on paper do not end up being ranked in the same order after on-campus interviews, reflecting the differences we alluded to above between real and paper presentations of self. Another intangible screening factor is how well the candidates are "liked." Here, social skills may be more important than technical expertise or paper qualifications. How people present themselves in a job interview, however, may not predict how well they will actually perform on the job. Everything else being equal (and sometimes not so equal), at this final stage of the hiring process the candidate who "gets along" best with the most influential members of the committee will typically triumph over others.

In the end, a job offer is made to one person. Although the hiring committee, the department, and the university may congratulate themselves for having selected the "best" person in the pool, the reality is that there is, in fact, no way to determine that with certainty. Do we routinely hire highly qualified candidates who are very meritorious? Absolutely. Have we always hired the *most* meritorious person for the job? Probably not, but we will never know for sure. The point of this extended example is to show that even within the professoriate, a profession in which academic qualifications and individual merit are highly extolled, there is no assurance that the "best" ultimately prevails. The hiring process is likely to be even more slippery for real estate agents, store clerks, janitors, and a host of other jobs for which the merit criteria may be less agreed upon and more difficult to measure and for which the screening processes are far less rigorous. When it comes to hiring the "best" or "most qualified," there are many slips betwixt the cup and the lip.

THE COSTS OF MEASURING UP

The American emphasis on merit and competition is not without its costs. In an insightful analysis of the American "performance ethic," sociologist James Mannon points out that in the "relentless quest to measure up to the innumerable standards of health, wealth, competence, and so on, Americans are becoming less autonomous, less authentic, and less free" (1997, 1). Beginning with the Apgar score for newborns, a numerical scale that indicates a baby's clinical vitality and well-being immediately after birth, Americans are subjected to a dizzying variety of "measures" purporting to indicate how they "rate" compared to others—IQ tests, standardized "aptitude" tests, achievement tests, grades, athletic scores, the "thin-to-win" norms presented in women's magazines, incomes as yardsticks of worth, and so on. These measures are often of dubious reliability, validity, and relevance to real life.

In *The Competition Paradigm* (2003), Pauline Vaillancourt Rosenau explains how competition among individuals in the pursuit of these standards can often lead to a host of ill effects, including irritability, insomnia, depression, impaired memory function, hypertension, cardiovascular disease, diabetes, and lowered immunity. Rosenau distinguishes between destructive and constructive forms of competition. Constructive competition is associated with four characteristics:

> First, winning must not be so important that it generates the extreme anxiety that interferes with performance. Second, all participants in the competition must see themselves as having a reasonable chance to win and thus remain motivated to give it an honest try, their best effort. Third, the rules of competition need to be clear and fair as to procedures and criteria for winning. Finally, those competing should be able to monitor how they are doing compared to others. (Rosenau 2003, 9)

Destructive competition, by comparison, does not satisfy these conditions. Destructive competition creates negative unintentional side effects, such as "cutting costs by polluting the environment, competing by reducing worker safety and protection measures, competing at misleading advertising, competing at socially irresponsible, damaging financial speculation" (Rosenau 2003, 13). At the individual level, destructive competition is repeatedly illustrated in the media. For example, in one 1970s movie comedy, people who "didn't earn their age" (in thousands) were simply defined as "losers." Survey research repeatedly shows that "income questions" are highly sensitive. This is at least partially because income is taken as a yardstick of self-worth and as a measure of prestige, so individuals don't want to admit they make a low income.

Unfortunately, much of the competition to get ahead in America is rigged and therefore falls into the destructive category, with all its attendant ill effects. The danger comes when a person's sense of self-esteem, inherent worth, and dignity are judged by societal standards that are often irrelevant by the rules of the game that are rigged. In short, if the race to get ahead is rigged and if individuals who do not get ahead are presumed to be personally deficient, however that is defined and to whatever ends, then devastating consequences can occur—both for individuals and society as a whole.

SUMMARY

This chapter has explored the meritocratic formula for getting ahead in America: being talented, having the right attitude, working hard, and having high moral standards. We have reviewed the evidence linking these "individual" traits with life outcomes. With the exception of high moral standards, all of them have some bearing on getting ahead in America. That is, individual capacity, certain attitudes, and hard work all probably do help people get ahead. High moral standards, however, may actually have the opposite effect by reducing options available to get ahead. While being made of the "right stuff" in general helps people get ahead, the reality is that these qualities exist in far greater quantity in the general population than is ever actually realized. Moreover, many individual traits often have social origins, and the effects of these traits are often much less than is presumed. By themselves, these traits are not typically enough to make the difference. It is not innate capacity alone, or hard work alone, or the proper frame of mind alone that makes a difference. Rather, it is the *combination* of opportunity and these other factors that makes a difference.

We also call into question the presumption that people know merit when they see it. How do we really know who is the most meritorious? Recall that it is a cardinal principle in meritocracy that the "most" qualified or "best" person should be hired for the job. Using an example from the process for hiring professors, we argue that it is often difficult or impossible to know who the best is. Finally, we discuss the costs of trying to measure up to sometimes artificial and irrelevant societal standards. In the frantic race to get ahead in a game in which the rules are rigged, the inherent value and dignity of all people, regardless of their individual merit or lack of it, may get lost in the shuffle.

REFERENCES

Ackmann, Martha. 2003. *The Mercury 13: The Untold Story of Thirteen American Women and the Dream of Space Flight*. New York: Random House.

Banfield, Edward C. 1970. *The Unheavenly City: The Nature and Future of Our Urban Crisis*. Boston: Little, Brown.

Bowles, Samuel, Herbert Gintis, and Melissa Osborne Groves. 2005. Introduction to *Unequal Chances: Family Background and Economic Success*, ed. Samuel Bowles, Herbert Gintis, and Melissa Osborne Groves, 1–22. New York: Sage.

Center for Economic Studies. 2011. "Estimates of the Shadow Economy in OECD Countries 2003–2011." CESifo DICE Report. http://www.cesifo-group.de/ifoHome/facts/DICE/Public-Sector/Public-Finance/Public-Revenues-without-Taxes-/dice-rep-shadow-econ/fileBinary/dice-rep-shadow-econ.pdf (accessed January 14, 2013).

Chambliss, William. 1989. "The Mundanity of Excellence." *Sociological Theory* 7:70–86.

Coakley, Jay. 2009. *Sports in Society: Issues and Controversies*. 10th ed. Boston: McGraw-Hill.

Coward, Barbara E., Joe R. Feagin, and Allen J. Williams Jr. 1974. "The Culture of Poverty Debate: Some Additional Data." *Social Problems* 21:621–34.

Della Fave, L. Richard. 1974. "The Culture of Poverty Revisited: A Strategy for Research." *Social Problems* 21:609–21.

Dunkleman, Allen J. 2000. "Our American Ideology of Success." Unpublished senior research project, University of North Carolina at Wilmington.

Ehrenreich, Barbara. 2001. *Nickel and Dimed: On (Not) Getting By in America.* New York: Metropolitan Books.

Farkas, George. 2003. "Cognitive Skills and Noncognitive Traits and Behaviors in Stratification Processes." In *Annual Review of Sociology*, vol. 29, ed. Karen S. Cook and John Hagan, 541–62. Palo Alto, CA: Annual Reviews.

Federal Bureau of Investigation. 2012. "Financial Crimes Report to the Public: Fiscal Years 2010–2011." Washington, DC: U.S. Government Printing Office.

Fischer, Claude S., Michael Hout, Martin Sanchez Jaankowski, Samuel R. Lucas, Ann Swidler, and Kim Voss. 1996. *Inequality by Design: Cracking the Bell Curve Myth.* Princeton, NJ: Princeton University Press.

Forbes. 2012a. "The Forbes 400." Forbes.com. http://www.forbes.com/forbes-400/list (accessed September 2012).

———. 2012b. "The World's Most Powerful Celebrities." Forbes.com. http://www.forbes.com/celebrities (accessed September 2012).

Gladwell, Malcolm. 2008. *Outliers: The Story of Success.* New York: Little, Brown.

Gould, Mark. 1999. "Race and Theory: Culture, Poverty, and Adaptation to Discrimination in Wilson and Ogbu." *Sociological Theory* 17:171–200.

Grammy, Abbas P. 2011. "The Underground Economy." Economic Research Center. *Premier Thoughts: The CSUB Business Blog.* http://www.csub.edu/kej/documents/economic_rsch/2011-11-28.pdf (accessed January 14, 2013).

Herrnstein, Richard, and Charles Murray. 1994. *The Bell Curve: Intelligence and Class Structure in American Life.* New York: Free Press.

Hoberman, John. 1997. *Darwin's Athletes: How Sport Has Damaged and Preserved the Myth of Race.* Boston: Houghton Mifflin.

Huber, Richard. 1971. *The American Idea of Success.* New York: McGraw-Hill.

Jencks, Christopher, Susan Bartlett, Mary Corcoran, James Crouse, David Eaglesfield, Gregory Jackson, Kent McClelland, et al. 1979. *Who Gets Ahead? The Determinants of Economic Success in America.* New York: Basic Books.

Kalleberg, Arene. 2011. *Good Jobs, Bad Jobs: The Rise of Polarized and Precarious Employment Systems in the United States, 1970s to 2000s.* New York: Sage.

Kane, John, and April D. Wall. 2006. *The 2005 National Public Survey on White Collar Crime.* Fairmont, WV: National White Collar Crime Center.

Lasky, Samantha. 2011. "Economic Mobility and the American Dream: Where Do We Stand in the Wake of the Great Recession?" Economic Mobility Project, Pew Charitable Trusts. http://www.pewstates.org/research/analysis/economic-mobility-and-the-american-dream-where-do-we-stand-in-the-wake-of-the-great-recession-85899378421 (accessed August 25, 2012).

Lewis, Oscar. 1959. *Five Families: Mexican Case Studies in the Culture of Poverty.* New York: Basic Books.

———. 1966. *La Vida: A Puerto Rican Family in the Culture of Poverty.* New York: Random House.

Longoria, Richard T. 2009. *Meritocracy and Americans' Views on Distributive Justice.* Lanham, MD: Lexington Books.

Mannon, James M. 1997. *Measuring Up: The Performance Ethic in American Culture.* Boulder, CO: Westview.

Maslow, Abraham. 1970. *Motivation and Personality.* 2nd ed. New York: Harper & Row.

McGee, Micki. 2005. *Self-Help, Inc.: Makeover Culture in American Life.* New York: Oxford University Press.

Messner, Steven F., and Richard Rosenfeld. 2007. *Crime and the American Dream.* Belmont, CA: Thomson Higher Education.

Murray, Charles. 2012. *Coming Apart: The State of White America, 1960–2010.* New York: Crown Forum.

National College Association of Athletics. 2012. "Probability of Competing in Athletics beyond High School." National College Association of Athletics, September 17. http://www. ncaa.org/wps/wcm/connect/public/Test/Issues/Recruiting/Probability+of+Going+Pro (accessed September 29, 2012).

New York Times. 2005. "Appendix: *New York Times* Poll on Class." In *Class Matters*, ed. *New York Times*, 244–76. New York: Times Books.

OECD (Organisation for Economic Co-operation and Development). 2012. "Average Annual Hours Actually Worked per Worker." http://stats.oecd.org/Index.aspx?DatasetCode= ANHRS (accessed October 10, 2012).

Parillo, Vincent N. 2005. *Diversity in America.* Thousand Oaks, CA: Pine Forge Press.

Peale, Norman Vincent. 1952. *The Power of Positive Thinking.* New York: Prentice Hall.

Pew Research Center. 2011. *Beyond Red vs. Blue: The Political Typology.* Pew Research Center for the People & the Press, May 4. http://www.people-press.org/2011/05/04/beyond-red-vs-blue-the-political-typology (accessed August 23, 2012).

Reiman, Jeffrey, and Paul Leighton. 2013. *The Rich Get Richer and the Poor Get Prison: Ideology, Class, and Criminal Justice.* 10th ed. Upper Saddle River, NJ: Pearson.

Rodman, Hyman. 1963. "The Lower Class Value Stretch." *Social Forces* 42:205–15.

Rosenau, Pauline Vaillancourt. 2003. *The Competition Paradigm: America's Romance with Conflict, Contest, and Commerce.* Lanham, MD: Rowman & Littlefield.

Schaefer, Richard T. 2005. *Race and Ethnicity in the United States.* Upper Saddle River, NJ: Prentice Hall.

Schlosser, Eric. 2003. *Reefer Madness: Sex, Drugs, and Cheap Labor in the American Black Market.* Boston: Houghton Mifflin.

Stanley, Thomas. 2000. *The Millionaire Mind.* Kansas City, MO: Andrew McMeel Publishing.

Starker, Steven. 2002. *Oracle at the Supermarket: The American Preoccupation with Self-Help Books.* Edison, NJ: Transaction Publishers.

Taylor, Jim, Doug Harrison, and Stephen Kraus. 2009. *The New Elite: Inside the Minds of the Truly Wealthy.* New York: American Management Association.

Valentine, Charles. 1968. *Culture and Poverty.* Chicago: University of Chicago Press.

Wiley, Norbert. 1967. "The Ethnic Mobility Trap and Stratification Theory." *Social Problems* 15:147–59.

Wolfe, Thomas. 1979. *The Right Stuff.* New York: Farrar, Straus & Giroux.

Chapter Three

The Silver Spoon

Inheritance and the Staggered Start

To heir is human.
—Jeffrey P. Rosenfeld, *Legacy of Aging*

A common metaphor for the competition to get ahead in life is the foot race. The imagery is that the fastest runner—presumably the most meritorious—will be the one to break the tape at the finish line. But in terms of economic competition, the race is rigged. If we think of money as a measure of who gets how much of what there is to get, the race to get ahead does not start anew with each generation. Instead, it is more like a relay race in which we inherit a starting point from our parents. The baton is passed, and for a while, both parents and children run together. When the exchange is complete, the children are on their own as they position themselves for the next exchange to the next generation. Although each new runner may gain or lose ground in the competition, each new runner inherits an initial starting point in the race.

In this intergenerational relay race, children born to wealthy parents start at or near the finish line, while children born into poverty start behind everyone else. Those who are born close to the finish line need no merit to get ahead. They already are ahead. The poorest of the poor, however, need to traverse the entire distance to get to the finish line on the basis of merit alone. In this sense, meritocracy applies strictly only to the poorest of the poor; everyone else has at least some advantage of inheritance over others that places them ahead at the start of the race.

In comparing the effects of inheritance and individual merit on life outcomes, the effects of inheritance come first, *followed by* the effects of individual merit—not the other way around. Figure 3.1 depicts the intergenerational relay race to get ahead. The solid lines represent the effects of inheritance on economic outcomes. The dotted lines represent the potential effects of merit. The "distance" each person needs to reach the finish line on the basis of merit depends on how far from the finish line each person starts the race in the first place.

It is important to point out that equivalent amounts of merit do not lead to equivalent end results. If each dash represents one "unit" of merit, a person born poor who advances one unit on the basis of individual merit over a lifetime ends up at the end of her life one unit ahead of where she started but still at or close to poverty. A person who begins life one unit short of the top can ascend to the top based on an equivalent one unit of merit. Each person is equally meritorious, but his or her end position in the race to get ahead is very different.

Heirs to large fortunes in the world start life at or near the finish line. Barring the unlikely possibility of parental disinheritance, there is virtually no realistic scenario in which they end up destitute—regardless of the extent of their innate talent or individual motivation. Their future is financially

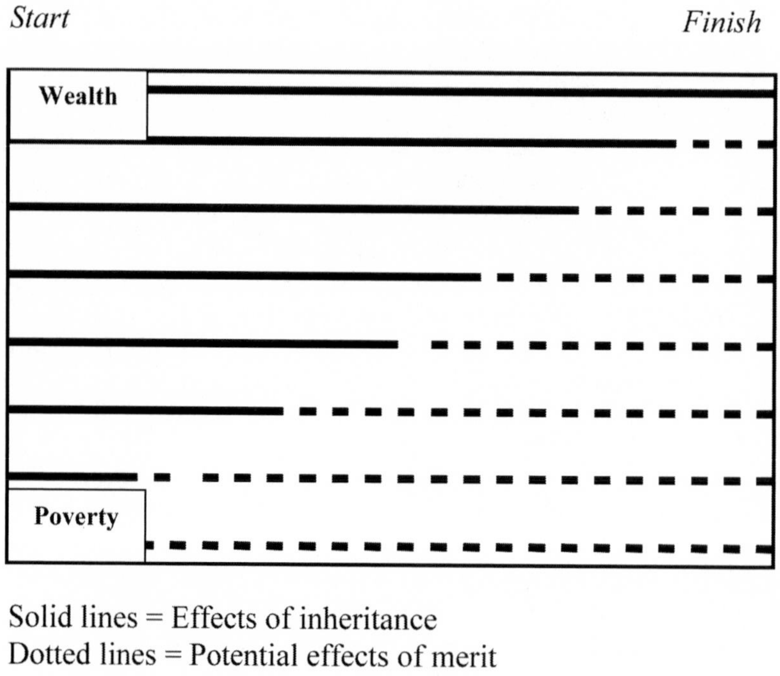

Start   *Finish*

Solid lines = Effects of inheritance
Dotted lines = Potential effects of merit

Figure 3.1. The Intergenerational Race to Get Ahead

secure. They will grow up having the best of everything and having every opportunity money can buy.

Most parents want the best for their children. Except in relatively rare cases of child abuse or neglect, most parents try to do everything possible to secure their children's futures. Indeed, the parental desire to provide advantages for children may even have biological origins. Under the "inclusive fitness-maximizing" theory of selection, for instance, beneficiaries are favored in inheritance according to their biological relatedness and reproductive value. Unsurprisingly, research shows that benefactors are much more likely to bequeath estates to surviving spouses and children than to unrelated individuals or institutions (Schwartz 1996; Willenbacher 2003). Moreover, most parents relish any opportunity to boast about their children's accomplishments. Parents are typically highly motivated to invest in their children's future in order to realize vicarious prestige through the successes of their children, which may, in turn, be seen as a validation of their own genetic endowments or child-rearing skills. Finally, in a form of what might be called "reverse inheritance," parents may be motivated to invest in children to secure their own futures in the event that they become unable to take care of themselves.

Regardless of the source of parental motivation, the point is that most parents clearly wish to secure their children's futures. The key difference among parents is not in parental motivation to pass on advantages to the next generation but in the capacity to do so, with some parents having more resources than others. For instance, at the turn of the twenty-first century in the United States, parents in the highest income quintile could spend $50,000 per child per year on food, housing, and other goods and services, but those in the bottom income quartile could only spend $9,000 per child per year (Moynihan, Smeeding, and Rainwater 2004). To the extent that parents are actually successful in passing on advantages to children, existing inequalities are reproduced across generations, and meritocracy does not operate as the basis for who ends up with what. Despite the pervasive ideology of meritocracy, the reality in America, as elsewhere, is inheritance first and merit second.

INCOME AND WEALTH INEQUALITY

In considering how parents pass on advantages to children in the race to get ahead, researchers have usually looked at occupational mobility, that is, at how the occupations of parents affect the occupations of children. The results of this research show that parental occupation has strong effects on children's occupational prospects. Some of this effect is mediated through education; that is, the prestige of parental occupation increases the educational attainment of children, which in turn increases the prestige of the occupations they attain. Looking at occupational prestige alone, however, underestimates the full extent of inequality in society and overestimates the amount of move-ment within the system. A fuller appreciation of what is at stake requires examination of the kind and extent of economic inequality within the sys-tem—who gets how much of what there is to get. Economic inequality in-cludes inequalities of both income and wealth. Income is typically defined as the total flow of financial resources from all sources (e.g., wages and sala-ries, interest on savings and dividends, pensions, and government transfer payments such as Social Security, welfare payments, and other government payments) in a given period, usually annually. Wealth refers not to what people earn but to what they own. Wealth is usually measured as net worth, which includes the total value of all assets owned (such as real estate, trusts, stocks, bonds, business equity, homes, automobiles, banking deposits, insu-rance policies, and the like) minus the total value of all liabilities (e.g., loans, mortgages, credit card and other forms of debt). For purposes of illustration, income and wealth inequalities are usually represented by dividing the popu-lation into quintiles and showing how much of what there is to get goes to each fifth, from the richest fifth of the population down to the poorest fifth. These proportions are illustrated in table 3.1.

In terms of income, in 2009 the richest 20 percent of households received a 50.8 percent share of all before-tax income, compared to only 5.1 percent received by the bottom 20 percent. As income increases, so does its level of concentration. The top 10 percent alone accounts for 36 percent, and the top 5 percent alone accounts for 25.9 percent of the total (Congressional Budget Office 2012, 5). Moreover, income has great staying power over time. That is, the same households in the top income group now are very likely to have been in the top income group in previous years (Mishel et al. 2012, 144).

Table 3.1. Share of Total Available Household Income and Total Net Worth, by Income Group, 2007

Income Group	Share of Income (%)	Share of Net Worth (%)
Top Fifth	54.6	85.0
Fourth Fifth	19.1	10.9
Third Fifth	13.3	4.0
Second Fifth	9.0	.2
Bottom Fifth	4.8	
Total	100.0	100.0

Source: Adapted from Congressional Budget Office (2012, 5) and Wolff (2010, 45).

Another indication of income inequality is revealed by a comparison of pay for the chief executive officers of major corporations with that of rank-and-file employees. CEO pay as a ratio of average worker pay increased from 18.3 to 1 in 1965 to 231 to 1 in 2011 (Mishel and Sabadish 2012), with much of the compensation package for CEOs coming in the form of stock options. Since CEO compensation is increasingly in the form of stock options, the ratio to worker pay in recent years is sensitive to changes in the market but always substantially higher than in previous decades; it is also substantially higher than the ratio of CEO-to-worker pay in other advanced industrial countries (Kalleberg 2011, 110).

When wealth is considered, the disparities are much greater. In 2010, the richest 10 percent of American households accounted for 74.5 percent of total net household wealth (Levine 2012a). The bottom 50 percent combined, by stark contrast, held 1.1 percent of all available net worth. At the bottom end of the wealth scale in 2007, 18.6 percent of households had zero or negative net worth, which is the highest it has been over the past twenty-four years (Wolff 2010, 10). In other words, a significant number of Americans either own nothing or owe more than they own.

As MIT economist Lester Thurow has observed, "Even among the wealthy, wealth is very unequally distributed" (1999, 200). In 2010, for instance, the top 1 percent of all wealth holders with an average household net worth of approximately $16 million and average annual income of over $1 million accounted for 35.4 percent of all net worth, 42.1 percent of financial wealth, and 17.2 percent of annual income (Wolff 2012, 58–60). The top 1 percent of the wealthiest households (representing about three million Americans) is significant not only for the amount of wealth held that sets this group distinctly apart from the rest of American society, but for the source of that wealth. Most of the wealth held by these top wealth holders comes not from wages and salary but from investments. In 2010 the top 1 percent of households held a staggering 61.4 percent of all business equity, 64.4 percent of all financial securities, 38 percent of all trusts, 48.8 percent of all stocks and mutual funds, and 35.5 percent of all nonhome real estate (Wolff 2012, 69). Because of the amount of ownership highly concentrated in this group, the top 1 percent of wealth holders are often referred to as "the ownership class" and are used as a proxy threshold for inclusion in the American "upper class."

In short, the degree of economic inequality in the United States is substantial by any measure. In fact, the United States now has greater income inequality and higher rates of poverty than other industrial countries (Wilkinson and Pickett 2009; Grusky and Krichell-Katz 2012; Mishel et al. 2012; Kerbo 2006; Smeeding, Ericson, and Jantti 2011; Salverda, Nolan, and Smeeding 2009; Sieber 2005). Moreover, the extent of this inequality is increasing. One standard measurement of the extent of inequality is the Gini coefficient, which measures the extent of the discrepancy between the actual distribution of income and a hypothetical situation in which each quintile of the population receives the same percentage of income. Values of the Gini coefficient range between zero and one, where zero indicates complete equality and one indicates complete inequality. Thus, the higher the number, the greater the degree of inequality. Using reports from the U.S. Census Bureau, Levine (2012b) demonstrates that the Gini coefficient for the United States has steadily and incrementally increased from 0.386 in 1968 to 0.469 in 2010—representing a 21.5 percent increase over a forty-two-year span.

Increases in wealth inequality are even more dramatic. The ratio of wealth of the top 1 percent of wealth holders to median wealth had increased from 125 times the median in 1962 to 225 times by 2009 (Mishel et al. 2012, 383). In short, the gap between those who live off investments and the large majority of people who work for a living has widened considerably in recent decades.

It is instructive to point out that this level of wealth inequality is greatly underestimated by the American public. A recent Duke University study showed that Americans estimate that the richest 20 percent of Americans account for 59 percent of the total wealth available, compared to the actual 84 percent (Norton and Ariely 2011). Moreover, in the same survey, Americans indicated that ideally the richest 20 percent *should* own 32 percent of the total wealth or about 50 percent less than they actually hold.

Consideration of wealth as opposed to just income in assessing the total amount of economic inequality in society is critical for several reasons. First, the really big money in America comes not from wages and salaries but from owning property, particularly the kind that produces more wealth. If it "takes money to make money," those with capital to invest have a distinct advantage over those whose only source of income is wages. Apart from equity in owner-occupied housing, assets that most Americans hold are the kind that tend to *depreciate* in value over time: cars, furniture, appliances, clothes, and other personal belongings. Many of these items end up in used-car lots, garage sales, and flea markets selling at prices much lower than their original cost. The rich, however, have a high proportion of their holdings in the kinds of wealth that *appreciate* in value over time. Second, wealth is especially critical with respect to inheritance. When people inherit an estate, they inherit accumulated assets—not incomes from wages and salaries. Inheritance of estates, in turn, is an important nonmerit mechanism for the transmission of privilege across generations. In strictly merit terms, inheritance is a form of getting something for nothing.

INTERGENERATIONAL MOBILITY

Defenders of meritocracy sometimes argue that the *extent* of economic inequality is not a problem as long as there is ample *opportunity* for social mobility based on individual merit. Overwhelming evidence, however, shows that a substantial amount of economic advantage is passed on across generations from parents to children (Ermisch, Jantti, and Smeeding 2012; Smeeding, Erikson, and Jantti 2011). The mechanisms by which parental privilege are transferred to children are varied, including direct advantages such as inheritance of material resources to indirect advantages such as increased capacity and opportunity for cognitive and physical development, better educational preparedness and opportunities, access to influential social networks, and access and exposure to prestigious cultural resources.

One way to measure the extent of intergenerational mobility is the correlation between parent and child incomes. Correlations can range from a low of zero to a high of one. If we had a pure merit system and assumed random transfer of genetic endowments across generations, we would expect a correlation of parent and adult child incomes to approach zero. On the other hand, in a strict caste system in which children inherit entirely the social position of parents and in which no mobility occurs, we would expect a correlation to approach one. The correlation between parents' and adult children's incomes in the United States is actually about 0.50 (Stiglitz 2012), a correlation midway between these extremes. This figure is much larger than in other industrial nations (Pew Economic Mobility Project 2011).

Table 3.2 shows the extent of intergenerational wealth transfers from parents to children as calculated by economists Kerwin Charles and Erik Hurst (2003). This study compares wealth of children and parents in wealth quintiles. These data show a great deal of "stickiness" between generations, especially in the top and bottom quintiles. For instance, 36 percent of children born to parents in the lowest quintile remain in the lowest quintile as adults, while, correspondingly, 36 percent of those born to parents in the top wealth quintile remain there as adults. Most movement that does take place between generations occurs as "short-distance" mobility between adjacent quintiles, especially in the middle quintile ranges. In short, most people stay at, or very close to, where they started, with most of the movement occurring as short-distance mobility in the middle ranges.

Another source of information on wealth transfers is the annual list of the four hundred wealthiest Americans published by *Forbes* magazine. A recent study of the 2011 *Forbes* list (United for a Fair Economy 2012) indicates that roughly 40 percent of those listed had inherited a sizable asset from a spouse or family member, defined as at least a medium-size business or wealth in excess of $1 million. Roughly 20 percent of those on the list inherited sufficient wealth of at least the $1 billion minimum required to make it on the list

Table 3.2. Intergenerational Wealth Transmission from Parents to Children

Child's Wealth Quintile	Parent's Wealth Quintile				
	Lowest (%)	Second (%)	Middle (%)	Fourth (%)	Top (%)
Lowest	36	26	16	15	11
Second	29	24	21	13	16
Middle	16	24	25	20	14
Fourth	12	15	24	26	24
Top	7	12	15	26	36
Total	100	100	100	100	100

Source: Charles and Hurst 2003.

through inheritance alone. Among the eleven wealthiest Americans on the 2011 *Forbes* list, six (ranked nos. 6, 9, 10, 11, 103, and 139) are heirs of Sam Walton, founder of the Walmart empire. The six Walton heirs have a combined estimated net worth of $93 billion, which is equal to the wealth of the bottom 41.5 percent of all American families. An earlier study of the 1982 *Forbes* list (Canterbery and Nosari 1985) also showed that at least 40 percent of that year's list inherited at least a portion of their wealth, and the higher on the list, the greater the likelihood that wealth was derived from inheritance.

Although there is some movement over time onto and off the *Forbes* list of the richest four hundred Americans, this does not mean that those who fall off the list have lost or squandered their wealth. Most likely, when wealthy individuals fall off the *Forbes* list, they have not lost wealth at all but rather have not gained it as quickly as others. Although those who fall off the four hundred list may have lost ground relative to others, they typically still have vast amounts of wealth and most likely remain well within the upper 0.01 percent of the richest Americans.

Research has shown that there is a remarkable level of stability among the listings in the Forbes 400. In one recent study of the *Forbes* list, over a sixteen-year period between 1995 and 2003, the percentage of those who remained on the list from one year to the next (excluding those who fell off the list because of death) ranged from a low of 84 percent in the 1998–1999 period to a high of 95 percent in the 2002–2003 period (Sauls 2012). Moreover, how individuals ranked within the list is also very stable from year to year. Over the same sixteen-year period, the correlation of rankings from one year to the next varied from a low of .82 in 2000–2001 to a high of .93 in 2009–2010, with an average of .89 for all years combined.

The increasing degree of concentration of wealth and the high stability of wealth over time is particularly significant given the large amount of wealth available for transfer across generations. A recent study estimates that baby boomers born between 1946 and 1964 are likely to inherit a total of $8.4

trillion in bulk estates (MetLife Mature Market Institute 2010). An earlier study estimated that over a fifty-five-year period from 1998 through 2052, a total of $41 trillion will be available for transfer ($25 trillion to heirs, $8 trillion to taxes, $6 trillion to charity, and $2 trillion to estate fees) (Havens and Schervish 2003). These vast amounts of wealth will not simply evaporate between generations, and indeed much of the intergenerational transfer will reach not only to the current generation of baby boomers but to their children as well, further solidifying the continuity of wealth inequality overtime. Indeed, the combination of increasing amounts and concentration of wealth at the top of the system and the stability of wealth and inequality across generations gives rise to what some observers suggest is the unfolding of a second Gilded Age of dynastic wealth in America (Grusky and Kricheli-Katz 2012; Freeland 2012).

Despite the evidence of wealth stability over time, much is made of the investment "risks" that capitalists must endure to justify returns on such investments. And to some extent, this is true. Most investments involve some measure of risk. The superwealthy, however, protect themselves as much as possible from the vicissitudes of "market forces"—most have professionally managed, diversified investment portfolios. As a result, established wealth has great staying power. In short, what is good for America is, in general, good for the ownership class. The risk endured, therefore, is minimal. Instead of losing vast fortunes overnight, the more common scenario for the super-rich is for the *amount* of their wealth to fluctuate with the ups and downs in the stock market as a whole. And, given the very high levels of aggregate and corporate wealth concentration in the economy, the only realistic scenario in which the ownership class goes under is one in which America as a whole goes under.

THE CUMULATIVE ADVANTAGES OF WEALTH INHERITANCE

Inheritance is more than bulk estates bequeathed to descendants; more broadly defined, it refers to the total impact of initial social-class placement at birth on future life outcomes. Therefore, it is not just the superwealthy who are in a position to pass advantages on to children. Advantages are passed on, in varying degrees, to all of those from relatively privileged backgrounds. Even minor initial advantages may accumulate during the life course. In this way, existing inequalities are reinforced and extended across generations. As Harvard economist John Kenneth Galbraith put it in the opening sentence of his well-known book *The Affluent Society*, "Wealth is not without its advantages and the case to the contrary, although it has often been made, has never proved widely persuasive" (1958, 13). Specifically, the cumulative advantages of wealth inheritance include those discussed below.

Childhood Quality of Life

Children of the privileged enjoy a high standard of living and quality of life regardless of their individual merit or lack of it. For the privileged, this not only includes high-quality food, clothing, and shelter but also extends to luxuries such as travel, vacations, summer camps, private lessons, and a host of other enrichments and indulgences that wealthy parents and even middle-class parents bestow on their children (Duncan and Murnane 2011; Lareau 2011; Smeeding, Erikson, and Jantti 2011). These advantages do not just reflect a higher standard during childhood but have important long-term consequences for future life chances. Children raised in privileged settings are much more likely to have better and more rapid physical, cognitive, emotional, and social development, better school readiness, and higher academic achievement. Conversely, children raised in poverty have higher risks for basically everything that is bad that can happen to them as adults later in life—dropping out of school, becoming victims of crime and violence, having more physical and mental health problems, having lower economic prospects, and having greater likelihood of familial disruption. The more severe these deprivations and the earlier they occur, the greater the negative consequences (Duncan and Murnane 2011; Smeeding, Erikson, and Jantti 2011). In short, the effects of early childhood development have a "long reach" into later life. It is important to emphasize that children of privilege do not "earn" a privileged childhood lifestyle; they inherit it and benefit from it long before their parents are deceased.

Knowing with Which Fork to Eat

Cultural capital refers to what one needs to know to function as a member of the various groups to which one belongs. (We address the issue of cultural capital more fully in chapter 4.) All groups have norms, values, beliefs, ways of life, and codes of conduct that identify the group and define its boundaries. The culture of the group separates insiders from outsiders. Knowing and abiding by these cultural codes of conduct are required to maintain one's status as a member in good standing within the group. By growing up in privilege, children of the elite are socialized into elite ways of life. This kind of cultural capital has commonly been referred to as "breeding," "refinement," "social grace," "savoir faire," or simply "class" (meaning upper class). Although less pronounced and rigid than in the past, these distinctions persist into the present. In addition to cultivated tastes in art and music ("highbrow" culture), cultural capital includes, but is not limited to, interpersonal styles and demeanor, manners and etiquette, and vocabulary. Those from more humble backgrounds who aspire to become elites must acquire the cultural cachet to be accepted in elite circles, and this is no easy task.

Those born to it, however, have the advantage of acquiring it "naturally" through inheritance, a kind of social osmosis that takes place through childhood socialization (Lareau 2011).

Having Friends in High Places

Everybody knows somebody else. Social capital refers to the "value" of whom you know. (We review the importance of social capital on life outcomes more fully in chapter 4.) For the most part, privileged people know other privileged people, and poor people know other poor people. Another nonmerit advantage inherited by children of the wealthy is a network of connections to people of power and influence. These are not connections that children of the rich shrewdly foster or cultivate on their own. The children of the wealthy travel in high-powered social circles; these connections provide access to power, information, and other resources. The difference between rich and poor is not in knowing people; it is in knowing people in positions of power and influence who can do things for you.

Early Withdrawals on the Family Estate

Children of the privileged do not have to wait until their parents die to inherit assets from them. Inter vivos transfers of funds and "gifts" from parents to children can be substantial, and in many cases represent a greater proportion of intergenerational transfers than lump-sum estates at death. Parents provide inter vivos transfers to children to advance their children's current and future economic interests, especially at critical junctures or milestones of the life cycle (Oliver and Shapiro 2006; Zissimopoulos and Smith 2011). These transfers continue beyond early childhood and include milestone events for adult children such as going to college, getting married, buying a house, and having their own children, or at crisis events such as income shocks related to job loss, divorce, or medical crisis. At each event, there may be a substantial infusion of parental capital—in essence an early withdrawal on the parental estate. The amounts transferred are highly skewed. One recent study of parents over the age of fifty (Zissimopoulos and Smith 2011), for instance, showed that in the United States over a sixteen-year period, the bottom 50 percent of parental households gave an average of only $500 to their adult children, but parents in the top 1 percent gave an average of $137,641 per child to their adult children. Moreover, households that give substantially to children give more as a percentage of their total income and wealth than other households, further reflecting the differential capacity of parents to transfer advantages across generations. For those with great wealth, inter vivos gifts to children also provide a means of legally avoiding or reducing estate taxes. In this way, parents can "spend down" their estates during their lives to avoid estate and inheritance taxes upon their deaths.

One of the most common current forms of inter vivos gifts is payment for children's education. (We address education more fully in chapter 5.) A few generations ago, children may have inherited the family farm or the family business. With the rise of the modern corporation and the decline of family farms and businesses, inheritance increasingly takes on more fungible or liquid forms, including cash transfers. Indeed, for many middle-class Americans, education has replaced tangible assets as the primary form by which advantage is passed on between generations. Also, with rising overall life expectancy, there is a longer period of time during the lives of parents and children in which inter vivos gifts can take place.

What Goes Up Doesn't Usually Come Down

If America were truly a meritocracy, we would expect fairly equal amounts of both upward and downward mobility. Until very recently and for most of American history, however, there have been much higher rates of upward than downward mobility. There are two key reasons for this. First, most mobility that people have experienced in America in the past century, partic- ularly occupational mobility, was due to industrial expansion and the rise of the general standard of living in society as a whole. Sociologists refer to this type of mobility as "structural mobility," which has more to do with changes in the organization of society than with the merit of discrete individuals. (We discuss the effects of social structure on life outcomes in more detail in chapter 6.) A second reason why upward mobility is more prevalent than downward mobility is that parents and extended family networks insulate children from downward mobility. That is, parents frequently "bail out," or "rescue," their adult children in the event of life crises such as sickness, unemployment, divorce, or other setbacks that might otherwise propel adult children into a downward spiral. In addition to these external circumstances, parents also rescue children from their own failures and weaknesses, includ- ing self-destructive behaviors. Parental rescue as a form of inter vivos trans- fer is not a generally acknowledged or well-studied benefit of inheritance. Indirect evidence of parental rescue may be found in the recent increase in the number of "boomerang" children, adult children who leave home only to return later to live with their parents. Kim Parker of the Pew Research Center (2012) reports that 39 percent of all young adults, ages eighteen to thirty- four, either were currently living with their parents or had moved back in temporarily in the past. The reasons for adult children returning to live at home are usually financial: adult children may be between jobs, between marriages, or without other viable means of self-support.

If America operated as a "true" merit system, people would advance solely on the basis of merit and fail when they lacked merit. In many cases, however, family resources prevent, or at least reduce, "skidding" among adult children. One of the authors of this book recalls that when he left home as an adult, his parents took him aside and told him that no matter how bad things became for him out there in the world, they would send him money to come home. This was his insurance against destitution. Fortunately, he did not take his parents up on their offer, but neither has he forgotten it. Without always being articulated, the point is that this informal familial insurance against downward mobility is available, in varying degrees, to all except the poorest of the poor, who simply have no resources to provide.

Live Long and Prosper

From womb to tomb, the more affluent one is, the less the risk of injury, illness, and death (Budrys 2010; Cockerham 2012; National Center for Health Statistics 2011; Weitz 2013). Among the many nonmerit advantages inherited by those from privileged backgrounds is higher life expectancy at birth and a greater chance of better health throughout life. For instance, research has found that individuals in the top decile of income have a life expectancy that is about seven years longer than individuals in the bottom decile (Peltzman 2009). There are several reasons for the strong and persistent relationship between socioeconomic status and health. Beginning with fetal development and extending through childhood, increasing evidence points to the impact of early childhood on adult health. Prenatal deprivations, more common among the poor, for instance, are associated with later life conditions such as retardation, coronary heart disease, stroke, diabetes, and hypertension. Poverty in early childhood is also associated with increased risk of adult diseases. This may be due in part to higher stress levels among the poor and less control over that stress. Cumulative wear and tear on the body over time occurs under conditions of repeated high stress. Another reason for the health-wealth connection is that the rich have greater access to quality health care. Even with the recent passage of the Patient Protection and Affordable Health Care Act in 2010 (more commonly referred to as Obamacare), access to quality health care in America is still largely for sale to the highest bidder. Under these conditions, prevention and intervention are more widely available to the more affluent. Finally, not only does lack of income lead to poor health, but poor health leads to reduced earnings. That is, if someone is sick or injured, he or she may not be able to work or may have limited earning power.

Overall, the less affluent are at a health disadvantage due to higher exposure to a variety of unhealthy living conditions. The less affluent, for instance, are also likely to have nutritional deprivations and, ironically, are also more likely to be obese. Obesity is related to poor nutrition linked to diets that are high in low-cost sugar and carbohydrates and low in high-cost fruits, vegetables, and other sources of protein. The less affluent are also more likely to be exposed to physical risks associated with crowding, poor sanitation, and living in closer proximity to chemical and biological sources of pollution (Brulle and Pellow 2006).

Part of the exposure to health hazards is occupational. According to the U.S. Department of Labor (2012), those in the following occupations (listed in order of decreasing risk) have the greatest likelihood of being killed on the job: fishers, timber cutters, airplane pilots, sanitation workers, roofers, structural metal workers, farmers and ranchers, truck and delivery drivers, electrical power-line workers, and taxicab drivers. With the exception of airline pilot, all the jobs listed are working-class jobs. Since a person's occupation is strongly affected by family background, the prospects for generally higher occupational health risks are in this sense at least indirectly inherited. Finally, although homicides constitute only a small proportion of all causes of death, it is worth noting that the less affluent are at higher risk for being victims of violent crime, including homicide.

Some additional risk factors are related to individual behaviors, especially smoking, drinking, and drug abuse—all of which are more common among the less affluent (Budrys 2010). Evidence suggests that these behaviors, while contributing to poorer health among the less affluent, are responsible for only about one-third of the "wealth-health gradient" (Smith 1999, 157). These behaviors are also associated with higher psychological as well as physical stress. Indeed, the less affluent are not just at greater risk for physical ailments; research has shown that the less affluent experience higher levels of stress and are at significantly higher risk for mental illness as well (Cockerham 2011; Weitz 2013). Despite the adage that "money can't buy happiness," social science research has consistently shown that happiness and subjective well-being tend to be related to the amount of income and wealth people possess (Frey and Stutzer 2002; Layard 2005; Schnittker 2008; Wilkinson and Pickett 2009). This research shows that people living in wealthier (and more democratic) countries tend to be happier and that rates of happiness are sensitive to overall rates of unemployment and inflation. In general, poor people are less happy than others, although increments that exceed average amounts of income are negligibly related to levels of happiness. That is, beyond relatively low thresholds, additional increments of income and wealth are not likely to result in additional increments of happiness. Although money may not *guarantee* a long, happy, and healthy life, a fair assessment is that it aids and abets it.

You Can't Take It with You

Whatever assets one has accumulated in life that remain at death represent a bulk estate. "Inheritance" is usually thought to refer to bequests of such estates. Because wealth itself is highly skewed, so are bequests from estates. Beyond personal belongings and items of perhaps sentimental value, most Americans at death have little or nothing to bequeath. There is no central accounting of small estates, so reliable estimates on the total number and size of estates bequeathed are difficult to come by. Prior to the current baby boom generation, only about 20 percent of all households reported having received a bequest (Joulfaian and Wilhelm 1994; Ng-Baumhackl, Gist, and Figueiredo 2003). As a likely result of the combination of post–World War II growth and prosperity and the frugality of the "Greatest Generation" who came of age during this period, new estimates suggest that as many as two-thirds of baby boomers will eventually receive some inheritance (MetLife Mature Market Institute 2010). However, as wealth is highly skewed, so too are estates. Among the two-thirds of baby boomers who expect to receive at least some inheritance, households in the top wealth decile anticipate an average inheritance of $1.1 million compared to an average of $9,000 for households in the bottom wealth decile (MetLife Mature Market Institute 2010). And, as we have seen, even among the top wealth decile, wealth is highly skewed so that "average" is likely highly skewed to a relatively small portion of very wealthy family fortunes receiving much larger sums. In short, although few are likely to inherit great sums, bequests from estates are nevertheless a major mechanism for the transfer of wealth and privilege across generations (McNamee and Miller 1989, 1998; Miller, Rosenfeld, and McNamee 2003).

Some may argue that those who receive inheritances often deplete them in short order through spending sprees or unwise investments and that the playing field levels naturally through merit or lack of it. Although this may occur in isolated cases, it is not the general pattern—at least among the superwealthy. Although taking risks may be an appropriate strategy for acquiring wealth, it is not a common one for maintaining wealth. Once secured, the common strategy for protecting wealth is to play it safe—to diversify holdings and make safe investments. The superwealthy often have teams of accountants, brokers, financial planners, and lawyers to "manage" portfolios for precisely this purpose. One of the common ways to prevent the quick spending down of inheritances is for benefactors to set up "bleeding trusts" or "spendthrift trusts," which provide interest income to beneficiaries without digging into the principal fund. Despite such efforts to protect wealth, estates may, in some families, be gradually diminished over generations through subdivision among descendants. The rate at which this occurs, however, is likely to be slow, especially given the combination among the wealthy of low birthrates and high rates of marriage within the same class.

Even in the event of reckless spending, poor financial management, or subdivision among multiple heirs, the fact remains that those who inherit wealth benefit from it and benefit from opportunities that such wealth provides, for as long as it lasts, regardless of how personally meritorious they may or may not be.

WHAT IS IT LIKE TO BE RICH?

In his 1926 short story "The Rich Boy," F. Scott Fitzgerald wrote, "Let me tell you about the very rich. They are different from you and me." By the very rich, we mean the 1 percent or so of Americans who own nearly 40 percent of all the net worth in America. Most of the very rich either inherited their wealth outright or converted modest wealth and privilege into larger fortunes. How different are they? By the sheer volume and type of capital owned, this group is set apart from other Americans. This group is further distinguished by common lifestyles, shared relationships, and a privileged position in society that produce a consciousness of kind (Domhoff 2009). In short, they are a class set apart in both economic and social terms. Using surveys and simulations, sociologist Lisa Keister (2000) created a demographic profile of the wealthiest 1 percent of Americans. Compared to all households, the wealthiest 1 percent are much more likely to be white (96 percent for the top 1 percent compared to 82 percent for the general population), between forty-five and seventy-four years of age (73 percent for the top 1 percent compared to 41 percent for all households), and college educated (68 percent for the top 1 percent compared to 22 percent for all households). As one might expect, the upper class is about equally divided between men and women, but men have historically played a more dominant role within the upper class (Chang 2010). Besides being almost exclusively white, the inner circle of the upper class has historically been predominantly Protestant and of Anglo-Saxon heritage. The acronym *WASP* (for white Anglo-Saxon Protestant) was first coined by sociologist E. Digby Baltzell, himself a member of the upper class, to describe its social composition. Although the upper class is gradually becoming less exclusively WASP (Zweigenhaft and Domhoff 2006), there is still a strong association of upper-class status with WASP background. Beyond these demographic characteristics, how else are the rich different from most other Americans?

Exclusivity

An important defining characteristic of the upper class is that it is exclusive. Wealth in America is highly concentrated. Money alone, however, does not grant full admission into the highest of elite circles. Full acceptance requires the cultural capital and cachet that only "old money" brings. And "old money" means inherited money. The exclusiveness of old money is exemplified by the *Social Register*, a list of prominent upper-class families first compiled in 1887. The list has been used by members of the upper class both to recognize distinction and as a guide for issuing invitations to upper-class social events. For years separate volumes of the *Social Register* were published in different cities throughout the United States. But since the Malcolm Forbes family took over the publication in 1976, the *Social Register* has been consolidated into one national book. To be listed, a potential member must have five letters of nomination submitted by those already on the list and not be "blackballed" by any current members. There is great continuity across generations among the names included in these volumes. One study (Broad 1996), for instance, shows that of the eighty-seven prominent founders of family fortunes listed in the 1940 *Social Register*, 92 percent had descendants listed in the 1977 volume. The percentage of descendants of these prominent families included in the 1995 volume, fifty-five years later, dipped only slightly to 87 percent. Highlighting connections to the past, almost half of those listed in 1995 attached Roman numerals to their surnames, such as II, III, IV, V, VI, and so on. Another common practice among upper-class families is to use maternal surnames as first names or middle names. The use of these "recombinant" names highlights connections to prominent families on both sides as well as patterns of intraclass marriage. Almost 50 percent of those listed in 1995 had such recombinant names. Most social clubs of the upper class also show connections to the past—if only because they have been in existence for a long time and their membership shows intergenerational continuity (Kendall 2008; Sherwood 2010).

It is not mere coincidence that the upper class has great reverence for the past. In a highly meritocratic culture, it is an ongoing challenge for those who inherit great wealth to justify their claim to it. The past, therefore, is a source of the justification of wealth for the upper class and a claim to status.

The children of the wealthy in America are not immune to the ideology of meritocracy that pervades the culture as a whole. Justification of the inheritance of wealth is a prevalent theme among those who were born into wealth (Aldrich 1988; Forbes 2010; Schervish, Coutsoukis, and Lewis 1994). As one inheritor of an oil fortune put it, "The feelings of guilt put me through much agony. For a long, long, long time, it gave me low self-esteem: who am I to deserve all of this good fortune?" (Schervish, Coutsoukis, and Lewis 1994, 118). Unlike the children of European aristocrats who felt entitled to privilege as a matter of birthright, American children of great wealth are victims of an ideology that, through no fault of their own, essentially invalidates them.

Isolation

In addition to exclusivity, the upper class in America is relatively anonymous and hidden from the public view. A second defining characteristic of the upper class in America is that it is isolated. The upper class is separated from the mainstream of society in a world of privacy: remote private residences, private schools, private clubs, private parties, and private resorts. With the exception of service staff, throughout their lives, upper-class individuals interact mostly with people like themselves. The geography of the upper class shows a distinct pattern of isolation, intentionally maintained and reinforced through land-use strategies that include incorporation, zoning, and restrictive land covenants (Higley 1995). Houses and mansions are tucked away in exclusive communities. Individual residences within these communities, often with long and meandering driveways, are typically set back from the public roads that connect them with the larger world. Once approached, the residences are fortresses of security, complete with bridges, fences, gates, guard dogs, and sophisticated electronic surveillance. Children raised within these confines are isolated as well, separated from the outside world by a series of private nannies, private tutors, private preparatory boarding schools, and private elite Ivy League colleges. Even travel within the upper class is often isolated—in private planes and limos and on private yachts. And even when resorting to more commercial forms of transportation, there is always the more isolated and pampered option of traveling "first class."

The upper-class tendency to isolate itself geographically from the rest of society has been emulated by the upper middle classes. The overall trend is toward greater socioeconomic residential segregation in American society as a whole (Massey, Rothwell, and Domina 2009). The creation of white-flight suburbs in the post–World War II era began a trend that has now extended to the rising popularity of "gated" communities (Blakely and Snyder 1997). Once restricted to the superwealthy and some retirement villages, gated communities are now for the merely privileged.

One reason for this self-imposed isolation is security. Those who have more have more to lose. Keeping potential criminals out, however, also has the effect of keeping the rich in. In addition to concerns about property theft or vandalism, the superwealthy are also concerned about the potential for kidnapping, which is a real concern for those of great wealth who might be targeted for ransom.

Class Endogamy

One aspect of this self-segregation is the strong tendency toward upper-class endogamy, or marriage within one's own social class (Cherlin 2009; Elmelech 2008, 55–57; Van Leeuwen, Mass, and Miles 2006; Carlson and England 2011). Despite the romantic ideal that "love is blind" and that love is mostly a random process in which anyone can fall in love at any place at any time (as portrayed in countless songs, novels, and movies), the social reality is that mate selection is a very structured process in which people tend to marry people who replicate their own social profile at rates far in excess of random chance alone. That is, people tend to marry people of similar age, education, race, religion, and social-class background. There are three primary possible reasons for this nonrandom convergence (Kalmijn 1998): (1) everything else being equal, people may prefer to marry people like themselves; (2) third parties (e.g., friends, family, and sometimes institutions such as religious groups or the state) may encourage or even require such convergence; and (3) apart from intentional personal preference or outside pressure, people may tend to marry people from within their own social milieu or social circles of acquaintances, which in turn would substantially increase the probability of marrying someone like themselves. Although in the modern era, third-party influence has been greatly reduced (although not eliminated), continued or even increased patterns of social segregation increase the probability of marital demographic convergence (homogamy) far beyond random chance alone. Kalmijn and Flap (2001) have identified five potential "meeting settings" that highly structure the prospects of marriage: work, school, residence, common family networks, and voluntary associations (such as religious, political, and other cultural organizations that individuals voluntarily belong to). In a preliminary study conducted in the Netherlands, Kalmijn and Flap (2001) found, for instance, that 42 percent of married couples had met in one of these five institutional settings. Of these settings, the one in which couples were most likely to have initially met was educational settings. Moreover, the higher the level of education achieved, the more likely couples would have met in those settings.

These findings are consistent with other research conducted in the United States that show high rates of educational endogamy, especially at very high and very low levels of educational attainment (Rosenfeld 2008; Schwartz and Mare 2005). To the extent that educational endogamy occurs and to the extent that access to education is class based (see chapter 5), the likelihood of class endogamy also increases. Class endogamy through education can occur in two ways. One way is that those of the same social-class background (class of origin) are more likely to go to the same kinds of schools and have the same levels of educational attainment. A second way is that those who are from lower social-class origins who are upwardly mobile are more likely to end up in educational and work settings that increase the prospect of marrying someone from a higher social class of origin compared to those who are not upwardly mobile. Historically, the prospect for upward mobility through marriage has been greater for women than men. In what might be referred to as the "Cinderella effect," early research seemed to show that women could sometimes trade attractiveness in a marriage market for access to higher-status men (Elder 1969). This presumed tradeoff, however, risks social derision, for instance, in situations in which substantially younger "trophy" wives marry especially high-profile wealthy or successful older men. Americans do not approve of "marrying for money" as a means of upward social mobility—although if one happens to fall in love with a rich person, so much the better. How extensive an intentional marrying-for-money strategy of upward mobility exists or how successful it might be are unknown, but such strategies would not in any event meet with social approval and would not generally be considered a legitimate part of the American Dream.

With greater gender equality and greater female participation in the labor force, it is likely that this avenue for upward mobility for females has declined. Evidence suggests, for instance, that as women's labor force participation has increased, men are likely to be competing for high-earning, highly educated women as women have traditionally competed for high-earning men (Schwartz and Mare 2005).

Given the high level of social isolation of the upper class, upper-class endogamy is likely to be especially high. Traditional upper-class social institutions such as the debutante ball, at which young upper-class women are first "presented" to "society," certainly increase these probabilities. As sociologist Digby Baltzell put it, "The debutante ritual is a *rite de passage* which functions to introduce the post-adolescent into the upper-class adult world, and to insure upper-class endogamy as a normative pattern of behavior, in order to keep important functional class positions within the upper class" (1992, 60). Other upper-class institutions include elite boarding prep schools, elite social clubs, and elite summer resorts, all of which provide settings and organized activities that bring upper-class young adults together. Combining upper-class and upper-middle-class familial assets through marriage and then transferring those assets to children born into these families further solidifies nonmerit economic advantage across generations.

Poor and working-class families on the other hand are much less likely to be married in the first place, much more likely to have children outside of marriage, and more likely to experience familial disruption through divorce—all of which have adverse economic consequences (Carlson and England 2011). Moreover all of these trends have accelerated in the past several decades. Some have argued that the increase in familial instability especially among the poor and working class is related to moral breakdown, which then is seen as itself a cause of economic instability (Murray 2012). Others (Cherlin 2009; Wilson 1987), however, point to the opposite direction of influence, that is, how economic instability creates familial instability. Research, for instance, indicates that even among poor and working-class populations in which marriage rates are low and out-of-wedlock births are high, marriage is still highly valued and preferred (Edin and Kefalas 2005; Cherlin, Cross-Barnet, Burton, and Garrett-Peters 2008). However, the recent reduction of manufacturing and construction jobs (see chapter 6) has increased economic instability among the poor and working class and has resulted in a shortage of what sociologist William Julius Wilson calls "marriageable men" with secure enough economic prospects who are not otherwise unemployed, underemployed, or incarcerated. These trends not only reduce the prospects for initial marriage but also contribute to circumstances in which existing marriages are less likely to survive.

Distinctive Lifestyle

In the late nineteenth century, America entered the Gilded Age, so named for its opulent and even ostentatious displays of great wealth. During the Gilded Age the rich competed with one another to flaunt their wealth. During this time, some of the great mansions were built, including George Vanderbilt's Biltmore Estate in Asheville, North Carolina, a 175,000-square-foot, 250-room, Renaissance-style chateau completed in 1895 and still the largest private house ever built in America (Frank 1999, 14). In some ways, America's wealthy of this period were insecure about their status and were envious of the more established European aristocracy. As a result, the newfound industrial wealth in the United States patterned itself after everything old and European. With the Great Depression, such displays were no longer considered in good taste. In subsequent decades, more subdued forms of luxury were preferred. Nevertheless, a lifestyle organized around formal parties, exclusive resorts and clubs, and such upper-class leisure activities as golf, tennis, horseback riding, and yachting persisted. Some segments of the upper class indulge themselves in support of the arts—theater, opera, orchestra, and other highbrow forms of cultural consumption. Some observers of upper-class life have noted a surge in luxury spending on cars, boats, and homes as well as for such items as premium wines, fancy home appliances, and even cosmetic surgery (Frank 1999, 14–32; 2007; Brooks 2000; Taylor 1989). It should be noted, however, that the rich are not all alike in their consumption behavior. One of the advantages of being rich is that you can choose to display wealth ostentatiously or crassly or not at all. Sam Walton, for example, founder of the Walmart empire, was known to ride around in his hometown of Bentonville, Arkansas, in a beat-up Ford pickup. For the most part, however, the consumption patterns of the wealthy set them apart as a distinct social class.

Political Power

In a substantial sense, the upper class in America is also a ruling class. Despite the ideology of democracy in which everyone has an equal say in deciding what happens, the reality is that those who have the most economic resources wield the most power. In *Gospels of Wealth: How the Rich Portray Their Lives*, sociologists Paul Schervish, Platon Coutsoukis, and Ethan Lewis describe the power of the wealthy to make things happen (and other things not happen) as "hyperagency."

To the extent that it is possible to convert wealth into political power, the upper class can exert influence on political outcomes far beyond their numbers alone. The specific mechanisms by which this influence is exerted have been well documented (Domhoff 2009; Gilens 2012; Hacker and Pierson 2010; Phillips 2003). Beyond direct forms of influence such as substantial campaign contributions and holding government positions, economic elites exert indirect, but no less important, forms of influence through the corporate community, a policy planning network comprising foundations, think tanks and lobbies, and the media—all of which are dominated by propertied interests. For all of the key measures of political power as identified by Domhoff (2009)—who decides policy, who wins in disputes, and who benefits from political outcomes—the interests of the wealthy usually prevail.

It should be pointed out, however, that the upper class is not a political monolith. That is, as with all groups, there are always internal differences of opinion. On the estate tax issue, for instance, several very prominent members of the upper class—including Bill Gates and Warren Buffett—have been outspoken critics of proposals to abolish estate taxes. Both maintain that it is entirely appropriate for the government to heavily tax recipients of large estates as a form of unearned income, and both plan to give the bulk of their accumulated fortunes to charitable causes rather than bequeath them to heirs. Similarly, there are other members of the upper class who advocate for more equitable distribution of societal resources, including a recently formed group known as Patriotic Millionaires for Fiscal Strength consisting of 250 millionaires who in 2010 petitioned Congress and President Obama to establish a more genuinely progressive tax system (Collins 2012, 82).

The power of the upper class, while considerable, falls short of complete control. Labor unions and numerous interest groups, including civil rights groups, consumer groups, and others, chip away at the edges of the system of privilege on behalf of their constituencies. But in the final analysis, although these groups and the general public as a whole win some of the battles, propertied interests continue to win the class wars. As financier Warren Buffett noted in response to those who question the fairness of the system as "class warfare," "There's class warfare, all right, but it's my class, the rich class, that's making war, and we're winning" (*New York Times* 2006).

SUMMARY

The United States has high levels of both income inequality and wealth inequality. In terms of the distribution of income and wealth, America is clearly not a middle-class society. Income and especially wealth are not evenly distributed, with a relatively small number of well-off families at one end and a small number of poor families much worse off at the other. Instead, the overall picture is one in which the bulk of the available wealth is concentrated in a narrow range at the very top of the system. In short, the distribution of economic resources in society is not symmetrical and certainly not bell shaped: the poor who have the least greatly outnumber the rich who have the most. Moreover, in recent decades, by all measures, the rich are getting richer, and the gap between the very rich and everyone else has appreciably increased.

The greater the amount of economic inequality in society, the more difficult it is to move up within the system on the basis of individual merit alone. Indeed, the most important factor in terms of where people will end up in the economic pecking order of society is where they started in the first place. Economic inequality has tremendous inertial force across generations. Instead of a race to get ahead that begins anew with each generation, the race is in reality a relay race in which children inherit different starting points from parents. Inheritance, broadly defined as one's initial starting point in life based on parental position, includes a set of cumulative nonmerit advantages for all except the poorest of the poor. These include enhanced childhood standards of living, differential access to cultural capital, differential access to social networks of power and influence, infusion of parental capital while parents are still alive, greater health and life expectancy, and the inheritance of bulk estates when parents die.

At the top of the system are members of America's ownership class— roughly the 1 percent of the American population who own about one-third of all the available net worth. The upper class is set apart from other Americans not only by the amount and source of the wealth it holds but by an exclusive, distinctive, and self-perpetuating way of life that reduces opportunities for merit-based mobility into it.

REFERENCES

Aldrich, Nelson W., Jr. 1988. *Old Money: The Mythology of America's Upper Class*. New York: Knopf.

Baltzell, E. Digby. 1992. *The Philadelphia Gentlemen: The Making of a National Upper Class*. New Brunswick, NJ: Transaction.

Blakely, Edward J., and Mary Gail Snyder. 1997. *Fortress America: Gated Communities in the United States*. Washington, DC: Brookings Institute Press.

Broad, David. 1996. "The Social Register: Directory of America's Upper Class." *Sociological Spectrum* 16:173–81.

Brooks, David. 2000. *Bobos in Paradise: The New Upper Class and How They Got There*. New York: Simon & Schuster.

Brulle, Robert J., and David N. Pellow. 2006. "Environmental Justice: Human Health and Environmental Inequalities." *Annual Review of Public Health* 27:102–24.

Budrys, Grace. 2010. *Unequal Health: How Inequality Contributes to Health or Illness*. 2nd ed. Lanham, MD: Rowman & Littlefield.

Canterbery, E. Ray, and Joe Nosari. 1985. "The Forbes Four Hundred: The Determinants of Super-Wealth." *Southern Economic Journal* 51:1073–83.

Carlson, Marcia J., and Paula England, eds. 2011. *Social Class and Changing Families in an Unequal America*. Stanford, CA: Stanford University Press.

Chang, Mariko Lin. 2010. *Shortchanged: Why Women Have Less Wealth and What Can Be Done about It*. New York: Oxford University Press.

Cherlin, Andrew J. 2009. *The Marriage-Go-Round: The State of Marriage and the Family in America Today*. New York: Vintage.

Cherlin, Andrew, Caitlin Cross-Barnet, Linda M. Burton, and Raymond Garrett-Peters. 2008. "Promises They Can Keep: Low-Income Women's Attitudes toward Motherhood, Marriage, and Divorce." *Journal of Marriage and Family* 70, no. 4: 919–33.

Charles, Kerwin Kofi, and Erik Hurst. 2003. "The Correlation of Wealth across Generations." *Journal of Political Economy* 111, no. 6: 1155–82.

Cockerham, William. 2011. *Sociology of Mental Disorder*. 8th ed. Upper Saddle River, NJ: Prentice Hall.

———. 2012. *Medical Sociology*. 12th ed. Upper Saddle River, NJ: Prentice Hall.

Collins, Chuck. 2012. *99 to 1: How Wealth Inequality Is Wrecking the World and What We Can Do about It*. San Francisco: Berrett-Koebler Publishers.

Congressional Budget Office. 2012. "The Distribution of Household Income and Federal Taxes, 2008 and 2009." http://www.cbo.gov/sites/default/files/cbofiles/attachments/43373-06-11-HouseholdIncomeandFedTaxes.pdf (accessed September 1, 2012).

Domhoff, G. William. 2009. *Who Rules America? Challenges to Corporate and Class Dominance*. New York: McGraw-Hill.

Duncan, Greg J., and Richard J. Murnane, eds. 2011. "Introduction: The American Dream, Then and Now." In *Whither Opportunity? Rising Inequality, Schools, and Children's Life Chances*, 3–23. New York: Sage.

Edin, Kathryn, and Maria Kefalas. 2005. *Promises I Can Keep: Why Poor Women Put Motherhood before Marriage*. Los Angeles: University of California Press.

Elder, Glen H., Jr. 1969. "Appearance and Education in Marriage Mobility." *American Sociological Review* 34, no. 4: 519–33.

Elmelech, Yuval. 2008. *Transmitting Inequality: Wealth and the American Family*. Lanham, MD: Rowman & Littlefield.

Ermisch, John, Markus Jantti, and Timothy Smeeding. 2012. *From Parents to Children: The Intergenerational Transmission of Advantage*. New York: Sage.

Forbes, John Hazard. 2010. *Old Money America: Aristocracy in the Age of Obama*. New York: iUniverse.

Frank, Robert H. 1999. *Luxury Fever: Why Money Fails to Satisfy in an Era of Excess*. New York: Free Press.

———. 2007. *Richistan: A Journey through the American Wealth Boom and the Lives of the New Rich*. New York: Crown.

Freeland, Chrystia. 2012. *Plutocrats: The Rise of the New Global Super-Rich and the Fall of Everyone Else*. New York: Penguin.

Frey, Bruno S., and Alois Stutzer. 2002. *Happiness and Economics: How the Economy and Institutions Affect Well-Being*. Princeton, NJ: Princeton University Press.

Galbraith, John Kenneth. 1958. *The Affluent Society*. New York: Mentor Press.

Gilens, Martin. 2012. *Affluence and Influence: Economic Inequality and Political Power in America*. Princeton, NJ: Princeton University Press.

Grusky, David B., and Tmar Kricheli-Katz, eds. 2012. *The New Gilded Age: The Critical Inequality Debates of Our Time*. Stanford, CA: Stanford University Press.

Hacker, Jacob S., and Paul Pierson. 2010. *Winner-Take-All Politics: How Washington Made the Rich Richer—and Turned Its Back on the Middle Class*. New York: Simon & Schuster.

Havens, John J., and Paul G. Schervish. 2003. "Why the $41 Trillion Wealth Transfer Estimate Is Still Valid: A Review of Challenges and Comments." *Journal of Gift Planning* 7, no. 1: 11–15, 47–50.

Higley, Stephen R. 1995. *Privilege, Power and Place: The Geography of the American Upper Class*. Lanham, MD: Rowman & Littlefield.

Joulfaian, D., and M. O. Wilhelm. 1994. "Inheritance and Labor Supply." *Journal of Human Resources* 29: 1205–34.

Kalleberg, Arene. 2011. *Good Jobs, Bad Jobs: The Rise of Polarized and Precarious Employment Systems in the United States, 1970s to 2000s*. New York: Sage.

Kalmijn, Matthijs. 1998. "Intermarriage and Homogamy: Causes, Patterns, Trends." *American Review of Sociology* 24:395–41.

Kalmijn, Matthijs, and Henk Flap. 2001. "Assortative Meeting and Mating: Unintended Consequences of Organized Settings for Partner Choices." *Social Forces* 79:1289–1312.

Keister, Lisa A. 2000. *Wealth in America: Trends in Wealth Inequality*. Cambridge: Cambridge University Press.

Kendall, Diana. 2008. *Members Only: Elite Clubs and the Process of Exclusion*. Lanham, MD: Rowman & Littlefield.

Kerbo, Harold R. 2006. *World Poverty: Global Inequality and the Modern World System*. Boston: McGraw-Hill.

Lareau, Annette. 2011. *Unequal Childhoods: Class, Race, and Family Life*. 2nd ed. Berkeley: University of California Press.

Layad, Richard. 2005. *Happiness: Lessons from a New Science*. London: Allen Lane.

Levine, Linda. 2012a. *An Analysis of the Distribution of Wealth across Households, 1989–2010*. Congressional Research Service, July 17, 2012. http://www.fas.org/sgp/crs/misc/RL33433.pdf (accessed September 1, 2012).

———. 2012b. *The U.S. Income Distribution and Mobility: Trends and International Comparisons*. Congressional Research Service, March 7, 2012. http://www.fas.org/sgp/crs/misc/R42400.pdf (accessed September 1, 2012).

Massey, Douglas S., Jonathan Rothwell, and Thurston Domina. 2009. "The Changing Bases of Segregation in the United States." *Annals, American Academy of Political and Social Science* 626:74–90.

McNamee, Stephen J., and Robert K. Miller Jr. 1989. "Estate Inheritance: A Sociological Lacuna." *Sociological Inquiry* 38:7–29.

———. 1998. "Inheritance and Stratification." In *Inheritance and Wealth in America*, ed. Robert K. Miller Jr. and Stephen J. McNamee, 193–213. New York: Plenum Press.

MetLife Mature Market Institute. 2010. *Inheritance and Wealth Transfer to Baby Boomers*. Westport, CT: Mature Market Institute.

Miller, Robert K., Jr., Jeffrey Rosenfeld, and Stephen J. McNamee. 2003. "The Disposition of Property: Transfers between the Living and the Dead." In *Handbook of Death and Dying*, ed. Clifton D. Bryant, 917–25. Thousand Oaks, CA: Sage.

Mishel, Lawrence, Josh Bivens, Elise Gould, and Heidi Shierholz. 2012. *The State of Working America*. 12th ed. Ithaca, NY: Cornell University Press.

Mishel, Lawrence, and Natalie Sabadish. 2012. "CEO Pay and the Top 1%: How Executive Compensation and Financial-Sector Pay Have Fueled Income Inequality." Inequality and Poverty, Economic Policy Institute. http://www.epi.org/publication/ib331-ceo-pay-top-1-percent (accessed January 8, 2013).

Moynihan, Daniel Patrick, Timothy M. Smeeding, and Lee Rainwater. 2004. *The Future of the Family*. New York: Sage.

Murray, Charles. 2012. *Coming Apart: The State of White America, 1960–2010*. New York: Crown Forum.

National Center for Health Statistics. 2011. *Health, United States, 2011 in Brief*. Hyattsville, MD: National Center for Health Statistics, U.S. Department of Health and Human Services.

New York Times. 2006. As quoted in an interview reported in "In Class Warfare, Guess Which Class Is Winning," by Ben Stein, November 26, 2006. http://www.nytimes.com/2006/11/26/business/yourmoney/26every.html (accessed August 30, 2012).

Ng-Baumhackl, Mitj, John Gist, and Carlos Figueiredo. 2003. "Pennies from Heaven: Will Inheritances Bail Out the Boomers?" Washington, DC: American Association of Retired Persons Public Policy Institute.

Norton, Michael I., and Dan Ariely. 2011. "Building a Better America: One Wealth Quintile at a Time." *Perspectives on Psychological Science* 6, no. 9: 9–12.

Oliver, Melvin L., and Thomas M. Shapiro. 2006. *Black Wealth/White Wealth: A New Perspective on Racial Inequality*. 10th anniversary ed. New York: Routledge.

Parker, Kim. 2012. "The Boomerang Generation Feeling OK about Living with Mom and Dad." Pew Research Center. http://www.pewsocialtrends.org/2012/03/15/the-boomerang-generation (accessed September 1, 2012).

Peltzman, S. 2009. "Mortality Inequality" *Journal of Economic Perspectives* 23, no 4: 175–90.

Pew Economic Mobility Project. 2011. "Does America Promote Mobility as Well as Other Nations?" Pew Charitable Trusts. http://www.pewstates.org/research/reports/does-america-promote-mobility-as-well-as-other-nations-85899380321 (accessed January 14, 2013).

Phillips, Kevin. 2003. *Wealth and Democracy: A Political History of the American Rich*. New York: Random House.

Rosenfeld, Jeffrey P. 1980. *Legacy of Aging: Inheritance and Disinheritance in Social Perspective*. Norwood, NJ: ABLEX.

Rosenfeld, Michael J. 2008. "Racial, Educational and Religious Endogamy in the United States: A Comparative Historical Perspective." *Social Forces* 87, no. 1: 1–31.

Salverda, Weimer, Brian Nolan, and Timothy M. Smeeding, eds. 2009. *Oxford Handbook of Economic Inequality*. Oxford: Oxford University Press.

Sauls, Adam. 2012. *A Longitudinal Study of American Economic Elites*. Unpublished MA thesis, University of North Carolina Wilmington.

Schervish, Paul G., Platon E. Coutsoukis, and Ethan Lewis. 1994. *Gospels of Wealth: How the Rich Portray Their Lives*. Westport, CT: Praeger.

Schnittker, Jason. 2008. "Diagnosing Our National Disease: Trends in Income and Happiness, 1973 to 2004." *Social Psychology Quarterly* 71, no. 3: 257–80.

Schwartz, Christine, and Robert D. Mare. 2005. "Trends in Educational Assortative Marriage from 1940 to 2003." *Demography* 42, no. 4: 621–46.

Schwartz, T. P. 1996. "Durkheim's Prediction about the Declining Importance of the Family and Inheritance: Evidence from the Wills of Providence, 1775–1985." *Sociological Quarterly* 26: 503–19.

Sherwood, Jessica Holden. 2010. *Wealth, Whiteness, and the Matrix of Privilege: The View from the Country Club*. Lanham, MD: Rowman & Littlefield.

Sieber, Sam D. 2005. *Second-Rate Nation: From the American Dream to the American Myth*. Boulder, CO: Paradigm.

Smeeding, Timothy, Robert Erikson, and Markus Jantti, eds. 2011. *Persistence, Privilege and Parenting: The Comparative of Intergenerational Mobility*. New York: Sage.

Smith, James P. 1999. "Healthy Bodies and Thick Wallets: The Dual Relation between Health and Economic Status." *Journal of Economic Perspectives* 13: 145–66.

Stiglitz, Joseph E. 2012. *The Price of Inequality: How Today's Divided Society Endangers Our Future*. New York: Norton.

Taylor, John. 1989. *Circus of Ambition: The Culture of Wealth and Power in the Eighties*. New York: Warner Books.

Thurow, Lester C. 1999. *Building Wealth: The New Rules for Individuals, Companies and Nations in a Knowledge-Based Economy*. New York: HarperCollins.

United for a Fair Economy. 2012. *Born on Third Base: What the Forbes 400 Really Says about Economic Equality and Opportunity in America*. Boston, MA. http://faireconomy.org/sites/default/files/BornOnThirdBase_2012.pdf (accessed January 24, 2013).

U.S. Department of Labor. 2012. "National Census of Fatal Occupational Injuries in 2011 (Preliminary Results)." Bureau of Labor Statistics. http://www.bls.gov/news.release/pdf/cfoi.pdf (accessed January 14, 2013).

Van Leeuwen, Marco, Ineke Mass, and Andrew Miles, eds. 2006. *Marriage Choices and Class Boundaries: Social Endogamy in History*. International Review of Social History Supplement 13. Cambridge, UK: University of Cambridge.

Weitz, Rose. 2013. *The Sociology of Health, Illness, and Health Care: A Critical Approach*. Boston: Wadsworth.

Wilkinson, Richard, and Kate Pickett. 2009. *The Spirit Level: Why Greater Equality Makes Societies Stronger*. New York: Bloomsbury Press.

Willenbacher, Barbara. 2003. "Individualism and Traditionalism in Inheritance Law in Germany, France, England, and the United States." *Journal of Family History* 28, no. 1: 208–25.

———. 2012. "The Asset Price Meltdown and the Wealth of the Middle Class." New York: New York University.

Wilson, William Julius. 1987. *The Truly Disadvantaged: The Inner City, the Underclass, and Public Policy*. Chicago: University of Chicago Press.

Wolff, Edward N. 2010. "Recent Trends in Household Wealth in the United States: Rising Debt and the Middle-Class Squeeze—an Update to 2007." Working paper no. 589, Levy Economics Institute of Bard College.

———. 2012. "The Asset Price Meltdown and the Wealth of the Middle Class." NBER Working paper no. 18559. The National Bureau of Economic Research.

Zissimopoulos, Julie M., and James P. Smith. 2011. "Unequal Giving: Monetary Gifts to Children across Countries and over Time." In *Persistence, Privilege and Parenting: The Comparative Study of Intergenerational Mobility*, ed. Timothy Smeeding, Robert Erikson, and Markus Jantti, 289–328. New York: Sage.

Zweigenhaft, Richard L., and G. William Domhoff. 2006. *Diversity in the Power Elite: How It Happened, Why It Matters*. New York: Rowman & Littlefield.

Chapter Four

It's Not What You Know But . . .

Social and Cultural Capital

It's not what you know but whom you know.
—Anonymous

We now turn our attention to two additional nonmerit factors, social capital and cultural capital. Social capital refers essentially to "who" you know, which is another type of nonmerit resource that individuals can exploit to advance their position in society. All individuals are embedded in networks of social relations; that is, everybody knows somebody. Social capital focuses attention on differential access to opportunities through social connections. Individual and family social connections mediate access to educational, occupational, and economic opportunity.

Cultural capital refers to knowledge of the norms, values, beliefs, and ways of life of the groups to which people belong. It is information, often esoteric, specialized, costly, and time consuming to accumulate, that, like social capital, mediates access to opportunity. It is a factor in social mobility because as people move into different segments of society, they need to acquire the cultural wherewithal to travel in different social circles. In essence, cultural capital is a set of cultural credentials that certify eligibility for membership in status-conferring social groups. To "fit in" and "look and know the part" is to possess cultural capital; to "stick out like a sore thumb" is to be without the cultural cachet necessary to blend in and be fully accepted into groups to which we belong or aspire to belong.

In this chapter we discuss these forms of capital and how they are related. We also examine the related phenomenon of social climbing, or deliberate attempts to enhance one's social standing by accumulating and conspicuously displaying particular forms of social or cultural capital.

SOCIAL CAPITAL: "WHO" YOU KNOW

Americans have a love/hate relationship with social capital. We love it when we can use it and it works for us, and we hate it when we have none or it works against us. If we "get a foot in the door" because we have a "contact" on the inside, we are grateful. Indeed, job-placement counselors encourage and coach job applicants to cultivate personal ties and to "network." If, however, we are bypassed for a job (or a promotion) for someone we perceive to be less qualified but who knows someone higher up in the food chain than we do, we feel victimized and are outraged.

Anyone who has ever filled out a job application knows that whom you know matters. Almost all job applications have a space for "references." References not only provide testimony to an applicant's character and ability, but they also signal a connection to the applicant. Apart from the merit of the candidate, applicants whose references are well known, prestigious, or powerful have an advantage over applicants whose references are none of those things. In some cases, an employer's interest in a job candidate may reflect the merit of the applicant's references rather than that of the candidate. Particularly in the professions, but also in other jobs, mentor-protégé relationships are critical—not just for training but when the time comes for job placement as well. Good mentors go to bat for their protégés and often risk their own stock of prestige and credibility to do so. Whom you know may become especially important when the quality of candidates is unknown or indistinguishable, which for neophytes just starting out with little or no track record is often the case.

The social science community is just beginning to catch up to the folk wisdom on this issue. One of the first systematic modern analyses of social capital was produced in the 1980s by the French sociologist Pierre Bourdieu (1986, 248). Bourdieu focuses attention on the benefits that accrue to individuals from their participation in groups and deliberate attempts by individuals to foster social relations for the purpose of creating this resource. Strategies that produce valuable social capital are not directly an indication or reflection of individual merit, especially in cases in which investments are made by others (e.g., parents, friends, or mentors). James S. Coleman (1988), an American sociologist, has also contributed much to the understanding of social capital and the examination of its effects. Coleman emphasizes the point that social capital is not a characteristic of people but is embedded in relations among people. The networks of these relations, in turn, have characteristics in and of themselves. These characteristics include the level of trust within the network, the extent of obligations and expectations of reciprocity among individuals within the network, the degree to which the network facilitates the exchange of information within it, and the type of sanctions used to enforce norms of sociability within the network. Since the source of social capital ultimately resides in groups and not individuals per se, individuals benefit not by "owning" social capital but by tapping into it. Thus, the social capital grapevine is available only in and through relationships and the groups in which these relationships occur.

One reason that social capital is dependent on the larger social context in which it occurs is that neither of its critical components, resources or access, is distributed evenly. For resources such as "insider information" to be converted into social capital, individuals must perceive that some specific resource is present within their social field and have some form of social relationship that provides access to that resource. Individuals can thus be said to have social capital when resources are present and accessible. Furthermore, it cannot simply be assumed that individuals utilize their social capital all the time or that they use it equally well or with equal effectiveness. With these qualifications in mind, a rapidly growing body of empirical research has confirmed what most people already suspect based on their own observations: connections matter. That is, social capital enhances the likelihood of a person's attaining educational, occupational, and entrepreneurial success.

The Strength of Weak Ties

A substantial body of research also confirms the direct effects of social capital on adult success (cf. Campbell and Rosenfeld 1985; Granovetter 1973; Lin 1999, 2000a, 2000b; Lin and Erickson 2008; Portes 1998; McDonald, Lin, and Ao 2009). Social capital affects access to job opportunities, mobility through occupational ladders, promotions, earnings, and entrepreneurial success. In analyzing the effects of social capital on adult success, sociologist Mark Granovetter (1973, 1983) documented the importance of what he referred to as the "strength of weak ties." In terms of having access to new sources of information, Granovetter showed that it is often better to have a larger number of casual acquaintances (weak ties) than to know just a few people very well (strong ties). Granovetter noted that maintaining close friendships (strong ties) requires time and energy. One cannot be "best friends" with a large number of people. The closer you are to a few people, the fewer people you can be close to. The disadvantage of such groups is that no one in the group is likely to know anyone else that the others within the group don't already know. Information flows within such groups, therefore, tend to be redundant. Unlike the strong ties that bind cliques of individuals who share mostly within-group information, weak ties are potential sources of new information because they bridge different cliques. In short, weak ties serve as an informal employment-referral system, placing people "in the loop" about jobs that come up and people who can help. Numerous follow-up studies (Granovetter 1983; Lin, Vaughn, and Ensel 1981; Lin, Ensel, and Vaughn 1981; Lin 1982; Lin and Dumin 1986; DeGraaf and Flap 1988; Lin and Erickson 2008; Kendall 2008) demonstrate that weak ties are "strong" in facilitating occupational attainment.

In short, whom you know matters. For example, in one early and now classic study of job placement, Granovetter (1974) showed that 56 percent of all job applicants found out about the job through a personal contact. An additional 19 percent of job applicants found out about the job through third-party contacts such as advertisements, employment agencies, university placement services, professional associations, or other formal means. Only 18 percent of the respondents in this study directly applied for a job without either a personal contact or third-party intervention. Many jobs are never advertised. Applicants may only know about an opening through an informal grapevine. Indeed, it is often the case, especially in the private sector, that only those jobs that are unattractive or difficult to fill are publicly advertised.

In a more recent study, Nancy DiTomaso (2013) conducted in-depth randomly selected interviews with 246 non-Hispanic whites between 25 and 55 years of age in New Jersey, Ohio, and Tennessee regarding their occupational histories. DiTomaso found that a substantial majority of her sample used some form of social capital (defined as a combination of information, influence, or access to opportunity) in securing jobs throughout their careers. The average proportion of jobs for which respondents received help from others throughout their careers was 68 percent, with about 60 percent getting help from others to secure their first job and between 70 and 80 percent getting help from others to secure subsequent jobs (DiTomaso, 2013, 73–74).

Importantly, DiTomaso found that people receiving these unearned advantages did not generally acknowledge or recognize these advantages as factors contributing to their occupational attainment:

> When asked about what had most contributed to what they had attained in their lives, the vast majority of the interviewees cited their own talent, hard work, and persistence. Hardly any interviewees pointed to the advantages that he or she had because of the ability to live in safe and resource-rich neighborhoods, attend high-quality schools, or be supported by an extensive private network of family and friends who could pass along information, use influence on their behalf, or provide them with jobs that would protect them from having to compete in the marketplace on an equal basis with those who did not have access to the same kinds of social resources. (DiTomaso 2013, 318–19)

Exclusion and Replication

All groups maintain boundaries between who is "in" and who is "out." All groups have criteria for both inclusion and exclusion. Privileged groups maintain privilege in part by restricting access to rewards they control by keeping insiders in and outsiders out. One of the consequences of social capital is that lack of it restricts entry into privileged groups and the resources they control. The flip side to being part of the grapevine and "in the loop" is that while it benefits members of one group, it typically excludes others, sometimes unconsciously or unwittingly. Numerous studies, for instance, have shown how social connections utilized by white ethnics in various trades have effectively kept racial minorities out (Waldinger 1995; Parks-Yancy 2006; Massey 2007). Ultimately, such informal networks reduce organizational efficiency since otherwise-qualified applicants for positions are never considered. Thus, strong associations within the group may restrict opportunity outside the group. This often occurs among groups that have experienced long histories of discrimination and exclusion. In such groups, there is safety in numbers because isolated members of the group can often become the most vulnerable targets for exploitation and oppression. This circumstance contributes to a heightened sense of in-group solidarity grounded in the common experience of subordination. Along with a heightened sense of in-group solidarity, long histories of oppression can also generate a sense of out-group hostility and suspicion. Within some segments of the African American community, for instance, oppositional identities and subcultures may develop (Ogbu 1978, 2008) in which academic success is looked at as definitely "uncool" and suspiciously defined as "acting white," effectively cutting off opportunities for advancement in the dominant mainstream of society.

The lack of social connections or truncated networks in areas of concentrated poverty such as inner cities contributes to occupational problems for their inhabitants (Wilson and Portes 1980; Wilson 1987, 1996; Massey 2007). Everyday survival in poor urban communities frequently depends on close interaction with kin and friends in similar situations. Since such ties seldom reach beyond the local community, the inhabitants are deprived of sources of information about employment opportunities elsewhere and ways to attain them. This problem is compounded by the departure of middle-class families from black inner-city areas, which has depleted the social capital of the remaining population and contributed to high levels of unemployment and welfare dependency (Wacquant and Wilson 1989; Wilson 1987, 1996).

Women, likewise, have also historically confronted restricted access to privileged social networks, sometimes derisively referred to as "the good old boy network" that has contributed to a "glass ceiling" of limited (nonmerit) opportunities for advancement (McDonald, Lin, and Ao 2009). The process of this restriction is often subtle and can come in many forms. Women in business settings, for instance, may be restricted from inner male sanctums such as the golf course, the racquetball court, the bar, the poker game, or other arenas of mostly male interaction in which insider information is shared and business deals are often cut outside of "official" work environments. Women, especially professional women, are also systematically disadvantaged with respect to senior mentors, as previously mentioned a critical social capital resource especially for those just starting out. Although women are now entering professions such as medicine, law, and the professoriate at rates that are close to parity with men, those who occupy the senior positions in the professions (judges, senior partners, full professors, chief surgeons, etc.) are overwhelming men, in part because so few women entered those professions a mere generation ago. Senior professional men are often reluctant to take on younger professional female protégés, and younger professional females are likewise reluctant to cultivate ties with senior professional men. Younger professional women are at a systematic (nonmerit) disadvantage in access to valuable information that could be imparted to them by those in their professions with the most experience and in access to the most critical professional resources such as sponsorship for assignments, positions, promotions, and the like.

One of the consequences of restricted access to privileged social capital for some groups more than others is that over time privileged groups tend to replicate their own social and demographic profile. If new positions are filled directly through contacts or where social connectedness is critical (such as through referrals or letters of reference), then the effective pool of eligibles for consideration is likely to be disproportionally drawn from the same social profile as those already occupying such positions. That is, the pools will likely replicate the same social milieu of those doing the hiring since people tend to associate with people like themselves.

Since access to social networks is so critical for job placement and since such access has historically been an effective basis for exclusion (both intended and unintended), most public institutions now require that job openings for any permanent position must be publically advertised. Moreover, in those job announcements, there is often an explicit EOC (Equal Opportunity Employer) statement expressly encouraging previously excluded groups such as women and minorities to apply. Such efforts to reduce the nonmeritocratic effects of social capital, however, are still the exception rather than the rule since most employment occurs in private settings where such efforts are typically not required or employed.

The Invisible Hand of Social Capital

Having friends in high places increases the likelihood of receiving useful information in routine exchanges even without actively seeking such information (Lin 2000a). People with networks yielding access to substantial job information will be more apt to be presented with opportunities to change jobs without an active search. In short, having friends in high places is associated with the routine flow of useful information—"the invisible hand of social capital." Only when such useful information is not available and not forthcoming would mobilization of social contacts become necessary. Those with friends in lower places, however, must call more often upon whatever contacts they have to actively seek out useful information (Lin 2000a, 792). This also explains why strong ties are less effective for minority-group members and why cross-gender ties are more useful for females than for males.

Thus, it is clear that not all individuals or social groups uniformly acquire social capital, acquire it in the same manner, or receive equivalent returns from its use. Class, status, gender, racial, and ethnic groups have different access to social capital because of their advantaged or disadvantaged structural positions and associated social networks. Individuals with higher socioeconomic origins are more likely to access better social resources in social networks or to find contacts with better social standing. Others, occupying inferior positions in the social hierarchy and accessing worse resources in social networks, attain lower status in their careers. People in lower-socioeconomic-status groups tend to be members of resource-poor networks that share a relatively restricted variety of information and influence. They tend to use local ties, strong ties, and family and kin ties. Since these ties are usually homogeneous in resources, this networking tendency reinforces poor social capital. People in higher socioeconomic groups tend to be embedded in resource-rich networks characterized by relative richness not only in quantity but also in kind—resource heterogeneity (Lin 1982, 2000a; Lin and Erickson 2008; Lin and Dumin 1986; Campbell, Marsden, and Hurlbert 1986).

NEPOTISM

The most blatant form of advantage through social capital is nepotism, often defined as the undue preference for close kin or friends where open merit-based competition should prevail. The beneficiaries of nepotism possess social capital—parents, siblings, other close kin, and friends—that is activated on their behalf and is quite independent of their individual merit or qualifications. In *In Praise of Nepotism: A Natural History* (2003), Adam Bellow (son of famous author and Noble laureate Saul Bellow) argues that nepotism has a biological basis (enhancing chances for survival by maximizing inclusive fitness). According to Bellow, nepotism is based on the "natural" preference for close kin and is found in one form or another in all human societies. He emphasizes that America is no exception, that despite its meritocratic ideology, nepotism is as American as apple pie, has been endemic throughout its history, and is actually resurgent in a new form that he calls the "new nepotism." Bellow documents the pervasiveness of nepotism in America from colonial times to the present, correctly pointing out that many exemplars of the "self-made man" were in fact beneficiaries of significant nepotism.

Nepotism, then, is a form of inherited and unearned advantage based on social capital that is independent of individual merit and that varies by social class. The most privileged classes tend to have the most valuable social capital. For the privileged, nepotism provides considerable advantage and is an important means by which privilege is transferred from one generation to the next, enabling the formation of dynasties of wealth and power. For the privileged, nepotism takes the form of essentially unearned access to high appointive or elective office, as well as to high-income and high-authority occupations. Nepotism operates in all social classes, but potential benefits decline as one moves down the social-class ladder. Thus, members of the working class are also recipients of nepotism, but its payoffs are less valuable simply because the working class tends to have lower social capital. Nepotism in the working class tends to be limited to access to apprenticeships, unions, or the more "desirable" working-class occupations. For example, in the capitalist class, a son may be placed in an upper-echelon position in the family business; in the working class, a son may get access to union membership or a "good" job running one of the machines at the mill where his father has worked for twenty years.

One of Bellow's least compelling arguments is that the "new nepotism" in America is compatible with principles of merit. Bellow contends that although one might initially secure a position through nepotism, today the recipient must continually display merit to keep the position, often working harder to demonstrate competence and hence worthiness. The problem with this line of reasoning is that although nepotism and meritocracy can coexist in a social system, they ultimately represent zero-sum principles of distribution. That is, the more nepotism operates, the less merit operates, and no nuanced argument can escape this fundamental contradiction. The initial advantage of placement, for instance, is a crucial one that summarily denies others access to opportunity regardless of their level of merit. Further, contrary to Bellow's argument, there is precious little evidence that the beneficiaries of nepotism display self-consciousness about the nonmerit basis of their opportunity or express feelings of "unworthiness." Instead, they are effectively socialized to expect to receive and to manage differential opportunity. They tend to "get the benefit of the doubt" and operate in what might be called a "climate of positive expectations" that produces self-fulfilling prophecies that legitimate the nepotism.

In sum, the operation of nepotism and variations in the quantity and quality of social capital provide unequal access to educational, occupational, and entrepreneurial success. These effects are independent of individual merit and are related to a great extent to the class-based social circles in which people travel. Beyond one's social milieu, some people may have better social skills than others and may be better able to cultivate social capital. The advantage of the social capital itself, however, is independent of a person's ability to perform certain tasks; that is, someone may be good at making friends and may use those friends to help get a job that itself has nothing to do with the ability to make friends. At minimum, nepotism provides access beyond a person's ability to do the job.

Despite Bellow's endorsement of the supposed advantages of nepotism, most public as well as some private employers expressly forbid hiring relatives or at least highly circumscribe the conditions under which this can occur. Even when the hiring of relatives is permitted, the usual rule is that anyone in the employing organization who is related to any job prospect must recuse themselves from the decision to hire. Antinepotism rules also usually forbid relatives in the same employing organization from having any supervisory or evaluative role over someone with whom they are related on the grounds that such activity would create a "conflict of interest" or even "the appearance of a conflict of interest."

CULTURAL CAPITAL: FITTING IN

The importance of something is sometimes most dramatically revealed by its absence. The lack of cultural capital, for instance, has been the gist of several classic comic moments on film. The musical comedy *My Fair Lady* is about the efforts—on a bet—of a stuffy professor played by Rex Harrison to coach a young London cockney girl played by Audrey Hepburn to "pass" as a British socialite. A similar theme is at work in the popular American film *Pretty Woman*, in which a wealthy businessman played by Richard Gere befriends a prostitute played by Julia Roberts, who, with some crash-course coaching from the manager of the Beverly Hills Wilshire Hotel, attempts, with limited success, to "pass" as his dignified and refined escort. In one particularly revealing restaurant scene, Julia Roberts' character begins to eat the salad at the beginning of the dinner only to be told that the salad comes at the end of the meal. Her exasperated response, "But that is the fork I knew!" exposes her lack of cultural capital. The lack of cultural capital is especially sharply drawn in the 1960s TV show *The Beverly Hillbillies*. In this situation comedy, a family of Tennessee hillbillies becomes instant millionaires. Although the hillbillies were portrayed as having enormous sums of economic capital, they were without upper-class cultural capital and wildly out of place among the rich and famous in Beverly Hills. These are, of course, exaggerated and fictionalized accounts, but they serve to illustrate what sociologists refer to as "cultural capital" (Lewin 2005).

Social inequality is not just about wealth and power but about culture as well. Claims that one group's culture ranks higher in social standing than another's can be based on almost anything—tastes in music, leisure, food, fashion—in short, anything that creates invidious status distinctions (Steinhaur 2005; Weber 1968; Veblen 1953). What is required is a claim of superiority and getting others to accede to it. Bourdieu (1986) has explored this dimension of inequality at length. For Bourdieu, cultural capital is cultural property, or, more specifically, the possession of knowledge and artifacts associated with groups. The source of cultural capital is located in, and transmitted through, what Bourdieu calls habitus, the whole panoply of practices, dispositions, and tastes that organizes an individual's participation within the culture of a group.

Acquiring Cultural Capital

The process of acquiring culture requires an investment of time and effort. As with the acquisition of a muscular physique or a suntan, others cannot do it for you. Knowledge of a group's way of life cannot be transmitted instantaneously by gift or bequest, purchase, or exchange. It is acquired over time through the process of socialization. In this sense, it is a form of hereditary transmission that is heavily disguised. Because the social conditions of its transmission and acquisition are more disguised than those of economic capital, it is likely to be unrecognized as a form of inherited capital and instead be claimed as individual competence. That is, the possession of cultural capital is generally claimed as "evidence" of individual merit, while its fundamental dependence on differential opportunities for its inheritance goes unrecognized. Like other forms of capital, its value is based on the fact that not everyone possesses it. The logic of scarcity secures material and symbolic advantages for those who possess it. That is, any given cultural competence derives a scarcity value from its position in the distribution of cultural capital and yields profits of distinction for its owner (e.g., being able to read in a world of illiterates).

The initial accumulation of cultural capital starts at birth, without delay, only for the offspring of families endowed with prestigious cultural capital. Indeed, the transmission of cultural capital through socialization is the most valuable hidden form of hereditary transmission of privilege (Kendall 2002, 2008). Cultural capital, therefore, receives proportionately greater weight in the justification of privilege (presumed merit) because more direct and visible forms of transmission (e.g., inheritance of economic capital) tend to be more strongly censored and controlled (e.g., getting something for nothing).

Research suggests that parents may influence children's cultural capital in three ways: children may acquire cultural skills "frictionlessly" by living in a home where parents possess considerable prestigious cultural capital; they may acquire it effortlessly in their friends' homes, whether or not their own parents are so oriented; or parents may invest strategically in cultural goods to improve their children's life chances (Mohr and DiMaggio 1995, 179). Middle-class or even working-class parents, for instance, may consciously invest in exposing children to prestigious forms of cultural capital beyond their own level of cultural capital and often even beyond their own economic means to do so through study-abroad experiences, enrichment camps, music lessons, and the like. What is more, young adults may, independently of their families, seek out cultural capital to escape their socioeconomic origins or to reject that which their family has provided. As opposed to the frictionless means of absorbing the culture one was initially socialized into, acquiring prestigious social or cultural capital from the outside is a much more daunting and difficult task.

In *Home Advantage*, an excellent ethnography, sociologist Annette Lareau (2000) convincingly demonstrates the numerous ways in which family–school connections operate to increase the relative successes of public school children. Specifically, the mothers of middle-class and more privileged children more effectively deploy social and cultural capital for the benefit of their children than do the mothers of working-class and less privileged children. For example, compared to the mothers of less privileged children, middle-class mothers are more educated and more likely to read to their children, tutor them, and help them with their homework. They are much more likely to regulate their children's extracurricular time and plan activities that help them build their own cultural capital: sports teams (soccer moms); lessons of all kinds (music, dance, cotillion); summer camps of all kinds, including sports camps; play dates; and the like. Middle-class moms are more likely to live in the same neighborhoods as their children's teachers and thus to know them "out of class," possibly as friends or members of the same clubs. They often have teachers in their own extended families. They are more likely to have become friends with their children's classmates' parents and can thus use these friendships for information about the effective deployment of social and cultural capital. In short, they have the advantages of knowing "the right thing to do" or "what works" with their children's teachers.

Meanwhile, the mothers of working-class and poorer children have few of these advantages. Being less educated themselves, the moms are less likely to read to their children. They feel less confident in interactions with teachers. More generally, their habitus suggests that the teachers are the experts, that it is the teachers' responsibility to teach the children, and thus these mothers are less likely to intervene. There is clearly less connection between families and schools, and the mothers allow their "children to be children." Outside school, the children are expected to entertain themselves and play with neighborhood friends in their own independent and unregulated activities. In general, the working-class habitus seems to produce less social and cultural capital, and the moms tend to use it in clumsy ways that teachers sometimes define as inappropriate and annoying. These and many other differences help to explain why the students of middle-class and more privileged families "do better" in schools and reap the credential rewards.

Further, in *Unequal Childhoods* (2003), Lareau convincingly shows the differential benefits that accrue to middle-class and privileged children compared to working-class and less privileged children. She finds that the middle-class parents engage in a process of "concerted cultivation" in which their kids are systematically and consciously provided with social and cultural capital. Thus, middle- and working-class families have different sets of "cultural repertoires" about how children should be raised and act as cauldrons in which children are socialized to develop different social and cultural capacities that produce subsequent differences in opportunity. In short, Lareau convincingly shows that social class and race are quite important for getting ahead in life, and specifically how they are important.

Cultural capital can also be objectified in material artifacts. Bourdieu (1986), for instance, argues that cultural capital can be certified in the form of academic qualifications and serve as a testimony of cultural competence for its bearer. This objectification, he says, is what makes the difference between the capital of the self-educated person, which may be called into question at any time, and the cultural capital academically sanctioned by legally guaranteed qualifications formally independent of the person of their bearer. With the academic qualification, a certificate of cultural competence confers on its holder a conventional, constant, legally guaranteed value with respect to culture. By conferring institutional recognition on the cultural capital possessed, the academic qualification also makes it possible to compare qualification holders and even to exchange them (by substituting one for another in succession). Furthermore, it makes it possible to establish conversion rates between cultural capital and economic capital by guaranteeing the monetary value of a given academic capital (e.g., the "going" starting salary for an MBA from the Wharton School of Business). This is important because what is being selected out is not practical knowledge necessary to do the job (which could be self-taught or acquired on the job) but the degree itself as a form of cultural capital. Degrees signify cultural capital and become filters for eligibility; in this sense, the lack of a degree creates an artificial barrier to mobility otherwise predicated on skill, ability, experience, or knowledge acquired through alternate means.

Cultural Capital and Jobs

In a revealing recent study of hiring in elite professional service firms (law, investment banking, and consulting firms), Lauren Rivera (2012) shows that employers not only sought out candidates who were competent but also similar to themselves in terms of common leisure pursuits, experiences, and self-presentational styles. Cultural matching along these lines factored prominently into hiring decisions and often outweighed concerns about absolute productivity. Competence counts in terms of minimum thresholds but may not be as important as cultural considerations. Indeed, more than half of the hiring agents in the study reported that fitting in was the most important criterion for consideration at the job interview stage, taking precedence over factors such as analytical thinking ability and communication skills. Rivera identified three ways through which cultural similarities affect candidate selection in the interview process. First, employers actively sought out candidates that "fit in" to the prevailing culture of the employing firm as indicated by the interests and activities of those already employed in the firm. Second, employers felt better able to understand and evaluate the background and experiences of candidates who had similar social backgrounds and experiences as they had. Third, similarities of experiences with particular candidates generated excitement on the part of evaluators who would then fight for those candidates in deliberations regarding final selection. In short, cultural criteria not only affect hiring outcomes in these elite professional settings but often trump strictly merit factors.

Old Money and New Money

Research on the upper class consistently demonstrates the importance of cultural capital in distinguishing "old money" from "new money" (Fabrikant 2005; Johnston 2005; Scott and Leonhardt 2005; Frank 2007). One institution that serves as a site for upper-class production, deployment, and intergenerational transmission of social and cultural capital is the upper-class social club. Sociologist Diana Kendall in *Members Only: Elite Clubs and the Process of Exclusion* (2008) and sociologist Jessica Holden Sherwood in *Wealth, Whiteness and the Matrix of Privilege: The View from the Country Club* (2010) convincingly document numerous ways that the upper class uses exclusive clubs to maintain upper-class advantage. First, the clubs serve as private domains for the conduct of business—on the golf course and at private parties, dinners, and other social affairs. Second, the clubs serve as sites for making connections by providing occupational and political networks. Third, these clubs have numerous functions at which politicians and upper-class members meet and share insider information about political policy and strategy and at which members provide politicians with money and support,

which William Domhoff (2009) has described well as a "policy-making process." Finally, these clubs provide resources for launching the next generation. For example, these clubs serve as sites for parties, organized activities
for children, debutante balls, and the exchange of information about elite
preparatory schools and elite colleges and universities.

Clearly, cultural capital reproduction routinely occurs not just in formal
settings such as schools but in informal setting such as social clubs and
exclusive upper-class resorts. Even within the same class categories, however, the circumstances and settings in which cultural capital is transferred may
vary. Muriel Egerton (1997), for instance, has shown that household cultural
climate varies according to parents' level of formal education and the employment situation of the father. In those families in which the father is
employed in an occupation for which cultural capital is recognized as important for success (e.g., one of the professions), there is investment in cultural
resources in the home, and such investment leads to children's acquisition of
cultural capital. Thus, occupational groups dependent for their authority on
cultural rather than economic capital invest more in legitimate culture in their
homes and transmit cultural capital more effectively to their children, and
occupational effects are evident beyond the impact of family income and
parents' education.

The reproduction of cultural capital has occurred with enough frequency
to have generated commonplace stereotypes of subcultural differences
among occupational groups, status groups, and social classes. Even within
social classes, subcultural differences are manifest. For example, within the
upper class, the *upper*-upper class, with its "old money" (dynastic wealth)
and its cultural capital displayed as refined manners, styles, and tastes (Fabrikant 2005), is contrasted with the *lower*-upper class, the nouveau riche,
whose members may possess as much or even more economic capital but are
"betrayed" by lack of cultural capital, as indicated by deficiencies in savoir
faire, unrefined manners, lack of style, and pedestrian tastes (Fabrikant 2005;
Steinhaur 2005; Frank 2007).

SOCIAL CLIMBING

Social climbing and snobbery have long been stock material for novelists and
are part of the American folklore of social ranking and mobility (Buckley
2005; McGrath 2005). The very existence of these terms reflects a cultural
recognition of unequally ranked socioeconomic groups or social classes and
individual efforts to move upwardly through them. In general discourse, the
terms *social climber* and *snob* tend to be used interchangeably. Both snobs
and social climbers engage in activities that exclude and usurp. Essentially,
social climbing may be defined as strategies and activities used to achieve

upward social mobility that come to be defined negatively because they are seen as violating accepted rules for the acquisition and use of social and cultural capital. To the extent that efforts for upward social mobility involve the inappropriate deployment of social and cultural capital, they run the risk of negative labeling as social climbing.

Social climbers, within the limits set by their economic capital, systematically cultivate social capital, then attempt to deploy it in the pursuit of upward social mobility. They cultivate social relationships and engage in those social activities that provide access to members of the group to which they seek membership. Such activities include the conscious construction of social networks that have a status appreciably higher than that of the networks of nonclimber peers. Climbers try to carefully select organizational memberships (the "right" clubs, churches, charities, boards, and the like), develop social relations, and cultivate friendships among members of the target group. They use numerous strategies, including "name dropping," segregating audiences when deemed necessary (Mills 1951; Goffman 1951, 1959, 1967), and refusing to associate with members of lower-ranked groups. They may even use their children as sources of social contacts or as symbols of attainment. The placement of children in exclusive preparatory schools and the selection of their children's friends and activities are means of translating economic capital into social capital.

Social climbers hope that if they associate with people of higher status, some of the higher status will "rub off" on them. Those who associate with social climbers, however, risk having their own status lowered by such associations. In this regard, Vance Packard, in his influential book *The Status Seekers* (1959), made a useful distinction between status lending and status declassing. Climbers may attach themselves to status lenders, individuals who voluntarily confer their status by association with lower-status individuals and organizations. Status declassing, however, reflects efforts by higher-status individuals to take on characteristics of the lower-status individuals with whom they are interacting. Higher-status individuals may "declass," as by professing a "we're just plain folks" perspective, if it is deemed socially useful for them to do so. Climbers, however, must recognize and avoid higher-status individuals who declass as a strategy to avoid conferring status and thus legitimating the climber's status claims. Similarly, climbers must avoid individuals who employ strategies of condescension. By temporarily but ostentatiously abdicating dominant status to "reach down," the higher-status individuals may profit from this relation of domination, which continues to exist, by denying it.

Social climbers also attempt to develop and use cultural capital in the pursuit of upward social mobility. But one impediment to social climbing lies in the very nature of cultural capital. Components of cultural capital can usually be acquired only through extended and informal socialization within the group. While it is possible for the climber to acquire cultural capital formally, as through education or systematic training, such formal acquisition is economically costly and typically results in a tense, subtly imperfect mastery that is always marked by the conditions of its acquisition (e.g., Julia Roberts' character in *Pretty Woman* not knowing which fork to use). The resulting uneasy, practiced, unnatural, or even stilted displays are easily detected by members of the target group and thus betray the climber as a poseur—as not truly "one of us" (Buckley 2005; Fabrikant 2005).

Status competition within groups may lead to changes in what status pacesetters define as prestigious. This is most evident in the fickle nature of what is considered currently "fashionable" within elite circles. The constantly changing nature of status symbols suggests the source of yet another impediment to social climbing. Self-assured and long-established members of any group come to feel that adherence to its own standard canons is beneath them. Their status is so secure that to indulge in those observances would only lower them. They can best announce and display their unassailability by changing the canons. They have adopted an apparently noninvidious way of life for the quintessentially invidious purpose of showing that they are above taking part in a game played by "lessers." Such changes in cultural capital increase the difficulty of its acquisition and penetration of the target group by climbers: it is more difficult to hit a moving cultural target than a stationary one.

Social climbing elicits negative reactions for a variety of reasons. For some, the evidence of single-minded, obsessive preoccupation with status or the transparent, crudely instrumental efforts to deploy social and cultural capital are simply annoying (Buckley 2005; Fabrikant 2005). What is more, the actions of social climbers can make individuals acutely aware of their own cultural and social capital deficiencies. The American Dream encourages individuals to maintain or, if possible, improve their social positions by acquiring social, cultural, and economic capital and using them to their advantage. But such activity is governed by generally understood and accepted rules, and the social climber's actions challenge or violate them. Violating the rules is sufficient basis for negative labeling and exclusion. "Not knowing" the rules is no excuse because knowing and adhering to the rules is a nonsubstitutable criterion of eligibility.

Further, the instrumental acquisition and deployment of social and cultural capital as a strategic means for the achievement of upward social mobility violates meritocratic notions. According to meritocratic ideology, individual merit is the only legitimate basis for mobility. Hence, the purposeful use of social and cultural capital as a means of social mobility is suspect to the extent that it is not the product of individual merit or that it is viewed as being a substitute for individual merit.

From another perspective, the actions of social climbers challenge the legitimacy of group ranking and the unequal distribution of social and cultural capital, and they lay bare class-based resentments and hostilities. Rejection and exclusion of the climber by the target group constitutes an exercise of power. In fact, the climber's own group may experience a threat to its status and attempt to impose sanctions on the climber because, at least by implication, the climber's actions constitute a negative evaluation of that group and therefore a threat to its status claims and solidarity.

In sum, the actions of social climbers run counter to the individualistic and meritocratic components of the American Dream and the normative structure that underlies it. Climbing behavior also calls attention to inequalities among groups in the distribution of various forms of capital. Social climbers highlight the social and cultural insecurities of those with whom they interact. For all these reasons, the actions of social climbers tend to be viewed, especially by those of higher status, as fraudulent and shameful.

From this, we can conclude several things. First, the possession of cultural capital is related to social-class background, but the correlation is difficult to measure. The privileged do tend to have more cultural capital than those of lower socioeconomic status, but many cases do not fit this pattern, and there are differences among individuals in their ability to effectively deploy what cultural capital they possess. Second, while the possession of cultural capital may be viewed as evidence of individual merit, it is in fact acquired in ways that can hardly be attributable to individual effort or merit as conventionally defined. That is, much cultural capital is the result of familial socialization— cultural capital is often "frictionlessly" and effortlessly inherited. In this sense, the acquisition of cultural capital is best conceptualized as a process of differential cultural inheritance, not one of differential achievement. Third, strategies of mobility and reproduction are constrained, but not wholly determined, by social class. Thus, cultural resources enter into individual and familial strategies for advancement in a variety of ways. For some, investment in cultural capital is a conscious and purposeful effort or strategy, either for one's own mobility or for that of one's children (Lareau 2000, 2003). Fourth, cultural capital contributes directly to the acquisition of education. Educational credentials (cultural capital in its institutionalized form) then become criteria for access to occupational opportunity (eligibility requirements for hiring and promotion). Below we offer two brief examples of the importance and advantages of social and cultural capital in the lives of two recent American presidents: George W. Bush and Barack Obama.

THE CASE OF GEORGE WALKER BUSH

George Walker Bush, the forty-third president of the United States and prior governor of Texas, exemplifies the advantages of social and cultural capital. A self-admitted mediocre student, Bush nevertheless ascended to political prominence and power aided considerably by pedigree and social connections.

George Walker Bush is the grandson of Prescott Sheldon Bush, a U.S. senator from Connecticut, and the son of George Herbert Walker Bush, who was the forty-first president of the United States. George H. W. Bush had also been a member of the U.S. House of Representatives, U.S. ambassador to the United Nations, chairman of the Republican National Committee, chief of the U.S. Liaison Office in the People's Republic of China, director of the Central Intelligence Agency, and vice president of the United States. George Walker Bush's brother, John Ellis "Jeb" Bush, has served as governor of Florida. In short, the Bush family has long been prominent in American politics.

Throughout his life, George W. Bush has been awash in both social and cultural capital. He has drawn heavily on the social capital of family friends, relatives, and contacts in high places. Despite his famous malapropisms and lapses in syntax, he has procured ample amounts of upper-class cultural capital, including prestigious academic credentials (high school diploma from Phillips Andover Academy, BA from Yale, and MBA from Harvard). George W. Bush is well known for his considerable charm and social skills. Having grown up in the high-powered atmospheres of both big government and big business (like his father before him, he was in the Texas oil business), George W. Bush is very comfortable traveling in these high-powered circles.

George W. Bush is not alone in this regard. There have been a number of dynastic political families in the United States, including the Adamses, the Roosevelts, the Rockefellers, and the Kennedys, all of whom had progeny whose careers were enhanced by their upper-class origins and the economic, social, and cultural capital that go along with them.

In and of themselves, connections do not diminish or demean the individual accomplishments of the sons and daughters of the rich and powerful. Such individual accomplishments, however, must be understood within the larger social context of differing advantages in which they occur. Certainly through no fault of their own, but equally through no merit of their own, the sons and daughters of the rich and powerful inherit, along with the family name, disproportionate access to prestigious and influential forms of social and cultural capital.

THE CASE OF BARACK HUSSEIN OBAMA

We cannot leave this topic before discussing a more current case. In 2008, Barack H. Obama became the forty-fourth president of the United States and the first African American president, and he was reelected in 2012. He served three terms in the Illinois state senate from 1997 to 2004. Following an unsuccessful bid for a seat in the U.S. House of Representatives in 2000, he was elected to the U.S. Senate in 2004. He delivered the keynote address at the Democratic National Convention in July 2004. Since his defeat of Hillary Clinton in the Democratic primary and Republican senator John McCain in the general election, some have described Obama's rise to national political power as meteoric.

Barack Obama's election is sometimes lauded as a reaffirmation of the American Dream—that superior individual characteristics, including intelligence and talent, ultimately prevail and that in the end aristocratic backgrounds and inheritance of privilege, such as was the case with George W. Bush, are not needed to ascend to the highest positions of political or economic power in America. In short, Obama's election has been heralded as proof that America now operates as a true meritocracy. What is more, because he is an African American, Obama's election is viewed by some as a final vindication of the civil rights revolution of the 1960s and 1970s.

While Barack Obama is certainly individually meritorious, a closer examination of his rise to political prominence suggests a more nuanced interpretation that includes a confluence of relevant factors in his upbringing and background. First, one might argue that Barack Obama is certainly not a "typical" African American, whatever that might mean. His family background has been at least middle class for two generations. Specifically, he is not the product of the poor or working-class African American families of the rural South or the inner cities of the industrial North, residential locations of those whom William Julius Wilson (1987) has called "the truly disadvantaged." Obama's biological father was African, from the Nyanza Province in Kenya; thus, he was an African and not an American of African descent. His mother was a white American of English and Irish descent from Wichita, Kansas (Obama 2006).

His parents met in 1960 while attending the University of Hawaii at Manoa. They separated when Obama was two years old and divorced in 1964. Obama's father went on to graduate school at Harvard and eventually returned to Kenya. He saw his son only once more before dying in an automobile accident in 1982. After her divorce, Obama's mother married an Indonesian student who was also attending college in Hawaii. In 1967, the Indonesian government recalled all students studying abroad, so the family moved to Indonesia. When he was ten years old, he returned to Honolulu to live with his maternal (white, middle-class) grandparents. Obama's mother returned to Hawaii in 1972 for several years and then moved back to Indonesia, where she worked as an anthropological fieldworker. She stayed there for most of the remainder of her life, returning to Hawaii in 1994, where she died in 1995.

Some might suggest that Obama is African and white and not "truly" African American. Certainly, much of his childhood was not "typical" of that of other African Americans, including exposure to substantial cultural diversity, international influences, the advantages of a well-educated and culturally diverse family, and considerable social and cultural capital.

For example, following high school, Obama moved to Los Angeles, where he studied at Occidental College (a "top-50 national liberal arts college," according to *U.S. News & World Report* ratings) for two years. He then transferred to Columbia University (a "top-50 national university," again according to *U.S. News & World Report* ratings), where he majored in political science with a concentration in international relations. He graduated with a BA from Columbia in 1983 and entered Harvard Law School in 1988. He was selected as an editor of the *Harvard Law Review* at the end of his first year and was elected president of the journal in his second year. After graduating with a JD magna cum laude from Harvard in 1991, he returned to Chicago, where he practiced law and also taught constitutional law at the University of Chicago Law School. Through his elite Ivy League education, Barack Obama further enhanced his cultural capital and acquired upper-class credentials.

Today, Obama and his family qualify as "marginally rich." His wife, Michelle, is from a modest family background, having grown up in an African American working-class family in Chicago. She was perhaps even more upwardly mobile than her husband. Michelle Obama graduated from Princeton University and Harvard Law School and became a successful lawyer in her own right as an attorney for a large Chicago hospital. In December 2007, *Money* magazine estimated the Obama family's net worth at $1.3 million. Their 2007 tax return showed a household income of $4.2 million, up from $1.6 million in 2005. The Obamas' net worth in 2012, as reported by *Forbes*, is approximately $6 million, slightly down from 2011 (Carlyle 2012).

In short, Barack Obama's election was certainly significant and represents an important symbolic breakthrough in American race relations. However, his experiences in many ways have been unusual, certainly not typical of those of most African Americans, and do not in themselves reduce the impediments and disadvantages encountered daily by racial minorities in the United States. Individual accomplishments and successes must be understood within this larger social context of differential advantage. Certainly through no fault of their own, but equally through no merit of their own, people like Barack Obama, even if not born to rich and powerful families, nevertheless often inherit disproportionate opportunity and access to prestigious and influential forms of social and cultural capital.

SUMMARY

This chapter has reviewed the evidence on the importance of "whom you know" (social capital) and "fitting in" (cultural capital) for getting and staying ahead in America. Social capital and cultural capital are ultimately resources. As with the possession of wealth, the possession of social and cultural resources is not necessarily evidence of individual merit. Wealth can be converted into social and cultural capital providing distinct nonmerit advantages that can be transferred to the children of the rich and powerful. We have explored the related phenomenon of social climbing. Conscious construction and use of social networks, conspicuous and invidious consumption, name dropping, and "showy" displays of highbrow culture are some of the techniques employed by social climbers in their attempts to attain higher status. Instead of gaining the prestige and rank that they desire, however, social climbers are often viewed as snobs within their own groups and as impostors by those in the groups to which they aspire to gain membership.

REFERENCES

Bellow, Adam. 2003. *In Praise of Nepotism: A Natural History*. New York: Doubleday.

Bourdieu, Pierre. 1986. "The Forms of Capital." In *Handbook of Theory and Research for the Sociology of Education*, ed. John G. Richardson, 241–58. New York: Greenwood Press.

Buckley, Christopher. 2005. "My Nanny Was a Dreadful Snob." In *Class Matters*, ed. *New York Times*, 234–36. New York: Times Books.

Campbell, Karen E., Peter V. Marsden, and Jeanne S. Hurlbert. 1986. "Social Resources and Socioeconomic Status." *Social Networks* 8:97–117.

Campbell, Karen E., and Rachel A. Rosenfeld. 1985. "Job Search and Job Mobility: Sex and Race Differences." *Research in the Sociology of Work* 3:147–74.

Carlyle, Erin. 2012. "Obama's Worth Nearly $6 Million—See Why He's Down since Last Year." *Forbes*. http://www.forbes.com/sites/erincarlyle/2012/05/16/obamas-worth-nearly-6-million-see-why-hes-down-since-last-year (accessed October 21, 2012).

Coleman, James S. 1988. "Social Capital in the Creation of Human Capital." *American Journal of Sociology* 94:S95–S120.

DeGraaf, Nan Dirk, and Hendrik Derk Flap. 1988. "With a Little Help from My Friends." *Social Forces* 67:452–72.

DiTomaso, Nancy. 2013. *The American Non-Dilemma: Racial Inequality without Racism*. New York: Russell Sage Foundation.

Domhoff, William G. 2009. *Who Rules America? Challenges to Corporate and Class Dominance*. 6th ed. Boston: McGraw-Hill.

Egerton, Muriel. 1997. "Occupational Inheritance: The Role of Cultural Capital and Gender." *Work, Employment and Society* 11:263–82.

Fabrikant, Geraldine. 2005. "Old Nantucket Warily Meets the New." In *Class Matters*, ed. *New York Times*, 166–81. New York: Times Books.

Frank, Robert. 2007. *Richistan: A Journey through the American Wealth Boom and the Lives of the New Rich*. New York: Crown.

Goffman, Erving. 1951. "Symbols of Class Status." *British Journal of Sociology* 2:294–304.
———. 1959. *The Presentation of Self in Everyday Life*. Harmondsworth, UK: Pelican.
———. 1967. *Interaction Ritual*. New York: Pantheon.
Granovetter, Mark S. 1973. "The Strength of Weak Ties." *American Journal of Sociology* 78:1360–80.
———. 1974. *Getting a Job: A Study of Contacts and Careers*. Cambridge, MA: Harvard University Press.
———. 1983. "The Strength of Weak Ties: A Network Theory Revisited." *Sociological Theory* 1:201–33.
Johnston, David Cay. 2005. "Richest Are Leaving Even the Rich Far Behind." In *Class Matters*, ed. *New York Times*, 182–91. New York: Times Books.
Kalmijn, Matthijs, and Gerbert Kraaykamp. 1996. "Race, Cultural Capital, and Schooling: An Analysis of Trends in the United States." *Sociology of Education* 69:22–34.
Kendall, Diana. 2002. *The Power of Good Deeds: Privileged Women and the Social Reproduction of the Upper Class*. Lanham, MD: Rowman & Littlefield.
———. 2008. *Members Only: Elite Clubs and the Process of Exclusion*. Lanham, MD: Rowman & Littlefield.
Lareau, Annette. 2000. *Home Advantage: Social Class and Parental Intervention in Elementary Education*. Lanham, MD: Rowman & Littlefield.
———. 2003. *Unequal Childhoods: Class, Race, and Family Life*. Berkeley: University of California Press.
Lewin, Tamar. 2005. "A Marriage of Unequals" and "Up from the Holler: Living in Two Worlds, at Home in Neither." In *Class Matters*, ed. *New York Times*, 51–62 and 63–72. New York: Times Books.
Lin, Nan. 1982. "Social Resources and Instrumental Action." In *Social Structure and Network Analysis*, ed. Peter V. Marsden and Nan Lin, 131–45. Beverly Hills, CA: Sage.
———. 1999. "Social Networks and Status Attainment." *Annual Review of Sociology* 23:467–88.
———. 2000a. "Inequality in Social Capital." *Contemporary Sociology* 29:785–95.
———. 2000b. *Social Capital: A Theory of Structure and Action*. Cambridge: Cambridge University Press.
Lin, Nan, and Mary Dumin. 1986. "Access to Occupations through Social Ties." *Social Networks* 8:365–85.
Lin, Nan, Walter M. Ensel, and John C. Vaughn. 1981. "Social Resources and Occupational Status Attainment." *Social Forces* 58:1163–81.
Lin, Nan, and Bonnie Erickson, eds. 2008. *Social Capital: An International Research Program*. New York: Oxford University Press.
Lin, Nan, John C. Vaughn, and Walter M. Ensel. 1981. "Social Resources and Strength of Ties: Structural Factors in Occupational Attainment." *American Sociological Review* 46:393–405.
Massey, Douglas S. 2007. *Categorically Unequal: The American Stratification System*. New York: Sage.
McDonald, Steve, Nan Lin, and Dan Ao. 2009. "Networks of Opportunity: Gender, Race, and Job Leads." *Social Problems* 56, no. 3: 385–402.
McGrath, Charles. 2005. "In Fiction, a Long History of Fixation on the Social Gap." In *Class Matters*, ed. *New York Times*, 192–201. New York: Times Books.
Mills, C. Wright. 1951. *White Collar*. New York: Oxford University Press.
Mohr, John, and Paul DiMaggio. 1995. "The Intergenerational Transmission of Cultural Capital." *Research in Social Stratification and Mobility* 14:167–99.
Obama, Barack. 2006. *Audacity of Hope: Thoughts of Reclaiming the American Dream*. New York: Random House.
Ogbu, John U. 1978. *Minority Education and Caste*. San Diego, CA: Elsevier.
———. 2008. *Minority Status, Oppositional Culture and Schooling: Sociocultural, Political, and Historical Studies in Education*. New York: Erlbaum.
Packard, Vance O. 1959. *The Status Seekers*. New York: David McKay.
Parks-Yancy, Rochelle. 2006. "The Effects of Social Group Membership and Social Capital Resources on Careers." *Journal of Black Studies* 36:515–45.

Portes, Alejandro. 1998. "Social Capital: Its Origins and Applications in Modern Sociology." *Annual Review of Sociology* 24:1–24.

Rivera, Lauren. 2012. "Hiring as Cultural Matching: The Case of Elite Professional Service Firms." *American Sociological Review* 77:999–1022.

Sherwood, Jessica Holden. 2010. *Wealth, Whiteness, and the Matrix of Privilege: The View from the Country Club*. Lanham, MD: Rowman & Littlefield.

Scott, Janny, and David Leonhardt. 2005. "Shadowy Lines That Still Divide." In *Class Matters*, ed. *New York Times*, 1–26. New York: Times Books.

Steinhaur, Jennifer. 2005. "When the Joneses Wear Jeans." In *Class Matters*, ed. *New York Times*, 134–45. New York: Times Books.

Veblen, Thorstein. 1953. *The Theory of the Leisure Class*. New York: Modern Library.

Wacquant, Loic, and William Julius Wilson. 1989. "The Cost of Racial and Class Exclusion in the Inner City." *Annals of the American Academy of Political and Social Sciences* 501:8–26.

Waldinger, Roger. 1995. "The 'Other Side' of Embeddedness: A Case Study of the Interplay between Economy and Ethnicity." *Ethnic and Racial Studies* 18:555–80.

Weber, Max. 1968. *Economy and Society*. Trans. and ed. Guenther Roth and Claus Wittich. Berkeley: University of California Press.

Wilkerson, Isabel. 2005. "Angela Whitiker's Climb." In *Class Matters*, ed. *New York Times*, 202–33. New York: Times Books.

Wilson, Kenneth L., and Alejandro Portes. 1980. "Immigration Enclaves: An Analysis of the Labor Market Experiences of Cubans in Miami." *American Journal of Sociology* 86:295–319.

Wilson, William Julius. 1987. *The Truly Disadvantaged: The Inner City, the Underclass, and Public Policy*. Chicago: University of Chicago Press.

———. 1996. *When Work Disappears: The World of the New Urban Poor*. New York: Knopf.

Chapter Five

Making the Grade

Education and Mobility

To those of you who received honors, awards, and distinctions, I say, well done. And to the C students, I say, you too can be president of the United States.
—George W. Bush, Yale commencement address, thirty-three years after his graduation

According to the American Dream, education identifies and selects intelligent, talented, and motivated individuals and provides educational training in direct proportion to individual merit. The amounts and kinds of education attained are taken as measures of merit and are used as criteria of eligibility for occupations and the material awards attached to them. In the American Dream, education is the "engine" of meritocracy. Most Americans believe that education is the key to success: to get ahead in life you need a "good education" (*New York Times* 2005; Lareau 2000, 2003; Pew Research Center 2011).

A vastly different view of the role of education sees education not as a cause but as an effect of social class. Children generally receive education in direct proportion to their social-class standing: upper-class children tend to get upper-class educations (e.g., at elite private prep schools and Ivy League colleges), middle-class children tend to get middle-class educations (e.g., at public schools and public universities), working-class people tend to get working-class educations (e.g., public schools and technical or community colleges), and poor people tend to get poor educations (e.g., inner-city schools that have high dropout rates and usually no higher education). In each case, children from these different class backgrounds are groomed for the different roles that they will likely fill as adults. In this way, education largely reproduces existing inequalities across generations.

In America, as in all contemporary industrial societies, education has come to play an important role in selecting people for positions in the occupational structure. The overall relationship between education and future income is clear: the more education, the greater the chances of higher income (see table 5.1).

The close connection between "getting ahead" and education, however, is relatively recent. In the mid-nineteenth century, the United States was a nation of small-property owners, farmers, and shopkeepers. Many could read and write, but most had little formal education. Although opportunity has been an essential part of the American Dream since its beginnings, it meant the possibility for a person to grow to full potential, unfettered by the limits of class background or older feudal relations. These beliefs had important noneconomic as well as economic connotations, referring to opportunities to develop competence, character, and satisfying social ties, as well as to attain material well-being. The idea of opportunity as the chance to "move up" in the world gradually became a part of the American Dream, but it did not become very important until later in the nineteenth century. Thus, at first opportunity was not associated with upward social mobility, much less with upward mobility through education.

During the second half of the nineteenth century, the ideal of the "self-made man" (and most then were men) emerged and became an increasingly important component of the American Dream. But at first it was business, not education, that was seen as the main road to opportunity. The self-made

Table 5.1. Median Annual Income for Persons 25 to 64 Years by Educational Attainment, 2006–2008

Education Level	Median Income ($)
Professional degree	79,977
Doctorate	73,575
Master's degree	53,716
Bachelor's degree	42,783
Associate degree	32,602
Some college, no degree	27,361
High school graduate	21,569
9th–12th grade	10,996
Less than 9th grade	10,271

Source: U.S. Census Bureau 2011.

man started and grew his business or farm through intelligence and hard work, not by getting more education than his competitors.

The expansion of schooling was the result of major changes in the structure of occupational opportunities. With continuing industrialization, technological change, the rise of large corporations, and the closing of the frontier, by the end of the nineteenth century opportunities for becoming a self-made man had declined precipitously (see chapter 7). America was no longer a nation of small-scale entrepreneurs, farmers, and shopkeepers. More people were becoming employees in increasingly large, bureaucratically structured work organizations. These new conditions generated the development of new occupations, and with them new pathways to success.

At first education seemed an unlikely avenue. Businessmen, many of whom were self-made men with little formal schooling—graduates of the "school of hard knocks"—typically thought that schooling made young people unfit for the "real world," or at least didn't prepare them very well for it. Gradually, however, education increasingly came to be viewed as a replacement for the faltering promise of the family farm or business entrepreneurship. Andrew Carnegie, for example, and other influential people of the time believed that schools and colleges should be made into "ladders upon which the aspiring can rise" (1899, 663). But at the end of the nineteenth century, America's schools hardly constituted a well-organized ladder to success. It was during the first few decades of the twentieth century that the patchwork of American schooling was reorganized into the ladder structure that people like Andrew Carnegie advocated, thereby providing a mechanism to sustain the American promise of opportunity at the very time when fundamental changes in the economy were threatening to destroy it (Brint and Karabel 1989, 3–6).

Between 1900 and 1940, the proportion of white-collar jobs in the American labor force almost doubled from 18 percent at the turn of the century to 31 percent by 1940. Over the next forty years, the proportion of professional and managerial jobs doubled from 14 percent in 1940 to 26 percent in 1979. Finally, from 1979 to 2009, this proportion increased again from 26 to 37 percent (U.S. Census Bureau 1972, 1990, 2009). These massive changes in the occupational structure created increasing incentives for investment in education and led first to an increasing proportion of the population completing high school and college (see table 5.2).

These and similar data show that more Americans are enrolled in higher education today than ever before, and their numbers are growing. With respect to high school completion, from 1980 to 2011, the overall rate increased from 85 to 89 percent (U.S. Department of Education 2012). Between 1996 and 2006, the proportion of prime-working-age adults (aged twenty-five to fifty-nine) who had completed college rose by roughly 14 percent in both metropolitan and nonmetropolitan areas (Kusmin 2008).

Table 5.2. Years of School Completed by Persons Age 25 and Over, 1910–2011

Year	High School Completion	BA or Higher
1910	13.5	2.7
1920	16.4	3.3
1930	19.1	3.9
1940	24.5	4.6
1950	34.3	6.2
1960	41.1	7.7
1970	55.2	11.0
1980	68.6	17.0
1990	77.6	21.3
2001	84.3	26.1
2007	85.7	28.7
2009	86.7	29.5
2011	87.6	30.4

Source: Adapted from U.S. Department of Education (2011a).

Also, from 1980 to 2011, the proportion of people twenty-five years and over receiving a BA-level degree or higher increased 13.4 percent from 17.0 to 30.4 percent.

After World War II, growth in corporate size and concentration continued, and opportunities for upward mobility through various forms of entrepreneurship continued to decline. As this occurred, young people began to see diplomas and degrees as an alternate and less risky means to upward mobility—as tickets to the newer white-collar jobs that had proliferated. This view was reflected in public support for the building of secondary schools and colleges and for provision of financial aid for those who wanted to attend college but lacked the economic means.

Between the end of World War II and today, the proportions of students attending college have increased significantly (see table 5.3). Part of what stimulated increased college enrollments following World War II was the Servicemen's Readjustment Act of 1944, more commonly referred to as the GI Bill. Under benefits provided to veterans of World War II, over two million of those returning attended U.S. colleges and universities, sharply increasing the percentage of the adult population that was college educated. Higher education has not completely replaced entrepreneurship as an avenue to economic success. However, building one's own business is an arduous task with high risk for failure. Given the uncertainties of entrepreneurship, even many businesspeople prefer that their children pursue the less risky path

Table 5.3. College Enrollment Rates of High School Graduates, 1960–2010

Year	Percent of High School Graduates Enrolled in College
1960	45.1
1965	50.9
1970	51.8
1975	50.7
1980	49.3
1985	57.7
1990	59.9
1995	61.9
2001	61.7
2006	66.0
2010	68.1

Source: Adapted from U.S. Department of Education (2011b).

of professional training rather than following in their footsteps as entrepreneurs.

In the modern era, parental investment in the futures of children through formal education has thus largely replaced the inheritance of the family farm or the family business as the major form of intergenerational transfer of privilege. In preindustrial societies, the small family business and especially the small family farm always had the disadvantage of being potentially reduced in value or sustainability when subdivided into smaller parts among multiple heirs, giving rise to the then common inheritance practice of primogeniture (the eldest male child inherited everything). With industrialization, however, inheritance of privilege was much less likely to take on the tangible form of discrete farms or businesses and more likely to be in the form of fungible assets such as savings, investments, and educational opportunities in which there is no per unit diminution of value in assets and equal transfer of assets to multiple heirs is easier.

FUNCTIONAL VIEWS OF EDUCATION

The expansion of formal education has substantially increased the importance of schooling in the process of social selection. In modern corporate America, with increasingly complex and bureaucratized work structures, educational credentials have become an important determinant of an individual's life chances. According to the American Dream, the educational system provides substantial opportunities for able and hardworking children from lower-status families to move up, while requiring children from higher-status families to at least prove themselves in school if they want to maintain their advantages. Among those who take this view, schools are likened to an elevator in which everyone gets on at the same floor but, depending on how well he or she does in school, gets off at a different floor corresponding to a particular level of occupational prestige and income.

James Bryant Conant, while serving as president of Harvard University, wrote two articles (1938, 1940) that summarized his view of the role of education in the process of social selection. He argued that democracy does not require a "uniform distribution of the world's goods" or a "radical equalization of wealth." Instead, it requires a "continuous process by which power and privilege may be automatically redistributed at the end of each generation" (Conant 1940, 598). He and other "meritocrats" considered schools to be the primary mechanism of redistribution. Doubting that talent was concentrated at the top of the social-class structure, they believed it was instead rather evenly distributed throughout. By giving every student, from the most humble to the most privileged, an equal educational opportunity at the beginning of life, society would be in a position to select those most qualified by intelligence and hard work to occupy the command posts at the top. In this way, an "aristocracy of talent" would be re-created fresh in every generation. This argument, which some have called "meritocratic aristocracy," neatly combines a principle of an "aristocracy" based on merit with a principle of democratic selection, or equality of opportunity.

In this view, the meritocratic foundation of the American Dream is its educational system—the primary engine of equality of opportunity. The educational system recognizes and rewards with diplomas and certificates those who work the hardest, have the most ambition and perseverance, and possess the most talent and intelligence. These credentials in turn constitute the only legitimate basis for access to desirable jobs and other rewards of society. In short, according to this formulation, the educational system recognizes and rewards the meritorious, regardless of the circumstances into which they are born, thus reducing inequalities based on nonmerit factors like birth or inheritance. The functional theory of education suggests that one of the important functions of educational systems in modern society is to prepare people to become independent, economically productive adults. This means providing the training and skills needed to fill occupations in America's modern and changing industrial economy. The educational requirements of jobs in industrial society constantly increase as a result of technological change. The proportion of jobs that require low skill declines while the proportion that requires high skill increases. What is more, the same jobs are continually upgraded in their skill requirements. The result is need-driven educational expansion: educational requirements for employment continually rise, and more and more people are required to spend longer and longer periods in school. The most obvious meritocratic aspect of this theory is its clear claim that the opportunity to acquire training and skills is directly proportional to individual merit: talent and ability. By implication, educational expansion should reduce socioeconomic inequality since educational opportunity is apportioned on the basis of individual merit, which is distributed equally among the social classes.

Human Capital Theory

Similar to the functional theory of education in sociology, the human capital theory in economics implies meritocratic arguments. Human capital theory (Schultz 1961; Becker 1993) suggests that human resources are a form of capital. Humans can invest in themselves to increase their capital, thereby increasing their productive capacities. According to this theory, as individuals invest in their own human capital, they know more and know how to do more and can therefore command higher premiums for their labor. In modern society, the education system is the most important means through which individuals can invest in their human capital (skills and knowledge). This argument has considerable appeal: the worker is no mere "wage earner" who holds no property and controls neither the work process nor the product of his labor; he or she is instead transformed into a capitalist. In this view, the worker is a holder of capital—human capital—and has the capacity to invest in him- or herself through education.

Status-Attainment Theory

Following the advent of computer-assisted data analysis, research attempting to empirically specify the mechanisms and processes of individual achievement accelerated. Although there had been prior studies of "who gets ahead" in America, sociologists Peter Blau and Otis Dudley Duncan's 1967 *The American Occupational Structure* produced an avalanche of research on the subject of social mobility—the overall amounts and patterns of movement in the occupational structure—as well as what has come to be called status attainment, the process whereby a set of interrelated factors operate to determine which individuals get ahead educationally and occupationally. The latter research has produced the Wisconsin school, so named because the Department of Sociology at the University of Wisconsin became the most important site devoted to the elaboration and extension of Blau and Duncan's initial work. The Wisconsin school, which has dominated the formulation of the questions and methods used to address the issue of status attainment, uses complex multivariate statistical techniques to examine an ever-increasing number of individual-level psychological and attitudinal characteristics that would seem to make a difference in the levels of education, status of occupations, and incomes that people eventually attain. These "status-attainment" studies develop and test models that measure the independent effects of various attributes, such as socioeconomic background (parental education, occupation, income), measured mental ability (IQ, for example), educational and occupational aspirations, and the influence of significant others on these aspirations by statistically holding other variables in the model constant.

In a nutshell, these studies indicate that a mixture of merit, or "achieved," and nonmerit, or "ascribed," traits helps explain variations in educational, occupational, and income attainment. Family background (socioeconomic status) is an important ascribed factor that indirectly affects educational attainment. In turn, educational attainment has a sizable effect on occupational attainment, but it is important to remember that educational attainment is itself influenced by ascribed factors, some of which are not included in these models.

Clearly, high-level educational credentials are an important key to obtaining prestigious and well-paid jobs, and research suggests that people who finish higher-level degrees have a "leg up" in the labor market, even if they are not otherwise advantaged. While status-attainment studies have made important contributions to our understanding of "who gets ahead," this essentially individualistic perspective has produced incomplete and sometimes misleading results. Individual-level psychological, attitudinal characteristics and "human capital" resources (e.g., intelligence, aspirations) are assumed by these models to be the most important factors relevant to the attainment of education, occupational status, and income. Status-attainment models, however, have tended to underestimate the effects of ascriptive factors; more importantly, they neglect the effects of impersonal economic forces—structures of occupational and industrial opportunity ("demand-side" variables)—that are beyond individuals' control and have a role in determining the payoff of human capital resources (see chapter 6).

In short, individuals are subject to complex and shifting structures of demand, the vicissitudes of history, accidents, employers' decisions (rational and irrational), and their own decisions (good and bad). While some of the unexplained variation in who gets ahead no doubt has to do with "being in the right place at the right time" and similar factors of good or bad fortune, we must remember that these are actually individual-level reflections of structurally based demand for talent, skill, and experience.

CONFLICT VIEWS OF EDUCATION

Meritocracy requires equality of educational opportunity. The schooling system, however, provides the most privileged in society with greater opportunities to succeed and fewer chances to fail than it does for those from less privileged backgrounds. This is so because it frequently fails to identify and reward the potential and achievements of those who do not inherit the social, cultural, and economic capital of the privileged classes.

French sociologist Pierre Bourdieu emphasized that schools are instruments of social and cultural reproduction, which are means of social-class reproduction (Bourdieu 1973; Bourdieu and Passeron 1990). According to Bourdieu, schools do not produce cultural capital or even the means to appropriate it. Instead, they recognize it, reward the possession of it, and certify its possession by differentially awarding educational credentials in proportion to the amount of cultural capital possessed. Children from lower classes with less cultural capital are eliminated from the system because of their cultural capital deficits, or they self-eliminate as they come to recognize their low objective chances of success within the system. Thus, school tends to reinforce the cultural capital inequalities based on differences in family socioeconomic status. In this way, the type and amount of education individuals receive is largely "reproduced" by social class across generations.

While social reproduction theory began in Europe as a critique of the social-class biases of the schooling system (cf. Bernstein 1961; Bourdieu 1973; Bourdieu and Passeron 1990), perhaps the most famous American example of reproduction theory is Samuel Bowles and Herbert Gintis's *Schooling in Capitalist America* (1976). They show that while cognitive skills are important in the economy and in predicting individual success, the contribution of schooling to individual economic success can be explained only partly by the cognitive development fostered in schools. They argue that schools prepare children for adult work rules by socializing them to function well and without complaint in the hierarchical structure of the modern workplace. Schools accomplish this by what they call the "correspondence principle," namely, by structuring the social relations of school—interactions and individual rewards—to replicate the environment of the workplace: the social relations of production.

Social reproduction theory identifies specific mechanisms by which educational attainment is largely reproduced across generations through unequal social and cultural capital, educational tracking, and educational funding.

Social Capital and Cultural Capital

Increasing evidence shows that early childhood development is critical to later academic success (Duncan and Murnane 2011; Ermisch, Jantti, and

Smeeding 2012). The research confirms that cognitive and sociobehavioral traits related to "school readiness" are highly related to socioeconomic background. In other words, upon entry into the school system, children from more privileged backgrounds are already ahead and children from disadvantaged backgrounds are already behind, and these gaps tend to persist into adulthood. As noted in chapter 4, children from privileged families are more likely to be the beneficiaries of home environments that promote cognitive development and provide the social and cultural capital needed to do well in school. Therefore, privileged children are already ahead of the less privileged in cognitive ability, social skills, and cultural capital when they enter school. They are also more likely to attend "good" schools that are staffed by competent and experienced teachers, provide an academic college-preparatory curriculum, and are populated by other privileged students (Duncan and Murnane 2011; Massey 2007; Shapiro 2004). Teacher expectations build on these initial advantages: teachers expect more of children from higher-class backgrounds, and differential treatment based on these expectations leads to better performance among these children (Rosenthal and Jacobson 1968; Rist 1970; Good and Brophy 1987).

Research consistently shows that "parental involvement" is a key factor to the educational success of children, and that the extent of parental involvement varies by social class, with more privileged parents having higher rates of involvement in their children's education. Parental involvement can take many forms, including reading to children, assisting with homework, meeting with teachers, being involved in school organizations and activities, and even volunteering time to assist teachers in educational projects and activities. Privileged parents can also afford to invest more heavily in enrichment goods and services such as books, computers, high-quality child care, music lessons, and summer camps. Moreover the spending gaps for such enrichment goods and services between high-income and low-income parents have increased over time. Duncan and Murname (2011), for instance, document that in 1972–1973, parents in the top income quintile spent about $2,700 more per year on child enrichment than did low-income families; by 2005–2006 this gap had nearly tripled to $7,500. Privileged parents are also more likely themselves to have high educational attainment and to be familiar with "how the system works" and to "work the system" to maximize advantages for their own children, intervening on their behalf, sometimes aggressively, with teachers, principals, and other administrators (Lareau and Weininger 2003). Such aggressive privileged parents are commonly referred to by teachers and school administrators as "helicopter" parents. As birthrates have declined, especially among the privileged, there is some speculation that privileged parents are even more aggressive in investing in the futures of the fewer children they now have compared to prior generations. In the past, more children meant an increase in the odds that at least some would succeed even without aggressive parental intervention. Parents may feel more pressure with fewer children to advance the futures of each of the one or two children they are likely to have. With fewer total children, they also have more resources available per child to do so.

School Tracking

Another practice that jeopardizes equality of educational opportunity and tends to reproduce existing inequalities across generations is tracking. Approximately five out of six U.S. public schools use some form of tracking in which children are placed in different groups, or tracks, that prepare some for college and others for vocations that do not require college. There has been much research into the factors that influence track placement and the outcomes of such placement, but conclusions are complex because of the variety of tracking systems in use. One early study showed that all factors that could conceivably be taken to measure cognitive ability and academic performance together explain less than half of the variation in track placement. While measured intellectual skills are the factors most directly responsible for track placement, recall that cognitive skills and academic performance are influenced by family socioeconomic status, especially in critical early stages of childhood development.

Tracking takes place through vocational education as well. Sociologists James Ainsworth and Vincent Roscigno (2005) found that there are significant class, race, and gender disparities in vocational educational placement, even after accounting for prior achievement and educational expectations. They found that vocational involvement increases the likelihood of dropping out of high school and significantly decreases college attendance. Their findings suggest that educational-institutional processes often assumed to be neutral have striking and negative effects on subsequent educational and occupational trajectories.

Regardless of the manner in which individuals are tracked within the educational system, the outcomes of tracking are fairly clear. First, track mobility is typically low. Once a child is placed in a low track, it is difficult to "move up," and for those placed in a high track, it is difficult to do poorly enough to "move down." In short, tracking affects teacher expectations as well as access to quality teachers and the courses needed for college eligibility. Tracking produces self-fulfilling prophecies. Children in higher college-preparatory tracks tend to improve in academic achievement over the years, while those in lower tracks tend to perform at levels that make them ineligible for higher education. Children in higher tracks are less likely to drop out of school, have higher educational aspirations, and are more likely to attend college. In short, tracking often works to reinforce class differences and has an independent effect of further differentiating children in terms of family background (Alexander, Cook, and McDill 1978, 57; Gamoran and Mare 1989; Oakes 1990).

School Quality and School Funding

Journalist Jonathan Kozol has vividly characterized the system of education in America as one of "savage inequalities" (1991) that operates in effect as a system of "apartheid schooling" (2006). Kozol dramatically describes dilapidated school buildings and facilities, inadequate textbooks and teaching materials, and often unsafe and unsanitary conditions in poor school districts, with much cleaner and superior equipment and settings in wealthy school districts. A large part of these differences can be attributed to unequal school funding. The public schools attended by children from higher-income families are better partially because a significant portion of school funding comes from local property taxes, which produce more revenue in privileged residential areas. Despite a growing body of research that repeatedly demonstrates the negative effects of reliance on local funding on student academic achievement, the reliance on local funding is increasing. For example, in the 1989–1990 school year, the proportion of total revenues for public elementary and secondary schools that came from local property taxes was 35.9 percent. By the 2008–2009 school year, that figure was 43.7 percent, an increase of 7.8 percent (U.S. Department of Education 2007, 2009). States, too, vary in the amount of funding made available to public schools.

But this is only part of the story. Schools in wealthier areas are "better" for reasons other than the amount of economic resources spent on students. Not only do high-income families, living in high-income residential areas, provide a strong tax base that can be tapped to fund quality schools, but such families also have the political clout needed to more effectively demand quality education for their children. Wealthy parents also often have the option of avoiding public schools altogether by sending their children to expensive elite private schools and academies. Further, as noted above, the children of high-income families bring considerable cognitive ability as well as social and cultural capital with them to the schools. Finally, the socioeconomic composition of the student body contributes to the formation of school climates or cultures that can prove beneficial or harmful to academic and subsequent occupational attainment. For example, students benefit from peers and "significant others" who exhibit high educational and occupational aspirations because they contribute to educational and occupational attainment. Thus, school quality varies not only by amounts and kinds of economic inputs but by the social, cultural, and intellectual composition of the student body, which varies according to the socioeconomic status of students' families.

These composition factors to some extent mitigate the effects of material conditions and school spending on academic performance. Early research by sociologists James Coleman et al. (1966) and Christopher Jencks et al. (1972), for instance, seemed to show that a number of measures of school quality did not show significant relationships with outcomes such as test scores and later college attendance. In other words, regardless of spending levels and the quality of schools, children from more privileged backgrounds do better than children from less privileged backgrounds. Parents with their own resources can to some extent compensate in other ways for inadequate schools to ensure their own children's academic success. Although the findings of more than forty years of research are somewhat mixed, they generally show that differences in educational, occupational, and income attainment are at least partially attributable to differences in school quality and that the net effects of school quality are substantial (Altonji and Mansfield 2011; Condron and Roscigno 2003; Conley 1999; Johnson 2006; Massey 2007; Shapiro 2004).

Parents clearly believe that there are real differences in school quality and that these differences affect their children's chances for future academic and occupational success. Parents are impressed by the varying reputations that schools develop and are willing to pay the higher costs of housing in residential areas served by "quality" schools (Shapiro 2004). But, of course, variation in income means that not all parents can equally afford these higher housing costs (Massey 2007). As a result, many parents go into considerable debt to advance their children's futures (Warren and Warren Tyagi 2003). In fact, one of the main causes of personal bankruptcy is defaulting on mortgages. We suggest that a sizable but unknown number of these bankruptcies represent cases of family attempts to procure quality education for their children.

Various attempts to reduce the race/class "achievement gap" have produced several policy proposals with limited success. Head Start programs, for instance, are designed to address cultural and learning deprivations that low-income and minority children often have upon entry into the school system that puts them at a competitive disadvantage. Research on the long reach of these deprivations into adulthood suggests that such early childhood interventions can be effective in reducing the achievement gap (Duncan and Murnane 2011). Magnet and charter schools, national standardized testing as means of evaluating teacher and school performance, and proposed choice and voucher plans have also been advanced as ways to close the achievement gap. The cost, source of control, and effectiveness of these various reforms are highly variable as well as controversial. For the most part such proposals are still experimental. In the meantime, the opportunity/achievement gap persists.

Higher Education

The pattern that produces class-based inequality of educational opportunity in K–12 extends to higher education. Upper-class students are disproportionately funneled into exclusive elite and private colleges, middle-class students are disproportionately funneled into public state universities, and working-class students are disproportionately funneled into community colleges. In these settings, students are in essence being groomed for future roles in the economy, with upper-class students being largely groomed for command positions in major social institutions, middle-class students being largely groomed for functionary positions as midlevel managers and administrators, and working-class students being largely groomed for technical and vocational roles. The inequalities reproduced across generations are substantial but far from complete. In part this is because some parents, regardless of class position, are more successful in promoting the futures of their children. And some children, regardless of class position, are more capable than others. Some of the most capable are also assisted by merit-based scholarship programs and concerted efforts by some institutions to diversify their student bodies. As a result, some rich kids fail, and some poor kids succeed. These exceptions, however infrequent, help to sustain at least the outward appearance of meritocracy and the American Dream.

The overall pattern of unequal access to educational opportunity is clear. Moreover the gap in educational opportunity between low- and high-income families is increasing. For instance, Martha Bailey and Susan Dynarski (2011) tracked rates of college completion by income quartile for two cohorts of students, one born 1961–1964 and one born 1979–1982. For the most recent cohort, 54 percent of those students from the highest income quartile completed college, compared to only 9 percent of those students from the lowest income quartile. Compared to the earlier cohort, the rate of college completion for the top income quartile had increased 18 percent, but the comparable increase for the lower income quartile was only 4 percent. The income gap is most pronounced at the nation's most elite institutions. Anthony Carnevale and Stephen Rose, for instance, found that 74 percent of students at the nation's top 146 colleges come from the richest income quartile, but only 3 percent come from the poorest quartile (Carnevale and Rose 2004, 106).

Other research shows that low-income students finish college less often than higher-income students even when the lower-income students score higher on skills tests. Comparing eighth-grade skills-test scores and eventual college graduation rates, Matthew Chingos of the Brookings Institution, for instance, found that only 26 percent of students from the poorest income quartile with *above*-average test scores completed college, compared with 30 percent of students completing college from the richest income quartile who had *below*-average test scores (*New York Times* 2012).

There are several ways in which the pattern of unequal access to educational opportunities in K–12 is extended to the university level. Initial advantages or disadvantages of class placement at birth not only create unequal starting points but, as we have seen, accumulate and are amplified over time. One of the ways this difference works to the disadvantage of those from lower socioeconomic backgrounds is through the use of standardized aptitude tests such as the SAT and ACT as criteria for admission to colleges and universities. As we have seen, such tests were designed initially to promote meritocratic criteria for admission to colleges and universities. As the companies that produce these tests are careful to point out, they are not measures of innate intelligence but are designed to measure one's "aptitude" for advanced study. However, recent research (Bowen, Chingos, and McPherson 2011) has shown that such tests are very poor predictors of the likelihood of completing college. High school grades are far better predictors of successful college completion. On average, high school grades have five times more predictive power than test scores on college completion. For highly selective colleges and universities, test scores are better predictors of college completion but still have only half the predictive power of high school grades. Moreover the predictive power of high school grades is increased once controls are added for the quality of high school attended. At one level, all of this stands to reason. Grades are measures of actual performance, and prior performance is a good measure of future performance. Standardized tests, on the other hand, do not capture intangibles such as creativity, motivation, and perseverance. What they do capture is socioeconomic background since it is well known that scores on such aptitude tests are highly correlated with family income, probably to a large extent due to the effects of social and cultural capital described earlier. To the extent that colleges use such tests as screening devices for admission, those from lower socioeconomic backgrounds are at a systematic disadvantage based on selection criteria that turn out to have little bearing on the actual likelihood of success.

Another rather direct way in which social-class advantage at the college level is reproduced across generations is through legacy admissions (Soares 2007; Stevens 2007; Golden 2003, 2006; Karabel 2005; Espenshade, Chung, and Walling 2004; Howell and Turner 2004). Legacy admissions refer to advantage or additional consideration extended to applicants because family members are alumni of the institution to which the student has applied. In essence, legacy admissions operate as essentially a nonmerit affirmative action program for the already privileged. Studies of these practices generally reveal a roughly two-to-one admission advantage for legacies compared with overall rates (Bowen and Bok 2009; Howell and Turner 2004). In his study of admission practices at Yale University from 1920 to 2000, Joseph Soares shows that legacies made up an average of 20 percent of the first-year class at Yale University, with more recent years (1990–2000) averaging somewhat less at about 13 percent (Soares 2007, 91). Finally, Thomas Espenshade, Chang Chung, and Joan Walling (2004), controlling for sex, citizenship, SAT score, high school GPA, race, athletic recruitment, and several other relevant variables, found that other things being equal, status as the child of an alumnus translated into an admissions bonus of about 160 SAT points, improving considerably the odds of admission.

In *Creating a Class: College Admissions and the Education of Elites* (2007), sociologist Mitchell Stevens summarizes the findings of a particularly revealing study which shows how other more subtle mechanisms beyond legacy considerations operate to reproduce class advantage. Stevens gathered participant-observation data working for a year and a half in the admissions office at an elite New England college. Unsurprisingly, Stevens found that admissions were highly competitive. He also found that creating a first-year class was quite complicated and involved the use of criteria that favored the already privileged. He shows that this task cannot be completed without "systematic preferences" and that racial affirmative action is minimal. For example, applicants are given preference if their parents can pay full tuition, if they attended a high school with a high-status zip code, if they are athletes (especially football players), and even if they are popular. Stevens thus explains how elite colleges and universities reproduce the nation's most privileged classes. He finds that individualized evaluation protocols do not create equal educational opportunity but reproduce class privilege. In competing for the limited seats at these institutions, the goal of parents is to raise children with the attributes most sought by elite colleges and universities: measurable academic and extracurricular accomplishment and athletic prowess, good looks, a slender body, and an outgoing personality. Admission to such colleges is taken as evidence of excellent parenting, intellectual prowess, academic talent, and considerable accomplishment and certifies elite status.

The costs of higher education are also a barrier to access for students and their families with modest means. As previously noted in chapter 1, the cost of higher education in the past several decades has risen faster than the overall cost of living. For the 2010–2011 academic year, the average annual cost for tuition, fees, room, and board was $13,564 at a public four-year college and $36,252 at a private not-for-profit four-year college (U.S. Department of Education 2011c). Despite these higher costs, rates of college attendance in the past several decades have increased. This has been possible through increased student debt. Federal Pell Grants for low-income students have not kept pace with these rising costs. In the mid-1970s, the maximum Pell Grant covered almost 60 percent of the costs of attending a four-year public university; by 2000–2001 this coverage was reduced to 40 percent (Century Foundation 2004). Meanwhile, states have sharply reduced the subsidy for tuition at state universities and colleges, passing on a greater burden of the cost to students. In 1989, 9 percent of households owed some student debt with an average of the equivalent of $9,634 debt per household (in 2011 dollars); in 2010, 19 percent of households owed some student debt with an average of $26,682 per household (in 2011 dollars) (Fry 2012).

Compared to the early 1900s when less than 5 percent of Americans were college educated, there has been a dramatic increase in the proportion of the adult population that is college educated. This has democratized access to higher education through government funding of higher education—the GI Bill and its ongoing iterations, the post–World War II expansion of state universities and community colleges, and federal Pell Grants and guaranteed student loans—and the willingness of private lenders to forego collateral loan requirements and instead to loan money to students against the prospects of future earnings. In other words, the expansion of higher education to a greater segment of the American population has been primarily accomplished through debt.

In *Borrowing Inequality: Race, Class, and Student Loans* (2004), Derek Price uses social reproduction theory to explain two trends in student financial aid that have come about in recent decades: a transition from mostly grants to primarily loans and the rising share of college costs that students and families pay. According to him the result has been an overreliance on student loans to finance higher education, which has contributed to an educational-attainment gap. This in turn contributes to social and economic class reproduction by differentially increasing student borrowing and debt among less privileged students and their families. He argues that as the college credential replaces the high school diploma as the required standard of educational "achievement," increasing student debt among the less privileged jeopardizes any subsequent advantage that these educational credentials might produce. In short, the current overreliance on student loans to finance higher education diminishes the value of higher education.

At the same time that there has been a debt-financed increase in students going to college, there has been a depressed job market for college graduates, resulting in higher rates of underemployment for new entrants in the labor market (Vedder, Denhart, and Robe 2013; Stone, Horn, and Zukin 2012). Economist Richard Vedder and his associates, for instance, estimate that in 2010, 48 percent of employed U.S. college graduates were in jobs that the Department of Labor Statistics suggests require less than a four-year college degree (Vedder, Denhard and Robe 2013, 12). As a result, there are both inflationary pressures to seek more advanced degrees to gain a competitive edge and increased skepticism about the value of return on the investment in higher education.

We conclude that higher education is not governed by strict principles of meritocracy but instead reflects, legitimizes, and reproduces class inequalities. This is because all the advantages of class that we have already discussed—inherited familial economic resources (which translate into "quality education" and high educational aspirations), social capital (which includes parental "connections" and positive peer influences), and cultural capital—collectively produce K–12 educational outcomes, including high grade point averages, high standardized and AP test scores, and high SAT scores, which are important selection criteria for America's "best" colleges and universities. Thus, the advantages of high class produce the credentials sought by America's elite universities. But additional advantages accrue to class privilege, ranging from the simple ability to pay for an elite private college or university education, to the financial ability to take advantage of "early-acceptance" programs at such institutions, to elaborate back-channel "slotting" operations in which highly connected and expert high school and prep school counselors work closely with admissions officials to virtually place higher-status students at these institutions. In short, America's system of higher education is clearly not an "engine of meritocracy" but rather a basic component in a system that reproduces unequal starting points from one generation to the next.

CREDENTIAL INFLATION AND THE PAPER CHASE

Over the past century, educational requirements for entry-level jobs have spread to a wide range of occupations, keeping step with advances in educational attainment. The desire for more opportunity may be enough to increase the numbers of students seeking higher levels of schooling, but it does not in itself increase the probability that such hopes will be realized. Only a tightening link between educational qualifications and jobs can do that. An important facet of the school's changing role in social selection has to do with the rise of what Randall Collins (1979) has called credentialism, the monopolization of access to the more rewarding jobs and economic opportunities by the holders of degrees and certificates.

In the process of credentials inflation, higher degrees come to be required even for some jobs that may not be very intellectually demanding or for which an advanced degree would hardly seem necessary. For example, a college degree may not actually be needed to "manage" a video store. But if the pool of applicants for such a position comes to include holders of college degrees, they will tend to be selected over those without degrees, and soon a college degree will become a requirement. Once credentials are established as a requirement for hiring, inflationary pressures are strong, because students and their families have a strong interest in obtaining resources—in this case educational credentials—that promise them greater opportunities. In short, the aspiration for upward mobility can "ratchet up" credential requirements above what they might otherwise be, producing credential inflation. The result has been the proliferation of specialized occupational jurisdictions that are off limits to anyone without the accepted educational credentials. Professional associations, governments, and educational institutions have each played a role in constructing occupations and carving the structure of occupations into a maze of occupational jurisdictions controlled by the holders of specialized credentials; all have a stake in the expansion of the "credential society" (Collins 1979; Brown 1995, 2001).

A related argument is that the growth of credentialism has been fueled primarily by the growth of large organizations and the incentives of those in positions of authority in these organizations to find efficient ways to process people and to fill positions. Those making hiring decisions can hardly have a deep knowledge of each of perhaps hundreds of applicants' job-relevant characteristics. Some "shorthand" is needed—objective "evidence" that can be presumed to indicate potential for success. Organizations have come to use educational credentials as an important component of this shorthand—as signals that their holders are more likely than other people to behave in organizationally valued ways. Thus, educational credentials have proven a cost-effective way to limit the pool of eligibles and to aid in the hiring of people presumed to have qualities that organizations value. For example, educational credentials may signal the ability of a job applicant to concentrate in a disciplined way on assigned problems, something that students must do repeatedly if they are to succeed in school. Other traits include reliability (simply showing up every day on time and in a work-ready state), the ability to handle nonroutine or self-directed work, and the ability to conform to the direction and desires of superiors. From the employers' point of view, it is a good bet that those who have survived all the paper writing and examinations of a college education, as well as its stifling bureaucratic organization, have developed these qualities to a greater degree than those who have not.

Furthermore, as one moves up organizational hierarchies, the qualities that schooling selects may be even more important (Bourdieu 1984; Bourdieu and Passeron 1990). According to Robin Blackburn and Michael Mann, organizational careers are "fundamentally an apprenticeship in cooperation. . . . The essential point about jobs at the top of the hierarchy is not an unusual degree of skill but the costliness to management of error and the likelihood of error being made" (1979, 108). Therefore employers are often less concerned with the possession of specific information and technical skills than with possession of cultural capital (arbitrary knowledge, manners and decorum, styles and tastes representative of privilege) and noncognitive characteristics such as discipline, steadiness, and responsibility, sometimes referred to as "soft skills."

Today, higher educational credentials are required for professional, technical, and managerial occupations and for most other nonclerical white-collar jobs in large private- and public-sector work organizations. These jobs represent a very large proportion of the most prestigious and best-paying jobs available. Even in the less credentialized sphere of business management, credentialism has grown rapidly. Almost no one is promoted up the ranks into top management today without a college degree, and an MBA from a top-ranked business school has become an important ticket of admission to the executive suite.

However, the widespread practice of using educational credentials as proxies for skills needed to do certain jobs is imperfect. Beyond literacy and basic computational skills, most of what people need to know to perform most work tasks is learned on the job, not in the classroom. Educational credentials are only an indirect means of assessing a person's capacity to perform such tasks. To the extent that educational signals used as convenient screening devices for job placement are inaccurate, true meritocracy is compromised. In such cases, education does not act as a vehicle of upward social mobility for the most deserving; instead, the *lack* of particular credentials operates as an artificial barrier to mobility.

Although credentialism has increased tremendously during the past century, certain spheres of the job structure have been affected less than others. For example, some people without educational qualifications continue to start and run successful farms and small businesses, and these continue to be handed down within families. In addition, access to jobs in numerous skilled trades (plumber, electrician) is regulated more by family networks and informal training than by formal education. However, these jobs represent a declining proportion of job opportunities in modern America, and even among them, state licensure, based on passing formal competency tests, is becoming the norm.

SUMMARY

Education is both a merit and nonmerit factor in getting ahead in America. It is a merit factor in the sense that students "earn" grades, credits, and diplomas. It is a nonmerit factor in the sense that competition for success is structured by an educational system that does not provide equality of opportunity.

Equality of educational opportunity is a crucial component of the American Dream, but it has never come close to existing in America. Family socioeconomic status and other ascribed characteristics directly and indirectly affect educational attainment. Schools both reflect and re-create existing inequalities in society. Schools reward children of the privileged by certifying and enhancing their social and cultural capital. On the other hand, schools punish children of lower socioeconomic status for their lack of such capital, consigning them to lower-quality teachers, curricula, tracks, and schools, as well as to the self-fulfilling prophecies of low expectations that these produce. As a result, less-privileged children are awarded fewer and lower-valued credentials, and inequality is largely reproduced across generations. Moreover, with increased job competition and increased credential inflation, class reproduction continues to occur, but at higher levels of educational attainment in the population as a whole.

REFERENCES

Ainsworth, James W., and Vincent J. Roscigno. 2005. "Stratification, School-Work Linkages and Vocational Education." *Social Forces* 84:257–84.

Alexander, Karl, Martha Cook, and Edward McDill. 1978. "Curriculum Tracking and Educational Stratification: Some Further Evidence." *American Sociological Review* 43:47–66.

Altonji, Joseph G., and Richard K. Mansfield. 2011. "The Role of Family, School, and Community Characteristics in Inequality in Education and Labor-Market Outcomes." In *Whither Opportunity? Rising Inequality, Schools, and Children's Life Chances*, ed. Greg. J. Duncan and Richard J. Murnane, 339–57. New York: Sage.

Bailey, Martha, and Susan M. Dynarski. 2011. "Inequality in Postsecondary Education." In *Whither Opportunity? Rising Inequality, Schools, and Children's Life Chances*, ed. Greg. J. Duncan and Richard J. Murnane, 117–31. New York: Sage.

Becker, Gary S. 1993. *Human Capital: A Theoretical and Empirical Analysis with Special Reference to Education*. New York: Columbia University Press.

Bernstein, Basil. 1961. "Social Class and Linguistic Development: A Theory of Social Learning." In *Education, Economy, and Society*, ed. A. H. Halsey, Jean Floud, and C. Arnold Anderson, 288–314. New York: Free Press.

Blackburn, Robin M., and Michael Mann. 1979. *The Working Class in the Labour Market*. London: Macmillan.

Blau, Peter, and Otis Dudley Duncan. 1967. *The American Occupational Structure*. New York: Wiley.

Bourdieu, Pierre. 1973. "Cultural Reproduction and Social Reproduction." In *Knowledge, Education, and Cultural Change*, ed. Richard Brown, 71–112. London: Tavistock.

———. 1984. *Distinction*. Cambridge, MA: Harvard University Press.

Bourdieu, Pierre, and Jean-Claude Passeron. 1990. *Reproduction in Education, Society, and Culture*. London: Sage.

Bowen, William G., and Derek Bok. 2009. *The Shape of the River: Long-Term Consequences of Considering Race in College and University Admissions*. Princeton, NJ: Princeton University Press.

Bowen, William G., Matthew M. Chingos, and Michael S. McPherson. 2011. *Crossing the Finish Line: Completing College at America's Public Universities*. Princeton, NJ: Princeton University Press.

Bowles, Samuel, and Herbert Gintis. 1976. *Schooling in Capitalist America*. New York: Basic Books.

Brint, Steven, and Jerome Karabel. 1989. *The Diverted Dream: Community Colleges and the Promise of Educational Opportunity in America, 1900–1980*. New York: Oxford University Press.

Brown, David K. 1995. *Degrees of Control: A Sociology of Educational Expansion and Occupational Credentialism*. New York: Teachers College Press.

———. 2001. "The Social Sources of Educational Credentialism: Status Cultures, Labor Markets, and Organizations." *Sociology of Education*, extra issue: 19–34.

Carnegie, Andrew. 1899. "Wealth." *North American Review* 148:653–64.

Carnevale, Anthony P., and Stephen J. Rose. 2004. "Socioeconomic Status, Race/Ethnicity, and Selective College Admissions." In *American's Untapped Resource: Low-Income Students in Higher Education*, ed. Richard D. Rahlenberg. New York: Century Foundation Press.

Century Foundation. 2004. "Left Behind: Unequal Opportunity in Higher Education." http://tcf.org/assets/downloads/tcf-leftbehindrc.pdf (accessed May 13, 2013).

Coleman, James S., Ernest Q. Campbell, Carol J. Hobson, James McPartland, Alexander M. Mood, Frederic D. Weinfold, and Robert L. Link. 1966. *Equality of Educational Opportunity*. Washington, DC: U.S. Government Printing Office.

Collins, Randall. 1979. *The Credential Society: A Historical Sociology of Education and Stratification*. New York: Academic Press.

Conant, James Bryant. 1938. "The Future of Our Higher Education." *Harper's Magazine* 176 (May): 561–70.

———. 1940. "Education for a Classless Society: The Jeffersonian Tradition." *Atlantic* 165 (May): 593–602.

Condron, Dennis J., and Vincent J. Roscigno. 2003. "Disparities Within: Unequal Spending and Achievement in an Urban School District." *Sociology of Education* 76 (January):18–36.

Conley, Dalton. 1999. *Being Black, Living in the Red: Race, Wealth, and Social Policy in America*. Berkeley: University of California Press.

Duncan, Greg J., and Richard J. Murnane. 2011. "Introduction: The American Dream, Then and Now." In *Whither Opportunity? Rising Inequality, Schools, and Children's Life Chances*, 3–23. New York: Sage.

Ermisch, John, Markus Jantti, and Timothy Smeeding, eds. 2012. *From Parents to Children: The Intergenerational Transmission of Advantage*. New York: Sage.

Espenshade, Thomas J., Chang Y. Chung, and Joan L. Walling. 2004. "Admission Preferences for Minority Studies, Athletes, and Legacies at Elite Universities." *Social Science Quarterly* 84, no. 2: 612–23.

Fry, Richard. 2012. "A Record One-in-Five Households Now Owe Student Loan Debt." Washington, D.C. Pew Research Center. http://www.pewsocialtrends.org/2012/09/26/a-record-one-in-five-households-now-owe-student-loan-debt/ (accessed May 15, 2013).

Gamoran, Adam, and Robert D. Mare. 1989. "Secondary School Tracking and Educational Inequality: Compensation, Reinforcement, or Neutrality?" *American Journal of Sociology* 94:1146–83.

Golden, Daniel. 2003. "Family Ties: Preference for Alumni Children in College Admission Draws Fire." *Wall Street Journal*, January 15.

———. 2006. *The Price of Admission: How America's Ruling Class Buys Its Way into Elite Colleges—and Who Gets Left Outside the Gates*. New York: Crown.

Good, Thomas, and Jere Brophy. 1987. *Looking in Classrooms*. New York: Harper & Row.

Howell, Cameron, and Sarah E. Turner. 2004. "Legacies in Black and White: The Racial Composition of the Legacy Pool." *Research in Higher Education* 455, no. 4: 325–51.

Jencks, Christopher L., Marshall Smith, Henry Acland, Mary Jo Bane, David K. Cohen, Herbert Gintis, Barbara Heyns, et al. 1972. *Inequality: Reassessment of the Effect of Family and Schooling in America*. New York: Harper & Row.

Johnson, Heather Beth. 2006. *The American Dream and the Power of Wealth: Choosing Schools and Inheriting Inequality in the Land of Opportunity*. New York: Routledge.

Karabel, Jerome. 2005. *The Chosen: The Hidden History of Admission and Exclusion at Harvard, Yale, and Princeton*. New York: Houghton Mifflin.

Kozol, Jonathan. 1991. *Savage Inequalities: Children in America's Schools*. New York: Crown.

———. 2006. *The Shame of the Nation: The Restoration of Apartheid Schooling in America*. New York: Crown.

Kusmin, Lorin. 2008. "Education's Role in the Metro-Nonmetro Earnings Divide." *Amber Waves*, April. http://www.ers.usda.gov/AmberWaves/February08/Features/EducationRole.htm (accessed February 24, 2009).

Lareau, Annette. 2000. *Home Advantage: Social Class and Parental Intervention in Elementary Education*. Lanham, MD: Rowman & Littlefield.

———. 2003. *Unequal Childhoods: Class, Race, and Family Life*. Los Angeles: University of California Press.

Lareau, Annette, and Elliot B. Weininger. 2003. "Cultural Capital in Educational Research." *Theory and Society* 32, nos. 5–6: 567–606.

Massey, Douglas S. 2007. *Categorically Unequal: The American Stratification System*. New York: Sage.

New York Times. 2005. "Appendix: *New York Times* Poll on Class." In *Class Matters*, ed. *New York Times*, 244–76. New York: Times Books.

———. 2012. "Affluent Students Have an Advantage and the Gap Is Widening." December 22, 2012. http://www.nytimes.com/interactive/2012/12/22/education/Affluent-Students-Have-an-Advantage-and-the-Gap-Is-Widening.html (accessed January 30, 2013).

Oakes, Jeannie. 1990. *Multiplying Inequalities: The Effects of Race, Social Class, and Tracking on Opportunities to Learn Mathematics and Science*. Santa Monica, CA: Rand.

Pew Research Center. 2011. *Is College Worth It?* Pew Social & Demographic Trends, May 15.http://www.pewsocialtrends.org/2011/05/15/is-college-worth-it/#executive-summary?src=prc-number (accessed September 23, 2012).

Price, Derek V. 2004. *Borrowing Inequality: Race, Class, and Student Loans*. Boulder, CO: Lynne Rienner.

Rist, Ray C. 1970. "Student Social Class and Teachers' Expectations: The Self-Fulfilling Prophecy in Ghetto Education." *Harvard Educational Review* 40:411–50.

Rosenthal, Robert, and Lenore Jacobson. 1968. *Pygmalion in the Classroom*. New York: Holt, Rinehart & Winston.

Schultz, Theodore W. 1961. "Investment in Human Capital." *American Economic Review* 51:1–17.

Shapiro, Thomas M. 2004. *The Hidden Cost of Being African American: How Wealth Perpetuates Inequality*. New York: Oxford University Press.

Soares, Joseph. 2007. *The Power of Privilege: Yale and America's Elite Universities*. Stanford, CA: Stanford University Press.

Stevens, Mitchell L. 2007. *Creating a Class: College Admissions and the Education of Elites*. Cambridge, MA: Harvard University Press.

Stone, Charley, Carl Van Horn, and Cliff Zukin. 2012. *Chasing the American Dream: Recent College Graduates and the Great Recession*. New Brunswick, NJ: Rutgers University, John J. Heldrich Center for Workforce Development. http://www.heldrich.rutgers.edu/sites/default/files/content/Chasing_American_Dream_Report.pdf (accessed January 23, 2013).

U.S. Census Bureau. 1972, 1990, 2009. *Selected Tables*. Washington, DC: U.S. Government Printing Office.

———. 2011. "Table 1, Annual Earnings by Level of Education and Work Status." "Education and Synthetic Work-Life Earnings Estimates." American Community Survey Reports. http://www.census.gov/prod/2011pubs/acs-14.pdf (accessed September 10, 2012).

U.S. Department of Education. 2007. "National Public Education Financial Survey," 1989–1990 and 2004–2005. National Center for Education Statistics, Common Core of Data (CCD). Washington, DC: U.S. Government Printing Office.

———. 2009. "National Public Education Financial Survey (NPEFS)," fiscal year 2009, version 1a. National Center for Education Statistics, Common Core of Data (CCD). http://nces.ed.gov/pubs2011/expenditures/tables/table_01.asp?referrer=report (accessed September 20, 2012).

———. 2011a. *Digest of Education Statistics*, 2011. Table 8. http://nces.ed.gov/programs/digest/d11/tables/dt11_008.asp (accessed September 10, 2012).

———. 2011b. *Digest of Education Statistics*, 2011. Table 209. http://nces.ed.gov/programs/digest/d11/tables/dt11_209.asp (accessed September 10, 2012).

———. 2011c. *Digest of Education Statistics*, 2011. Table 351. http://nces.ed.gov/programs/digest/d11/tables/dt11_351.asp (accessed September 10, 2012).

———. 2012. *The Condition of Education 2012* (NCES 2012–045), indicator 48. National Center for Education Statistics.

Vedder, Richard, Christopher Denhart, and Jonathan Robe. 2013. *Why Are Recent College Graduates Underemployed? University Enrollments and Labor Market Realities*. Washington, DC: Center for College Affordability and Productivity. http://centerforcollegeaffordability.org/uploads/Underemployed%20Report%202.pdf (accessed January 30, 2013).

Warren, Elizabeth, and Amelia Warren Tyagi. 2003. *The Two-Income Trap: Why Middle-Class Mothers and Fathers Are Going Broke*. New York: Basic Books.

Chapter Six

Being in the Right Place at the Right Time

The Luck Factor

I think we consider too much the good luck of the early bird, and not enough
the bad luck of the early worm.
—Franklin Delano Roosevelt

My aspiration now is to get by luck what I could not get by merit.
—Mason Cooley, U.S. aphorist

In thinking about who ends up with what jobs, Americans tend to first think
about what economists call the "supply side." In labor economics, the supply
side refers to the pool of workers available to fill jobs. The ideology of
meritocracy leads Americans to focus on the qualities of individual workers:
how smart they are, how qualified they are, how much education they have,
and so on. These "human capital" factors, however, represent only half of the
equation. The other half, the "demand side," is about the number and types of
jobs available. How many jobs are available, their location, how much they
pay, and how many people are seeking them are important but often ne-
glected considerations in assessing the impact of merit on economic outcomes. In this chapter we explore the implications of the demand side and of
being in the right place at the right time.

FROM FARMER TO FACTORY WORKER TO
RETAIL SALES CLERK

The history of the American labor force can be summarized by tracing the evolution of three jobs: farmer, factory worker, and retail sales clerk. Figure 6.1 depicts historical changes in the American labor force comparing farming, manufacturing, and service occupations. In colonial times, the vast majority of American workers were farmers. Many worked their own small family farms. Corporations did not exist. America for the most part was an agrarian and land-based society. With the beginning of the Industrial Revolution in the mid-nineteenth century, what the average worker did for a living began to change. Farming became progressively more mechanized. Herbicides, pesticides, tractors, harvesters, and other heavy equipment gradually replaced field hands. America could grow more food with less human labor. By the end of the nineteenth century, urban factories were booming. Displaced farm laborers moved in large numbers from the rural countryside to urban centers in search of factory jobs.

More Americans were now factory workers, operating machines that turned raw goods into finished products. Most were machine operators; some were skilled craftsmen—electricians, millwrights, tool and die makers, and the like. Corporations replaced family businesses, and the rate of self-employment sharply declined. By the middle of the twentieth century, manufacturing had reached its peak. Manufacturing jobs, while still employing a significant proportion of the labor force in the United States, began to decline. The rate of decline accelerated in the latter part of the twentieth century as manufacturing increasingly shifted overseas, where labor was cheaper, less unionized, and less regulated. At the same time, farming occupations as a proportion of the total labor force fell off even more precipitously. In the

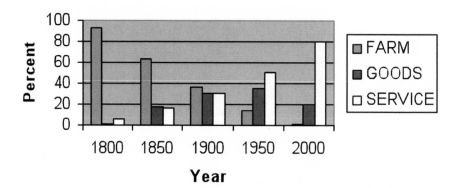

Figure 6.1. Employment by Industry. *Source:* U.S. Census Bureau 1975, 2001.

wake of these changes, the growth of the service sector of the economy exploded and now far outstrips farming and manufacturing as a source of employment. The service sector includes a mixed bag of occupations ranging from hairstylists, to insurance agents, to sales clerks, to computer programmers—all having to do in some way with processing either information or people or both. Instead of being a field hand on the farm or a machine operator in the factory, the typical worker in America is now a sales clerk in a department store.

These changes are significant in terms of how people "experience" intergenerational mobility. Each generation encounters a different array of "slots" to be filled. The changes in the "tasks" that need doing are not a reflection of individual merit. They are the result of changes in technology and concomitant changes in the division of labor, in economic and political policy, and in the global economy. Sociologists refer to mobility caused by changes in the division of labor in society as "structural mobility."

For most of the twentieth century, the types of slots available represented a generalized occupational upgrading. Unskilled farm labor, the backbone of an agrarian economy, was being replaced by factory and office work. Factory work included many blue-collar skilled and semiskilled jobs—an upgrade in terms of both earnings and social status. Compared to farming and manufacturing, office work in the service sector was cleaner, less dangerous, and less physically demanding and often conferred higher social status. The general standard of living also rapidly increased. Most of the upward "movement" individuals experienced compared to their parents and grandparents was the result of these structural changes, not individual merit. The college-educated computer programmer whose father was a factory worker with a high school education, whose father before him was a farmer with a grade school education, is not necessarily smarter, more motivated, or of higher moral caliber than his father or grandfather. Each faced very different opportunity structures. Fueled by the ideology of meritocracy, however, individuals swept up in these waves of social change are often quick to falsely attribute their rise in social standing to individual merit alone.

Beginning in the early 1970s, the ground shifted. Several trends coalesced to radically alter the American occupational landscape. First, U.S. industrial corporations were beginning to feel the pinch of increasing foreign competition. In the immediate aftermath of World War II, the United States emerged from the conflict as the only industrialized nation that had not had its industrial infrastructure damaged or destroyed. Under these conditions, the United States easily dominated global markets. As part of the postwar recovery effort, the United States helped rebuild Germany and Japan. Germany and Japan, among other nations, were now emerging as serious global competitors. In 1973, an oil embargo imposed by the Organization of Petroleum Exporting Countries (OPEC) sharply increased production costs, which was especially detrimental to nations and industries with the oldest and least efficient production facilities. The automobile industry in the United States, which had been the backbone of America's postwar industrial might, suffered dramatically from these changes. Using the most modern production facilities, Japan and Germany, producing smaller, more fuel-efficient, and higher-quality automobiles, made significant inroads into the American automobile market. Similar scenarios were played out as well in other industries, including steel, textiles, and chemicals, all of which had been part of America's postwar industrial strength.

To compensate for these losses, American industry sought new strategies. In what economists Bennett Harrison and Barry Bluestone (2000) characterize as "the Great U-turn," American corporations responded to these new competitive pressures through massive corporate "restructuring." Several strategies were pursued simultaneously, including shifting sites of production, encouraging supply-side government policy, "outsourcing," and "downsizing." To reduce production costs, corporations aggressively shifted production and technical-support services abroad. New communications technologies and declining transportation costs accelerated the globalization of markets. The trade deficit for the United States dramatically increased as imports exceeded exports, placing downward pressure on wages and benefits. Domestically, factory production shifted away from the urban industrial centers in the north-central and northeastern parts of the United States to the South and Southwest. All of these moves reduced production costs by relocating factory production as well as many technical-support services to new domestic and international locations with lower wages, less unionization, and less government regulation.

As part of the pressure to keep factories and service-support centers open or operating in the United States, those that did remain often extracted wage and benefit "concessions" and "givebacks" from workers. Corporations aggressively moved to break up existing unions and to prevent new ones from forming, further depressing wages and benefits, especially for blue-collar workers. As part of "downsizing" campaigns, corporations replaced permanent, higher-paid workers with "outsourced" contract labor and dramatically increased part-time temporary and contingent labor, partly as a strategy to avoid the benefit compensation otherwise mandated for full-time workers (Hatton 2011).

At the same time, corporations pressed for changes in government policy. Corporate America found a sympathetic sponsor for these changes in Republican presidential administrations, which lowered corporate and personal income taxes for the wealthy, deregulated large segments of the economy, trimmed the nonmilitary federal workforce, and sharply reduced welfare and other government programs targeted toward the poor. Operating in a new climate of relaxed government regulation, big business entered into a frenzy of megamergers, takeovers, and acquisitions. Most mergers resulted in lay-offs, as combined entities realized savings from increased economies of scale. Billions of dollars were taken out of the economy to finance megamergers. Through mergers and stock manipulations, investors could make money without necessarily increasing production or creating new jobs. When the dust cleared, there were fewer but bigger corporations. Personal investment income increased. Wages and benefits decreased or remained stagnant. Corporate profits and the salaries of corporate CEOs soared. Inequality increased. Social mobility declined. Job and income instability increased.

Millions of American workers were caught up in the tidal force of these structural changes. Hardest hit were male blue-collar factory workers. From 1992 to 2011, the manufacturing sector lost over nine million jobs (U.S. Department of Labor 2012a). In addition, as part of the overall downsizing strategy, middle-level management jobs were trimmed while new computer technologies automated routine information-processing tasks. In the postwar period, it had been possible for many working-class Americans with only a high school diploma to realize the American Dream by working in factories and corporate offices with good pay, good benefits, and long-term job stability. With "deindustrialization" and "downsizing," many of these workers were laid off (Uchitelle 2006). New jobs were created, but these were mostly in the "soft," low-wage, low-skill service sector.

Reflecting on her interviews with these workers, economist Paula Rayman put it this way:

> During the early 1980s, many workers in America who thought they had it made in the major industrial corporations of auto, steel, and aircraft found themselves unemployed. . . . They had done everything right: worked hard, done a fair day's work for a fair day's pay. But through no fault of their own, they found themselves cast out of work. And even though they were unemployed because of economic decisions not in their control, they felt personal shame for their failure to hold a job. The personalization of job-loss experiences in the United States is common to many employees from many industries. The Horatio Alger myth is very powerful: the belief that if you rise up, it is due to your own efforts, and if you sink, it is due to your own failures. There is not a powerful story that supports the view that an individual's job history reflects larger situational and organizational forces. In America, the stories are private, based on the individual, not social or based on institutional contexts. (2001, 70–71)

The American economy has been transformed from auto, steel, and oil to fast food, day care, and shopping malls. Table 6.1 shows the Department of Labor's projection of the twenty-five fastest-growing jobs in America that will produce the most new job slots between 2010 and 2020. With few exceptions, most of these "growth jobs" are in the low-wage service sector.

Chapter 6

Table 6.1. Occupations with Highest Projected Growth, 2010–2020

Occupation	N^a	Percent^b	Median Annual Earnings ($) 2010	Education or Training
Registered nurses	711,900	26	64,690	Associate's degree
Retail salespersons	706,800	17	20,670	Less than high school
Home health aides	706,300	69	20,560	Less than high school
Personal care aides	607,000	70	19,640	Less than high school
Office clerks, general	489,500	17	26,610	High school diploma or equivalent
Combined food preparation and serving workers, including fast food	398,000	15	17,950	Less than high school
Customer service representatives	338,400	15	30,460	High school diploma or equivalent
Heavy and tractor-trailer truck drivers	330,100	21	37,770	High school diploma or equivalent
Laborers and freight, stock, and material movers, hand	319,100	15	23,460	Less than high school
Postsecondary teachers	305,700	17	62,050	Doctoral or professional degree
Nursing aides, orderlies, and attendants	302,000	20	24,010	Postsecondary nondegree award
Child-care workers	262,000	20	19,300	High school diploma or equivalent

Occupation	Number of jobs[a]	Percent change[b]	Median pay	Education
Bookkeeping, accounting, and auditing clerks	259,000	14	34,030	High school diploma or equivalent
Cashiers	250,200	7	18,500	Less than high school
Elementary school teachers, except special education	248,800	17	51,660	Bachelor's degree
Receptionists and information clerks	248,500	24	25,240	High school diploma or equivalent
Janitors and cleaners, except maids and housekeeping cleaners	246,400	11	22,210	Less than high school
Landscaping and groundskeeping workers	240,800	21	23,400	Less than high school
Sales representatives, wholesale and manufacturing, except technical and scientific products	223,400	16	52,440	High school diploma or equivalent
Construction laborers	212,400	21	29,280	Less than high school

Source: U.S. Department of Labor (2012b).

a Number of jobs in thousands

b Percent change

Included in the list are low-paid service jobs such as food preparation and service workers, retail sales representatives, cashiers, office clerks, personal and home care aides, home health aides, janitors and cleaners, nursing aides and orderlies, waiters and waitresses, landscaping and groundskeeping workers, receptionists and information clerks, maids and housekeepers, and child-care workers. Sixteen of the twenty fastest-growing jobs in America typically require only either "short-term on-the-job training," "moderate-term on-the-job training," or "work experience in a related occupation." Only one requires a bachelor's degree (elementary school teachers), and only one (postsecondary teachers) requires a graduate degree. Reflecting the continued anticipated aging of the population, the number-one growth job in America is registered nurse, which minimally requires an associate's degree. Significantly, the second-fastest-growing job in America is retail salesperson, emblematic of the shift to an increasingly service-based economy. It is also instructive to note that the median income of these twenty-five fastest-growing jobs combined is $24,625 (authors' calculation based on U.S. Department of Labor data in table 6.1), which is barely above the $22,811 poverty threshold for a family of four (U.S. Census Bureau 2012c), further indicating that the combined direction of this growth is toward less well-paying jobs.

In short, the United States has evolved into what Yale University political scientist Jacob Hacker (2008) has described as a "service-sector nation," with attendant increases in job and income insecurity, involuntary job losses, part-time and contingent work, and declines in employment benefits such as health care and pension plans.

ALL DRESSED UP AND NOWHERE TO GO

Even if every adult in America were college educated, the "demand" for college-level jobs would remain the same. We would simply have more college-educated workers filling jobs that do not require college degrees and higher rates of underemployment in society as a whole. As levels of educational attainment in the population have increased, and as the economy has fallen short of producing jobs that require more education, rates of underemployment have increased. In a comprehensive analysis of labor-force trends, economists John Schmitt and Janelle Jones (2012) note that the percentage of the workforce with a college degree or more increased from 19.7 percent in 1979 to 34.3 percent in 2010. Furthermore, the median age of workers increased from thirty-four in 1969 to forty-one in 2010, indicating more cumulative work experience in the labor force as a whole. Over the same period, however, the share of "good-paying" jobs (defined as jobs that pay at least $37,000 per year, have employer-provided health insurance, and provide an employer-sponsored retirement plan) decreased from 27.4 percent of the labor force to 24.6 percent of the labor force. Taking into account the demographic changes in age and educational attainment, Schmitt and Jones estimate that relative to 1979, the economy has lost about one-third of its capacity to generate good jobs and that college graduates are less likely to have a good job now than three decades ago.

Since the level of educational attainment in the population is expected to continue to increase more sharply than the demand for more educated workers in the future, the incidence of individuals being employed in jobs less than commensurate with their level of educational attainment is likely to accelerate even further (Livingstone 2009; Wolf 2003; Vedder, Denhart, and Robe 2013). Economist Richard Vedder and his associates (2013), for instance, found that by 2010, 48 percent of employed U.S. college graduates were in jobs that require less than a four-year college education. They note that many occupations that require less than a college degree already have significant percentages of college graduates in them such as office clerks (17.6 percent), secretaries and administrative assistants (16.8 percent), retail sales clerks (24.6 percent), cashiers (10.2 percents) and bartenders (16.5 percent), and waiters and waitresses (14.3 percent). Between 2010 and 2020, using Department of Labor Statistics estimates, they anticipate that jobs requiring at least a bachelor's degree will grow by 14.3 percent, but the number of college graduates will increase by 31 percent; in other words, there will be nearly three new college graduates for every new job requiring a college degree (Vedder, Denhart, and Robe 2013).

In short, there has been a steady upgrading of human capital with college graduates on the supply side of the labor market, but the creation of good jobs on the demand side has grown only modestly, increasing the probability that individuals will end up in jobs not commensurate with their experience and education. An example of this broader national trend can be illustrated at our own university. The College of Arts and Sciences, the largest academic unit at our university, consists of the dean's office, twenty-one academic departments, and three interdisciplinary programs. Within the College of Arts and Sciences, there are a total of thirty-six "administrative associates," more commonly referred to as "secretaries." The position requires a minimum of a high school diploma. Among these thirty-six administrative associates, 66 percent have college degrees. Significantly, all are female. Moreover, the percentage of administrative associates within the College of Arts and Sciences that have bachelor's degrees has increased from 58 percent in 2008 to 66 percent in 2012. We do not have systematic data on the percentage of administrative assistants with college degrees in earlier years, but it is our impression that this percentage has substantially and steadily increased since the university was first established in 1946. The high rate of college graduates in these positions is substantially higher than for the nation as a whole and reflects a "soft" labor market in our tourist- and service-oriented coastal community, the surplus of college graduates in a college town, and the premium placed on educational credentials by the employing organization. But it also reflects the highly competitive job market for college graduates, particularly those who are geographically restricted by family or other obligations.

In *The Education-Jobs Gap* (1998), sociologist David W. Livingstone provides a comprehensive study of this general trend. Livingstone identifies five different types of underemployment: the talent-use gap, subemployment, credential underemployment, performance underemployment, and subjective underemployment. The *talent-use gap* refers to the opportunity gap between rich and poor to attain university degrees. Assuming equal levels of potential talent in the population as a whole, those from wealthier backgrounds are at least twice as likely to receive college degrees. In other words, long before people enter the labor force, potential talent is already wasted through differential access to higher education. *Subemployment* refers to a variety of nonvoluntary substandard conditions of employment, such as being unemployed but looking for work, working part time but wanting to work full time, and working full time at wages below the poverty level. An estimated 14 to 24 percent of the U.S. labor force, depending on cyclical variation, falls into this category. *Credential underemployment*, which refers to the condition in which a person's level of formal education exceeds that which is required for the job, affects an estimated 20 percent of the labor force. This type of underemployment, however, is constantly adjusted as employers raise educational requirements for positions, often beyond their real skill demands. A better measure of the overall extent of underemployment in the labor force is *performance underemployment*, which refers to the gap between the skills of the job holder and the actual skill demands of the job. This type of underemployment affects an estimated 40 to 60 percent of the currently employed labor force and has been steadily increasing for the past twenty-five years. Finally, Livingstone considers *subjective underemployment*, which refers to workers' perceptions that they hold jobs beneath their ability levels. Livingstone estimates that 20 to 40 percent of the labor force holds this view.

The implications of these findings are clear. There is no general shortage of talent or skill in the labor force. In fact, the situation is exactly the opposite. The economy is not producing enough jobs that match the skill and talent available in the labor force.

THE NONREVENGE OF THE NERDS

The extent of underemployment is inconsistent with the arguments of the postindustrial-society thesis first advanced by American sociologist Daniel Bell (1976). Observing a shift toward more white-collar employment, Bell theorized that American society had moved beyond industrialization. The emergent "postindustrial" society placed a high premium on formal and technical knowledge. According to this thesis, technical experts would come to dominate America and other advanced societies. Science and technology would be the key to the postindustrial future. In short, the future would belong to the nerds. In some ways, Bell's predictions seem to have been realized with the advance of the computer age. The computer has become the leading edge of the information society. Computer-related industries, populated by young, technically competent experts, flourished in the digital e-boom of the 1980s and 1990s.

The postindustrial society would presumably create demand for a more highly educated labor force. While it is true that the computer age ushered in a new genre of occupational specialties, it is also true that the bulk of the expansion of new jobs, as we have seen, has actually been very low tech. The assumption of the need for a more highly educated labor force outpaced the reality. While computerization created some new jobs with high skill requirements, other jobs have been automated or "deskilled" by computerization. Sales clerks, for instance, no longer need to calculate change. In fast-food chains, keyboards on cash registers sometimes display pictures rather than numbers. By the beginning of the twenty-first century, even computer-programming jobs, the supposed leading edge of the postindustrial boom, experienced sharp job losses. Between 2000 and 2004, 180,000 computer-programming jobs, or about one-quarter of the occupation's total employment, were lost (Hacker 2008, 77).

These jobs fell victim to two trends adversely affecting many other sectors of the labor force: automation and outsourcing. Many routine programming jobs were automated as advanced "canned" software programs were developed, eliminating the need to write programs in more complex and labor-intensive BASIC code. In addition, the ease of high-speed Internet connections and digital communication facilitated the outsourcing of many programming and technical-support jobs, especially to India.

Other professional-level jobs, while not eliminated by new technologies, have been greatly routinized. One example of these trends is pharmacy, a profession that formerly required a bachelor's degree as the first degree for pharmacy practice, but since 1990 a graduate doctoral-level degree (PharmD) has been designated by the American Association of Colleges of Pharmacy as the new first professional degree. Although pharmacists sometimes prepare or compound medications, most drugs now are prepared by manufacturers and prepackaged. Pill counters count out pills, and computer records check for warnings, side effects, and possible drug interactions. Pharmacy technicians often do much of this routine work, which is then "checked" by the licensed pharmacist before dispensing. While an important part of the health-care delivery system, the majority of what most pharmacists do in their jobs is often highly routinized.

In a careful study of labor-force changes through the 1970s, sociologist Randall Collins (1979) estimated that only 15 percent of the increase in educational requirements for new jobs could be attributed to the need for a more educated workforce. Most of the rest of the increase in educational requirements could be attributed to credential inflation—requiring higher levels of educational attainment unrelated to the actual skill demand of jobs (see chapter 5). As the labor force became more educated, employers simply increased their educational requirements. The result was an inflationary spiral of educational credentials.

Not having a credential (as opposed to the skills required to do a job) can be a nonmerit barrier to mobility. That is, if employers require a college degree for jobs that do not actually need a college graduate for their performance, then not having the credential per se can operate against more experienced or skilled candidates. The vast majority of jobs that college graduates hold, in reality, require literacy and not much else. The formal credentials people hold, as Livingstone states, represent only "the tip of the learning iceberg"; fully 70 percent of what people need to know to do their jobs they learn informally on the job (1998, 38).

As the pace of technological change increases, continuing and on-the-job training becomes even more important. To this extent, credentials, which are more available to those from more privileged backgrounds, become artificial barriers to true meritocracy. Collins notes that even some of the most technically demanding jobs—physician, engineer, lawyer—could be learned, and historically were, through apprenticeship training. For practical purposes, there is no evidence to suggest that learning about something by seeing it diagrammed on a blackboard in a classroom is superior to learning the same thing through direct observation and application on the job. Indeed, learning theory suggests that the reverse is probably the case. Colleges have begun to respond to employers' pleas for more practical occupational training by offering more "vocational" majors and embracing more "active" modes of learning, including internships and practica.

In a recent analysis of labor-force trends, economists Lawrence Mishel and his associates (2012) note, for instance, that the availability of more technologically advanced consumer products does not necessarily correspond to increased labor-force demand for more technologically advanced occupational skills:

> We are often told that the pace of change in the workplace is accelerating, and technological advances in communications, entertainment, Internet, and other technologies are widely visible. Thus it is not surprising that many people believe that technology is transforming the wage structure. But technological

advances in consumer products do not in and of themselves change labor market outcomes. Rather, changes in the way goods and services are produced influence relative demand for different types of workers, and it is this that affects wage trends. Since many high-tech products are made with low-tech methods, there is no close correspondence between advanced consumer products and an increased need for skilled workers. Similarly, ordering a book online rather than at a bookstore may change the type of jobs in an industry— we might have fewer retail workers in bookselling and more truckers and warehouse workers—but it does not necessarily change the skill mix. (2012, 295)

Moreover, they dispute the claim that recent increases in wage inequality are the result of a growing gap between the *need for* versus the *availability of* more educated and skilled workers in the labor force:

Technological change certainly has generated the need for a more educated workforce, and the workforce has indeed become far more educated. The share of the workforce without a high school degree has fallen sharply, and many more workers have college degrees (33.2 percent of the workforce had a four-year college or advanced degree in 2011, up from 18.7 percent in 1979). . . . Investment and technological change generally are associated with the need for more workforce skill and education—but this was true for the entire 20th century, and it therefore does not explain why wage inequality began to grow three decades ago. A convincing technology story must show that the impact of technology accelerated *relative to earlier periods* in order to explain why wage inequality started to grow in the 1980s, 1990s, and 2000s, and did not grow in prior decades. (2012, 299)

One of the problems in matching educational credentials with job demands is the length of training and the changing nature of the job market. The job market is difficult to predict in the long run, and this is a problem for those pursuing jobs that require long periods of formal training. Current "vacancies" and "high demand" may diminish by the time the training period is over. The market has ebbs and flows on both the supply and demand side. When demand is high, the market responds by attracting new entrants. Large numbers of new entrants can glut a market, resulting in oversupply, particularly if demand also dries up. In essence, people can be all dressed up with no place to go. One could argue that the truly meritorious would read market trends correctly and respond accordingly. The reality, however, is that markets, particularly long-term markets, are highly unpredictable. As rates of change increase, predictability declines. Most job experts agree that the job market is much more fluid now than it was for prior generations. Over a lifetime, the average worker now makes many more job changes both in terms of type and place of employment than his or her predecessors. In short, any one worker's location in the labor force at any one point is at least as much the result of market demands as individual merit.

BABY BOOMERS AND BABY BUSTERS

When a person is born matters for his or her life chances. Malcolm Gladwell begins his highly acclaimed book, *Outliers: The Story of Success* (2008), with a description of a study of the birth dates of professional hockey players. The study, by psychologists Roger Barnsley and A. H. Thompson (1988), found that professional hockey players disproportionately had birth dates in the early months of the year, especially January, February, and March. As it turns out, the birth date for age placement in youth hockey leagues in Canada is January 1. So that means that players playing in the same league at the same "age" could actually be as much as a year apart, with those being born in the earlier months nearly a year older than those being born in later months. At preadolescence, the age difference means a lot in terms of size, coordination, and maturity. At successive levels of advancement, the "best" players are selected for more competitive teams. Initially, the older players have a significant competitive advantage over younger players and advance more quickly. As they are advanced, they receive more advanced coaching and are encouraged to continue further. In this sense, success begets success, which is built upon an initially nonmerit advantage. Gladwell refers to this multiplier of initial advantage using a term coined by sociologist Robert Merton as "the Matthew effect," referring to a biblical verse in the Gospel of Matthew: "For unto everyone that has shall be given, and he shall have abundance. But from him that has not shall be taken away even that which he hath."

Even for the senior author of the hockey study, there was a serendipitous element to his discovery. He and his wife were attending a major junior league hockey game when his wife noticed the odd apparent coincidence of the preponderance of early birth months in the program listing the player's birth dates and initially brought it to her husband's attention.

Being in the right place at the right time is partly a matter of when people are born and when they enter the labor market. Quite apart from individual ability, how many people are chasing how many and what kind of jobs in what location is of major consequence. The best scenario is one in which a person is part of a small birth cohort and enters the labor force during a period of economic expansion; the worst scenario is one in which a person is part of a large cohort entering the labor force during a period of economic retrenchment. Consistent with the Matthew effect described earlier, the first full-time job after completion of formal education matters for future mobility since first jobs set career trajectories. Getting started on a branch higher up the tree in the first place will likely put one higher up from the ground at the end.

The best way to document the effects of cohort differences on mobility chances is to conduct a longitudinal study of different cohorts entering the labor force at different times and follow the careers and work histories of individuals in those cohorts over time. In a comprehensive analysis of this type, Annette Bernhardt and her colleagues (2001) followed two cohorts of white males. They traced career paths of the first cohort that entered the labor force in the mid-1960s and followed it through the end of the 1970s to the early 1980s. The second cohort entered the labor force in the late 1970s and early 1980s and was followed through the mid-1990s. The systematic comparison of career paths and work histories of these two cohorts provides a way to compare differences in initial job opportunities and opportunities for advancement encountered by these cohorts, independent of differences in individual abilities. Comparing cohorts, their key findings are that (1) economic mobility has declined and has become more unequal, (2) job instability has increased, and (3) the low-wage career trap has expanded its grip.

Bernhardt et al. found that 90 percent of white male workers in the most recent cohort are doing worse now than their counterparts at corresponding ages from the earlier cohort. Median wage growth has fallen by 21 percent, and the distributions of remaining gains have become more unequal. While a small core of the most recent cohort is holding its own, for the most part the net wage decline is a "race to the bottom" (Bernhardt et al. 2001, 174). The growth of income inequality in recent decades is not associated with individuals surging ahead but rather with a few holding on while most have lost ground. The small core of workers holding their own are mostly college graduates. But even here, nearly two-thirds of all college graduates in the more recent cohort fared worse than college graduates in the previous cohort.

Those college graduates in the recent cohort who did do well were not clustered in the high-technology areas—as would be predicted by the postindustrial-society thesis—but in the "paper-tiger" industries of finance, insurance, and real estate. In the recent cohort, those with associate's degrees and certificates from vocational, technical, and community colleges barely did better than high school graduates, further calling into question the idea that a gap in technical skills is the driving force behind growing wage inequalities.

Bernhardt et al. also document a 14 percent increase in job instability in the recent cohort, regardless of education level. Not only has there been an increase in job instability, but the wage penalties for changing jobs have increased. Those who manage to stay put in stable jobs tend to do better in the long run. Instability early in an individual's work history hurts workers' prospects for future stability: "Wage growth (or lack of it) early in the career can cascade into long-term changes in wage trajectories, so that a little inequality early on is likely to generate greater inequality down the line"

(Bernhardt et al. 2001, 109). Part of the reason for the general increase in job instability is the shift to service work, which traditionally pays less, has higher rates of turnover, and provides fewer benefits and fewer opportunities for advancement. But in the wake of downsizing, restructuring, and mergers, job instability has even increased in the manufacturing sector. The result is the end of an era in which employees could reasonably count on stable employment with a single employer for an entire career.

In terms of the distribution of "slots" to be filled in the labor force, Bernhardt et al. document an increase in low-wage jobs with little opportunity for advancement:

> The prevalence of low-wage careers has more than doubled, increasing from 12% in the original cohort to 28% in the recent cohort. These are not teenagers taking after-school jobs at McDonald's to earn spending money, but rather mature workers chronically cycling through bad jobs over the long run, and we find that they have two things in common. One is that they are increasingly trapped in just a handful of industries, such as retail trade, personal services, entertainment and recreation, and business and repair services. These industries offer few opportunities for wage growth, promotion, and training, making it difficult for workers to escape their grasp. The other is their inability to find stable full-time employment by the time they reach their mid-thirties—indicating a type of job churning that becomes increasingly harmful as workers grow older. (2001, 176)

Numerous other observers (cf. Blau 1999; Bluestone and Harrison 2000; Frank 2007; Fraser 2001; Hacker 2008; Harrison and Bluestone 1988; Hytrek and Zentfraf 2008; Kalleberg 2011; Levy 1998; Massey 2007; Palley 1998; Perrucci and Wysong 2008; Rayman 2001) have reached similar conclusions. Despite its relatively large size, the baby-boomer cohort has done better than the smaller baby-buster cohort that followed it. Although there is some disagreement about the causes of the recent job changes, all are in agreement that the ground has shifted and that there are fewer opportunities for good jobs now than for prior generations of workers. Simply put, beyond considerations of individual merit, it matters when you were born and what the labor force looks like when you enter it. But timing is only part of the story; being in the right place also matters.

THE RUST BELT AND THE SUN BELT

Throughout the first half of the twentieth century, the South lagged well behind other regions of the country. In 1947, for instance, family incomes in the South were 40 percent smaller than in other regions (Levy 1998, 127), partially because portions of the South were still largely underdeveloped industrially. This large gap was also due in part to the long history of racial discrimination that depressed the wages of a high proportion of poor rural blacks who lived there. But wages were also lower for southern whites compared to whites living in other regions with similar jobs and similar levels of education. Beginning in the 1960s, the South began to close the income gap on the rest of the county, and by the early 1990s, the gap between the South and other regions had closed to within about 20 percent (Levy 1998, 136). Economist Frank Levy points to several factors responsible for this change: the civil rights movement, which reduced economic discrimination; the extension of the interstate highway system and the development of network television, which helped link the South to other regions; and the spread of air-conditioning, making the South more amenable to the "climatically challenged" (1998, 133). The availability of cheap land, low wages, low taxes, and low levels of unionization also encouraged industrial development in the South. During the same period, deindustrialization of the Northeast and Midwest (the Rust Belt) depressed wages, especially in the manufacturing sectors. Despite these changes, significant regional gaps in income and poverty rates remain. Table 6.2 depicts median household income differences and family poverty rates among regions in the United States in 2011.[1]

Median household income ranges from a high of $53,864 in the Northeast to a low of $46,899 in the South, representing a 12.9 percent gap. Likewise, family poverty rates vary from a low of 13.1 percent in the Northeast to a high of 16 percent in the South, representing an 18.1 percent gap. In short, despite recent trends toward closing gaps, how much one is likely to earn and the likelihood of being poor still depend significantly on the region of the nation in which one happens to live.

As regional variations in wages and poverty rates have declined over time, wage differentials and poverty rates between people living in cities and people living in suburbs have increased. In 1959, median wages in the city trailed wages in the suburbs by only 11 percent; by 1996 the gap had increased to 27 percent (Levy 1998, 113). By 2011, median inner-city wages were 40.7 percent lower than median suburban wages (U.S. Census Bureau 2012c). Several factors have contributed to this ongoing increase. The

Table 6.2. Regional Differences in Median Income and Poverty Rates, 2011

Region	2011 Median Income ($)	2011 Poverty Rate (%)
Northeast	53,864	13.1
West	52,376	15.8
Midwest	48,722	14
South	46,899	16

Source: U.S. Census Bureau 2012a, 2012b.

post–World War II era witnessed a surge in suburban development. This exodus was fueled by the relative prosperity of the postwar period combined with government subsidies in the form of highway construction and Veterans Administration housing loans for returning veterans. More privileged whites, followed by black beneficiaries of the civil rights revolution, fled the inner cities in large numbers. Increasingly, the inner cities were populated by "left behinds"—people with no viable means of escape—the elderly and minority poor, and new ethnic immigrants (Wilson 1987). Many of the white-collar workers who worked in the urban high-rise offices during the day retreated to suburban bedroom communities at night. With urban manufacturing on the decline, fewer jobs for the unskilled and semiskilled remained. With factories and the middle class leaving inner cities, the tax base of big cities declined, resulting in a deterioration of public services. As urban unemployment and subemployment in the regular economy grew, "work" in the irregular economy—drugs, prostitution, gambling, and so on—also increased. All of these changes focused national attention on inner cities, which became lightning rods for social problems such as poverty, drugs, and crime.

Apart from one's particular job or how well one does it, where one works makes a difference in how much one is paid. The same job in the South or in inner cities may not pay as well in other regions or in the suburbs. Differences in pay based on place can be illustrated by comparing salaries of public school teachers. Teachers perform fundamentally the same job regardless of where they teach, requiring for the most part the same qualifications—a bachelor's degree and a teaching certificate—but rates of teacher pay vary considerably by state. The average public school teacher pay during the 2010–2011 school year in the United States was $54,965 (U.S. Department of Education 2011). However, the range of pay was considerable. Table 6.3 shows the states with the five highest average teacher salaries and those with the five lowest average teacher salaries. Average 2010–2011 teacher salaries ranged from a high of $71,277 in New York to a low of $34,508 in South Dakota (U.S. Department of Education 2011). In other words, teachers in South Dakota earn only about 48 percent of what teachers in New York earn for doing essentially the same job, requiring essentially the same qualifications. Even adjusting for cost-of-living differences among states, substantial pay differentials remain. Defenders of meritocracy might suggest that the really good teachers will gravitate to New York, where the pay is higher, and the least meritorious teachers will gravitate to South Dakota, where the pay is the lowest. Pay, however, is not the only motivating factor in where people choose to work. Ties to family and community, personal preference, access to information about job openings (social capital), and local labor markets generated by employer preferences to hire locally are all also clearly factors.

In addition to the community in which the work is performed, the characteristics of the employing organization and the industrial location of the job

Table 6.3. Average Teacher Salary, 2010–2011

Rank	State	Average 2010 Salary ($)	Percent of U.S. Average
Highest Five States			
1	New York	71,277	129.6
2	Massachusetts	69,619	126.6
3	California	68,067	123.8
4	New Jersey	65,666	119.5
5	District of Columbia	65,290	118.7
Lowest Five States			
46	Florida	45,783	83.3
47	Utah	45,654	83.1
48	Missouri	45,497	82.7
49	North Dakota	43,395	78.9
50	South Dakota	34,508	62.7

Source: U.S. Department of Education 2011.

also matter. Beyond the characteristics of individual workers, pay, benefits, and working conditions vary across employers and industries (Stainback and Tomaskovic-Devey 2012; Flynn 2003; Tolbert, Horan, and Beck 1980; Averitt 1968; Weeden 2002; Kalleberg 2011). Large, capital-intensive, high-profit firms with large market shares tend to pay employees the most. Government employment offers less pay but often provides high levels of job security. Level of government (federal, state, county, municipal) also makes a difference, with the federal level generally providing the best packages for employees. The small-business sector, by contrast, generally offers the lowest pay, the fewest benefits, and the poorest working conditions. A janitor, for instance, who works in an office building for a major corporation is likely to earn more than a janitor who works in a county public school building, who, in turn, is likely to earn more than a janitor who works in a local restaurant. Again, defenders of meritocracy might argue that the "best" and the hardest-working janitors will end up working for the major corporations, but there is no evidence to support such a claim. This is because such a claim assumes far more predictability and rationality in how workers are matched with jobs than actually exists. Workers do not systematically work for employing organizations that will pay the most for what they can do. For a variety of reasons, such as a job's availability at a particular place at the particular time someone is seeking it, many people somewhat haphazardly end up working for whom they are working and doing the work they are doing.

Most people who have been in the labor force for any extended period, if honest, would acknowledge unanticipated twists and turns along the way that, quite independently of their personal level of merit, resulted in their current location in the labor force. Christopher Jencks et al. (1979, 306–11) identified three sources of wage variation among otherwise indistinguishable workers. First, the business cycle can create market uncertainties, making it impossible for workers to know in advance how many weeks in a year they may end up working in any given job. In this scenario, among similarly skilled workers doing the same kind of work, some might be laid off and others not. Second, large firms often create pay scales for occupational slots, not the people who fill them. A firm's complicated wage structure is not especially responsive to market changes, so at any point, some individual workers may be paid over and others under the real market rate. Finally, neither employing organizations nor individual workers have all the information necessary to optimize decisions that affect wages. Employing organizations do not always know the minimum they can pay to attract workers with sufficient skill to do the job, and workers do not always know how high a wage they can command. As a result, some employers pay more than necessary, and some workers accept less than they could get. As Jencks et al. note, "These suboptimal bargains mean that identical workers do not always earn identical amounts" (1979, 310).

In the end, there is a great deal of what statisticians call "noise" when it comes to accounting for how much people are paid for the work they do. The best models account for only about half of the variance in income attainment and about two-thirds of the variance in occupational attainment. Some of the variance "unexplained" by these models could come from a combination of leaving out factors that matter and from less-than-perfect measures of the factors included. But some of the unexplained or residual variation is also likely due to simple random variation—or, in more everyday language, "luck."

THE RANDOM-WALK HYPOTHESIS

So far in this chapter, our discussion has revolved around education, jobs, and income. We have argued that the "going rate" of return for the jobs that people hold depends, at least in part, on factors that lie outside the control of individual workers themselves. Getting ahead in terms of the occupations people hold and the pay they receive involves an element of luck—being in the right place at the right time. There is also an element of luck in the acquisition of great wealth. Indeed, luck may be even more of a factor in wealth attainment than income attainment. The luck factor in wealth acquisition, as we have seen, begins at birth. By an "accident of birth," some are born into great wealth while most are not. Since no one "chooses" their parents, those born into privilege may be thought of as "lucky." But what of "self-made" individuals who acquire great wealth without being born into it? In *Building Wealth* (1999), economist Lester Thurow identifies thirteen "rules" for wealth building. Rule number thirteen states, "Luck is necessary. Talent, drive, and persistence by themselves aren't enough to get wealthy." Elaborating on this rule, Thurow writes,

> Although Bill Gates has as much wealth as the bottom 40% of American households, he has no known talents (IQ, business acumen, willingness to take risks) equal to the combined talents of those 110 million people. There are many other individuals just as smart, just as good businessmen, and just as good at everything else who do not have his wealth. Acquiring great wealth is best seen as a conditional lottery. Luck is necessary. One does have to be in the right place at the right time. . . . Ability is not enough. (1999, 205)

Thurow's point is clear enough: luck matters. Thurow observes that wealth creation comes from taking advantage of "disequilibriums," or shake-ups, in market conditions. Change brings about conditions of disequilibrium, and those conditions in turn create new opportunities for the creation of new wealth. Thurow identifies three types of disequilibrium: technological, sociological, and developmental. Technological disequilibrium refers to forms of new wealth created through advances in technology (computers) or the development of related products and services surrounding the advance of new technologies (e.g., computer software). Sociological disequilibriums are those created by behavioral or social change unrelated to technology. Thurow offers the example of the aging of the American population and how this demographic change creates new economic opportunities in products and services disproportionately consumed by the elderly (e.g., cruise lines, medical and assisted-living services). Finally, developmental disequilibrium refers to unequal conditions of development in different countries that create opportunities to introduce products and services available in one place that are not yet available in another place.

To some extent, those who are the most clever or most insightful might be better able to anticipate various market shakeups. However, the "random-walk hypothesis" developed by economists seems to account best for who ends up with the right idea, the right product, or the right service. The argument is simply that striking it rich tends to be like getting struck by lightning: many are walking around, but only a few get randomly struck. Large fortunes tend to be made quickly, taking early advantage of market shakeups. The window for striking it rich is very narrow since once it is open, others quickly rush in.

LOTTERY LUCKY

Another way to strike it rich in America is to win a lottery. The odds of getting rich by hitting the lottery jackpot, however, are long indeed. Lotteries offer the worst odds of any form of legalized gambling (Gudgeon and Stewart 2001). Lotteries generally pay back fourteen cents on the dollar, compared to ninety cents for typical casino games. The most popular lottery game is the 6/49 Draw. In this game, players pick six numbers from one to forty-nine and hope that they match the winning draw. The odds of winning with each ticket on the 6/49 Draw are 13,983,816 to 1. Among the largest lump-sum payments to a single ticket winner on a government-sponsored lottery went to Andrew Whittaker of West Virginia, who won $314.9 million in a Powerball drawing on December 25, 2002. Opting, as most large prize winners do, to take a lump sum, Whittaker received an after-tax prize of $114 million. In April of 2012, Merle and Patricia Butler of Illinois took home $110 million after taxes. Such winnings are a considerable amount for most people, but not nearly enough to place one onto the Forbes 400 wealthiest Americans list.

For a handful of very lucky Americans, then, winning the lottery can mean the fulfillment of the "rags-to-riches" American Dream (Kaplan 1978). It is a nonmerit form of rapid mobility, but mobility nevertheless. The media hype surrounding this type of mobility encourages the idea that America is a land of opportunity in which anyone at any time might become instantly wealthy.

Both conservatives and liberals have opposed lotteries. Conservatives sometimes oppose lotteries as a form of vice along with all other forms of gambling; liberals sometimes oppose lotteries because they exploit the poor. The poor are the least able to afford tickets and the most vulnerable to the lure of instant wealth. Despite these reservations, lotteries hold great romantic appeal and have become a popular American pastime. As of 2012, forty-four states, the District of Columbia, and Puerto Rico have lotteries. Even multistate lotteries have been developed. As weeks go by without winners, the pots increase in value, which in turn attracts more players. An estimated 75 percent of Americans have purchased a lottery ticket at least once, and 42 percent of men and 34 percent of women buy tickets weekly (Gudgeon and Stewart 2001).

State-sponsored lotteries are only one form of "gaming." Legalized gambling in casinos is available in Las Vegas and Atlantic City and on some Native American reservations. Offshore cruise lines whose sole purpose is to provide sites for gambling have flourished. They all market the same product: the hope of instant wealth. Among hopefuls, a few do win big, with great fanfare and excitement. The longer the odds, the larger the purse. The hoopla surrounding the "winners" is part of the marketing strategy to encourage players to play more. But the reality is that most players either lose or, occasionally, win just a little. The odds favor the house, ensuring over the long run that the house is ultimately the biggest winner of all. The house edge is the difference between the true odds of winning and the odds that the house actually pays when someone wins. The difference is usually in the neighborhood of 10 percent, assuring a profit stream for the house in the long run. A toss of the coin, for instance, has a fifty-fifty even chance of winning. If you bet a dollar to win, the house would pay 90 cents on the dollar for the bet.

Perhaps the largest but least recognized forum for legalized gambling in the United States is the stock market. For all practical purposes, investing in stocks and bonds is equivalent to gambling. The biggest difference between playing the stock market and other forms of gambling is that the odds for winning in the stock market are much better, although the return is usually much less. The odds of "winning" in the stock market can be increased beyond random chance by knowing as much as possible about the companies in which one invests and by being able to predict market changes. Knowing about companies and markets, in part, is a matter of social and cultural capital—being in a loop composed of people with accurate and current information. As recent investment scandals have underscored, these odds can be increased illegally through insider trading. Apart from such schemes, however, there is still an element of investor risk. Indeed, the willingness to take chances and to risk capital is the primary justification for capitalism. If it were possible to predict the future with certainty, then there would be no risk. But as long as the future remains unpredictable, luck is a factor.

Historian Jackson Lears, in his book *Something for Nothing: Luck in America* (2003), has identified an ongoing tension in America between what he refers to as "the culture of control" and "the culture of chance." Lears contends that the "culture of control," with its early colonial roots in the Protestant ethic and its emphasis on rational self-control, has dominated the American cultural landscape even to the point of denying luck altogether:

> Despite fresh evidence that hard-working people can easily lose everything to corporate confidence men, the insistence that "you make your own luck"—that you are personally responsible for your own economic fate—remains a keystone of our public life. There is of course a core of truth to this idea: disciplined effort is essential to success at most endeavors. But that does not mean that people necessarily get what they deserve. In recent decades, that notion has been repeated so often and so simplemindedly that it has become part of the general buzz of background noise in our society. (2003, 21)

Despite the dominance of the "culture of control," the "cultural of chance" has coexisted alongside it, particularly with regard to risking capital as an essential element of American capitalism:

> Yet the defenders of diligence have never entirely vanquished the devotees of chance. At least since Tocqueville compared American society to a "vast lottery," our business mythology has celebrated risk-taking, knowing when to hold and when to fold, taking advantage of "the breaks." Especially in flush times, it has not always been easy to distinguish gambling from speculation or investment, and even Horatio Alger knew that luck was as important as pluck in achieving success. The gambler, endlessly starting over with every hand of cards, has embodied the American metaphysic of reinventing the self, reawakening the possibilities from one moment to the next. The gambler and the entrepreneur have been twinned. (Lears 2003, 4)

Having money to invest or gamble in the first place is also a factor—and an important one. Small investments, no matter how good the rate of return, are unlikely to generate great wealth. Like many other aspects of getting ahead in America, it takes money to make money. And the really big money in America, as we have seen, comes not from working for a living but from return on capital investments.

SUMMARY

Merit hard-liners tend to deny or downplay the role of luck in getting ahead in America. Defenders of meritocracy often claim, "Individuals make their own luck," or, sarcastically, "The harder I work, the luckier I become." Despite such claims, the evidence suggests otherwise. In this chapter, we have identified several factors beyond individuals' immediate control that affect their life chances. While individuals do have some control over how skilled they are, they have no control over what kinds of jobs are available, how many, and how many individuals are seeking those jobs. These labor-market conditions occur independently of the capacities of discrete individuals—how smart or talented they are, how hard they work, or how motivated they are to get ahead. Most economists agree that labor-market conditions have fundamentally shifted since the early 1970s. A combination of circumstances prompted American corporations to sharply reduce manufacturing facilities in the United States, relocate facilities to the Sun Belt and overseas, consolidate through mergers, avoid unionization, "downsize" operations, "outsource" labor, and engage in other sweeping changes that collectively had a dramatic impact on the American labor force.

Although more Americans are getting more education, the economy is not producing enough jobs with good pay, good benefits, security, and opportunities for advancement commensurate with the higher levels of education attained. In essence, many American workers are all dressed up with no place to go. Compared to previous generations of workers entering the labor force, the most recent generation of workers faces fewer opportunities, greater job instability, and a greater chance of being stuck in dead-end jobs.

Beyond occupational success, being in the right place at the right time also matters for acquiring wealth. Striking it rich—be it through inheritance, entrepreneurial ventures, investments, or the lottery—necessarily involves at least some degree of just plain dumb luck. The simple fact is that there is far more intelligence, talent, ability, and hard work in the population as a whole than there are people who are lucky enough to find themselves in a position to take advantage of these qualities.

REFERENCES

Averitt, Robert T. 1968. *Dual Economy*. New York: Norton.

Barnsley, R., and A. H. Thompson. 1988. "Birthdate and Success in Minor Hockey: Key to NHL." *Canadian Journal of Behavioral Science* 20, no. 2: 167–76.

Bell, Daniel. 1976. *The Coming of Post-Industrial Society*. New York: Basic Books.

Bernhardt, Annette, Martina Morris, Mark Handcock, and Mark Scott. 2001. *Divergent Paths: Economic Mobility in the New American Labor Market*. New York: Sage.

Blau, Joel. 1999. *Illusions of Prosperity: America's Working Families in an Age of Economic Insecurity*. New York: Oxford University Press.

Bluestone, Barry, and Bennett Harrison. 2000. *Growing Prosperity: The Battle for Growth with Equity in the Twenty-First Century*. Boston: Houghton Mifflin.

Collins, Randall. 1979. *The Credential Society: A Historical Sociology of Education and Stratification*. New York: Academic Press.

Flynn, Nicolet. 2003. "The Differential Effect of Labor Market Context on Marginal Employment Outcomes." *Sociological Spectrum* 123, no. 3: 305–30.

Frank, Robert H. 2007. *Falling Behind: How Rising Inequality Harms the Middle Class*. Berkeley: University of California Press.

Fraser, Jill Anresky. 2001. *White-Collar Sweatshop: The Deteriorations of Work and Its Rewards in Corporate America*. New York: Norton.

Gladwell, Malcolm. 2008. *Outliers: The Story of Success*. New York: Little, Brown.

Gudgeon, Chris, and Barbara Stewart. 2001. *Luck of the Draw: True-Life Tales of Lottery Winners and Losers*. Vancouver, WA: Arsenal Pulp Press.

Hacker, Jacob S. 2008. *The Great Risk Shift: The New Economic Insecurity and the Decline of the American Dream*. New York: Oxford University Press.

Harrison, Bennett, and Barry Bluestone. 1988. *The Great U-Turn: Corporate Restructuring and the Polarizing of America*. New York: Basic Books.

Hatton, Erin. 2011. *The Temp Economy: From Kelly Girls to Permatemps in Postwar America*. Philadelphia, PA: Temple University Press.

Hytrek, Gary, and Kristine M. Zentfraf. 2008. *America Transformed: Globalization, Inequality and Power*. New York: Oxford University Press.

Jencks, Christopher, Susan Bartlett, Mary Corcoran, James Crouse, David Eaglesfield, Gregory Jackson, Kent McClelland, et al. 1979. *Who Gets Ahead? The Determinants of Economic Success in America*. New York: Basic Books.

Kalleberg, Arne L. 2011. *Good Jobs, Bad Jobs: The Rise of Polarized and Precarious Employment Systems in the United States, 1970s to 2000s*. New York: Sage.

Kaplan, Roy. 1978. *Lottery Winners: How They Won and How Winning Changed Their Lives*. New York: HarperCollins.

Lears, Jackson. 2003. *Something for Nothing: Luck in America*. New York: Penguin.

Levy, Frank. 1998. *The New Dollars and Dreams: American Incomes and Economic Change.* New York: Sage.

Livingstone, D. W. 1998. *The Education-Jobs Gap: Underemployment or Economic Democracy.* Boulder, CO: Westview.

———, ed. 2009. *Education and Jobs: Exploring the Gaps.* Toronto: University of Toronto Press.

Massey, Douglas S. 2007. *Categorically Unequal: The American Stratification System.* New York: Sage.

Mishel, Lawrence, Josh Bivens, Elise Gould, and Heidi Shierholz. 2012. *The State of Working America.* 12th ed. Ithaca, NY: Cornell University Press.

Palley, Thomas. 1998. *Plenty of Nothing: The Downsizing of the American Dream and the Case for Structural Keynesianism.* Princeton, NJ: Princeton University Press.

Perrucci, Robert, and Earl Wysong. 2008. *The New Class Society: Goodbye American Dream?* 3rd ed. Lanham, MD: Rowman & Littlefield.

Rayman, Paula. 2001. *Beyond the Bottom Line: The Search for Dignity at Work.* New York: Palgrave.

Schmitt, John, and Janelle Jones. 2012. "Where Have All the Good Jobs Gone?" Center for Economic and Policy Research. http://www.cepr.net/documents/publications/good-jobs-2012-07.pdf (accessed January 20, 2013).

Stainback, Kevin, and Donald Tomaskovic-Devey. 2012. *Documenting Desegregation: Racial and Gender Segregation in Private-Sector Employment since the Civil Rights Act.* New York: Sage.

Thurow, Lester C. 1999. *Building Wealth: The New Rules for Individuals, Companies and Nations in a Knowledge-Based Economy.* New York: HarperCollins.

Tolbert, Charles, Partick Horan, and E. M. Beck. 1980. "The Structure of Economic Segmentation: A Dual Economy Approach." *American Journal of Sociology* 85: 1095–1116.

Uchitelle, Louis. 2006. *The Disposable American? Layoffs and Their Consequences.* New York: Knopf.

U.S. Census Bureau. 2012a. *Historical Income Tables.* Washington, DC: U.S. Government Printing Office, table H-6, "Regions—All Races by Median and Mean Income: 1975 to 2011."

———. 2012b. *Historical Poverty Tables.* Washington, DC: U.S. Government Printing Office, table 9, "Poverty by Region."

———. 2012c. *Income, Poverty, and Health Insurance Coverage in the United States: 2011.* Washington, DC: U.S. Government Printing Office, table 1, "Income and Earnings Summary Measures by Selected Characteristics: 2010 and 2011."

———. 2012d. "Poverty Thresholds for 2011 by Size of Family and Number of Related Children under 18." Washington, DC: U.S. Government Printing Office. http://www.census.gov/hhes/www/poverty/data/threshld/index.html (accessed November 9, 2012).

U.S. Department of Education. 2011. *Digest of Education Statistics, 2011.* Table 84. http://nces.ed.gov/programs/digest/d11/tables/dt11_084.asp (accessed September 27, 2012).

U.S. Department of Labor. 2011. "Table 9, Percent Distribution of the Civilian Labor Force 25 to 64 Years of Age by Educational Attainment and Sex, 1970–2010." U.S. Bureau of Labor Statistics. http://www.bls.gov/cps/wlf-databook-2011.pdf (accessed October 2, 2012).

———. 2012a. "Business Employment Dynamics." Series ID: BDS0000000000100030120004LQ5. U.S. Bureau of Labor Statistics. http://data.bls.gov/timeseries/BDS0000000000100030120004LQ5?data_tool=XGtable (accessed October 2, 2012).

———. 2012b. "Table 2, Occupations with the Largest Numeric Growth, Projected 2010–20." *Occupational Outlook Handbook, 2012–13 Edition, Projections Overview.* U.S. Bureau of Labor Statistics. http://www.bls.gov/ooh/about/projections-overview.htm (accessed October 2, 2012).

Vedder, Richard, Christopher Denhart, and Jonathan Robe. 2013. *Why Are Recent College Graduates Underemployed?* Washington, DC: Center for College Affordability and Productivity. http://centerforcollegeaffordability.org/uploads/Underemployed%20Report%202.pdf (accessed February 1, 2013).

Weeden, Kim. 2002. "Why Do Some Occupations Pay More Than Others? Social Closure and Earnings Inequality in the United States." *American Journal of Sociology* 108:55–101.

Wilson, William Julius. 1987. *The Truly Disadvantaged: The Inner City, the Underclass, and Public Policy*. Chicago: University of Chicago Press.

Wolf, Alison. 2003. *Does Education Matter? Myths about Education and Economic Growth*. London: Penguin Global.

Chapter Seven

I Did It My Way

The Decline of Self-Employment and the Ascent of Corporations

I ate it up, and spit it out. I faced it all and I stood tall, and did it my way.
—Lyrics from "My Way," cowritten by Paul Anka and Frank Sinatra, as performed by Frank Sinatra

An important part of the American Dream is the opportunity to strike out on your own, be your own boss, own a business, and be the master of your own fate. Self-employment, in many ways, epitomizes the American Dream. Being self-employed exemplifies independence, initiative, self-reliance, and rugged individualism—virtues held in high regard in American society. The entrepreneur who builds a business from scratch and turns it into a success is an American icon. Celebrated historical examples abound—Andrew Carnegie (Carnegie Steel), Henry Ford (Ford Motor Company), Thomas Edison (General Electric), and, more recently, Ray Kroc (McDonald's), Sam Walton (Walmart), Bill Gates (Microsoft), and Steve Jobs (Apple).

The image of the rugged individualist fit well with conditions in early American society. Estimates are that in colonial America over 80 percent of the labor force was self-employed (Phillips 1958, 2). Most were farmers who owned their small family farms. Others were craftsmen, shopkeepers, and artisans. A few were fee-for-service professionals such as lawyers and physicians. Even the most prosperous of businesses employed relatively few workers, at least by modern standards. Among the small segment that was not self-employed, the largest contingent comprised slaves and indentured servants.

Wealth and property were primarily tied to the land, and the land was vast and only sparsely populated. After independence, the federal government acquired vast tracks of land on its western frontier. The government had acquired so much land that it was willing to give some of it away to white settlers who would stake a claim. For example, as a result of the Homestead Act of 1862, the U.S. government gave nearly 1.5 million families title to 246 million acres of land, nearly the size of California and Texas combined (Shapiro 2004, 190). At least for white settlers, America was literally the land of opportunity. The idea of rugged pioneers setting out against all the odds to stake their own claims and conquer the West became a deep and abiding image in the American psyche.

Self-employment also fit well with the principles of free-market capitalism. Economic self-interest, individual ownership, and unbridled competition became the cornerstones of the new economy. Self-employment resonated with the experience of the new nation. Americans were on their way to "doing it my way."

Since those early days, however, economic conditions have changed dramatically. Large bureaucratically organized corporations now dominate the American economic landscape. Despite these colossal shifts in the economy, many Americans continue to cling to the romantic image of the lone inventor and the individual entrepreneur as backbones of the American economy. In this chapter, we chronicle these changes and discuss their impact on the prospects for meritocracy.

MOM AND POP, WHERE ART THOU? THE DECLINE OF SELF-EMPLOYMENT

Estimating historical rates of self-employment can be tricky business (Aronson 1991, 137–42; Wright 1997, 142–45). Despite problems of comparability, counting, and classification, the overall historical pattern is clear. No matter how you calculate them, rates of self-employment in America have declined sharply (Aronson 1991; Hipple 2004; Phillips 1958; Mishel, Bernstein, and Allegretto 2007; Wright 1997). Self-employment as a percentage of the total labor force has plummeted from an estimated 80 percent in 1800 (Phillips 1958, 2), to 34 percent in 1900 (Wright 1997, 124), to 18 percent in 1950 (Hipple 2004, 14), to just 7.3 percent in 2006, and a slight rise to 10.9 percent in 2009 (Hipple 2010, 17). The recent uptick is likely due to the impact of the Great Recession during which many workers who lost their jobs in the paid labor force reluctantly turned to some form of self-employment to try to stay afloat.

Early declines in self-employment were mainly the result of the Industrial Revolution and the mechanization of agriculture, which displaced many small family farms. At the same time, opportunities for wage employment increased in the growing industrial sector. Although the decline of self-employment was most rapid in agriculture, self-employment declined in the nonagricultural sector as well. Goods manufactured in smokestack factories replaced handmade goods produced in craft shops. Supermarkets and chain convenience stores replaced mom-and-pop groceries and dry-goods stores. Giant suburban malls with "big-box" corporate chain outlets replaced the mom-and-pop shops and specialty stores. Chain motels and hotels replaced mom-and-pop roadside inns. Fast-food and franchise restaurants replaced mom-and-pop diners. HMOs and joint specialty practices replaced the "hang-out-a-shingle" solo family doctor. While remnants of traditional local independent businesses remain, each of these arenas of the economy has become increasingly bureaucratized, moving gradually away from sole proprietorships to partnerships to larger corporate establishments.

The U.S. Department of Labor (2012a) reports that for 2011, the occupations with the most self-employed workers included farmers and ranchers (860,000); child-care workers (489,000); carpenters (422,000); supervisors of retail salespersons (420,000); construction managers (361,000); landscapers and groundskeepers (308,000); hairdressers, hairstylists, and cosmetologists (307,000); construction laborers (228,000); painters and construction and maintenance workers (222,000); and real estate agents (217,000). Significantly, farmers, ranchers, and agricultural managers, who in 2000 accounted for one in ten of all self-employed workers in the United States, are projected to incur the most job losses between 2010 and 2020.

Even the current small percentage of self-employed counted in the regular labor force may be inflated, at least in terms of how self-employment has traditionally been conceived. For instance, individuals who own franchises licensed through major corporations strongly identify as self-employed (Bills 1998). Franchises operate in such diverse areas as motels, restaurants, convenience stores, gas stations, clothing outlets, and even funeral homes. An estimated 40 percent of retail sales are made through franchise outlets (Everett 2006). One-fourth of these outlets are owned by the parent franchisor company, while the majority are owned or partly owned by franchisees (Blair and Lafontaine 2005). Although franchisees may be owners or part owners of such establishments, they are not entrepreneurs in the traditional sense. They do not create new business concepts; nor do they develop new products. They often rely on the franchisor to provide training, financing, and marketing. Most franchisees are contractually bound to follow standardized procedures and operations established by the franchisor. Franchisees are therefore neither fully independent owners nor fully dependent wage employees. Instead, they represent a kind of in-between status most often referred to as "dependent self-employment" (Bills 1998; Muehlberger 2007).

Another dependent type of self-employment includes those who are self-employed but have only one client. Such enterprises may be spin-offs of parent businesses that are established separately for tax purposes. Instead of representing true entrepreneurial activity, such employment may be a new way for employers to hire outsourced workers under arrangements of home-work, freelancing, or subcontracting (Wright 1997, 140). Large construction firms, for instance, frequently subcontract trade work to individuals or small companies, often for less pay and benefits than the firm would pay its own full-time employees. Increasingly, large farmers in Texas and the Southwest use subcontractors to supply labor in an effort to avoid legal problems hiring undocumented Mexican immigrants (Massey 2007). Although individual craft workers or owners of the subcontracting companies may be "self-employed," they are often largely or wholly dependent on a single client, reducing their leverage and true autonomy.

Professionals in group practices may also identify themselves as self-employed or declare themselves self-employed for tax purposes, but they are not sole practitioners in the classical sense. There are clear advantages for professionals who work in these settings, such as taking turns being "on call" for the practice, having colleagues immediately available to consult, sharing expensive equipment and overhead costs, and hiring accountants, receptionists, nurses, and billing agencies. But their work and conditions of employment are increasingly bureaucratized and subject to control by others.

While these arrangements may inflate reported rates of self-employment, other forms of self-employment that go unreported have the opposite effect. Those who work "under the table" or "off the books" in what is alternately referred to as the "irregular economy," "the shadow economy," or the "black market" confound the estimates (Dallago 1990; Greenfield 1993; Leonard 1998; Naylor 2002; Schlosser 2003; Venkatesh 2006; Williams 2006; Williams and Windebank 1998). Individuals who work in the irregular economy may be self-employed or work for someone else. They may be in the irregular economy involuntarily because of lack of regular employment, or they may be voluntarily engaged in "hidden" entrepreneurial activity. Much of the economic activity that occurs in this sector is intentionally engaged in illegally to avoid taxation and regulation. Forms of work in this sector are varied, ranging from housewives watching other people's children in their homes for undeclared pay, to undocumented immigrants working in a variety of settings, to handymen doing home improvement and repair, to people participating directly in criminal activities such as theft, fencing, drug dealing, gambling, prostitution, loan sharking, smuggling, or, more recently, Internet or cybercrime. The full extent of these activities is unknown.

In many ways, the irregular economy is a bastion of unadulterated free enterprise. It is, in effect, unregulated and untaxed and creates opportunities for ambitious, risk-taking entrepreneurs. For some, the irregular economy has long been one of the few sources of employment or mobility in economically depressed areas (Fusfeld 1973; Naylor 2002; Venkatesh 2006). Some research, for instance, indicates that successful drug dealing early in life increases the likelihood of legitimate self-employment in later years (Fairlie 2002). Although employment in the irregular economy may, for some, be a vehicle of upward mobility and, in some cases, a pathway to eventual employment in the regular economy, it is not generally considered a legitimate part of the American Dream.

BETWIXT AND BETWEEN: THE CONTRADICTORY CLASS POSITION OF THE SELF-EMPLOYED

The class position of self-employed workers is at best ambiguous. Karl Marx initially distinguished two main social classes in capitalist societies: those who own the means of producing wealth (bourgeoisie) and those who sell their labor to others (proletariat). The bourgeoisie, however, include several subcategories (Wright 1997). One group of bourgeoisie, *rentier capitalists*, own businesses and hire the labor of others but do not themselves work for an income. Another group of bourgeoisie, *entrepreneurial capitalists*, both work in the businesses they own and hire the labor of others. *Petty bourgeoisie*, on the other hand, own their own businesses and work in them but do not hire the labor of others.

The vast majority of the self-employed in the United States are true petty bourgeoisie; that is, they tend not to have paid employees. In 2009, for instance, 86 percent of all self-employed workers had no paid employees (Hipple 2010, 30). Of the remaining 13.6 percent of self-employed workers who had paid employees, most had very few. More than three-fourths of self-employed workers who had paid employees had fewer than four, and only 3.8 percent had more than twenty.

Petty bourgeoisie and entrepreneurial capitalists occupy what sociologist Erik Olin Wright refers to as "contradictory" locations within the class structure. In some ways these groups share characteristics with capitalists, and in some ways they share characteristics with wage laborers. Like capitalists, the petty bourgeoisie own their own businesses, but unlike capitalists, the petty bourgeoisie do not hire or control the labor of others. Entrepreneurial capitalists and the petty bourgeoisie share with the proletariat the characteristic of working for an income. But unlike the proletariat, the work of entrepreneurial capitalists and the petty bourgeoisie is not supervised or controlled by others.

In later stages of industrial development, these class divisions become even more blurred. Some sociologists, for instance, make a distinction between the "old middle class" and the "new middle class" (Mills 1951). The old middle class consisted mostly of entrepreneurial capitalists and the petty bourgeoisie, that is, small-business owners, family farmers, and solo fee-for-service professionals.

The old middle class was considered generally respectable, mostly well to do, and fiercely independent. However, in later stages of industrialization, a new middle class of managers, administrators, and technicians emerged. The new middle class came about with the advent of the "managerial revolution" and the "separation of ownership from control" (Berle and Means 1932). In the early part of the twentieth century, more and more owners withdrew from day-to-day control of their businesses and began to hire managers to run them. As businesses became larger and more complex, layers of bureaucracy were added, and the ranks of management grew. Remnants of the old middle class remain, but it is outnumbered and overshadowed by the ascendance of the new middle class.

CHARACTERISTICS OF THE SELF-EMPLOYED

Compared to the wage-labor force, self-employed workers tend to be older, white, and male (Aronson 1991; Hipple 2010). Self-employed workers are older by an average of about ten years (Aronson 1991, 6). Age differences in rates of self-employment are especially acute in both upper and lower age groups. In 2009, for instance, workers over sixty-five were over three times *more* likely than their wage-labor counterparts to be self-employed, while workers twenty to twenty-four were almost three times less likely to be self-employed than their wage-labor counterparts (Hipple 2010, 23). Older workers are more likely than younger workers to have both the work experience and the accumulated capital required to start businesses. Also, in some cases older workers may opt for self-employment as an alternative to retirement or as a way to control the amount and pace of work as physical stamina declines.

Self-employed workers are somewhat more likely to be male than female. In 2009, 8.3 percent of men were self-employed compared with 5.6 percent of women (Hipple 2010, 21). Rates of self-employment among women, however, have increased in the last several decades (Aronson 1991, 5; Arum 1997; McCrary 1998). This growth of self-employment among women is associated with several factors. First, rates of self-employment tend to be higher in the growing service sector of the economy, where women have historically been overrepresented. Although some of the increase of female self-employment has occurred in the high-wage professional part of the service sector (e.g., physicians and lawyers), most of the increase has occurred in the low-wage nonprofessional part of the sector (e.g., child-care workers, hairdressers) (McCrary 1998). Second, some women may select self-employment because it affords them greater scheduling flexibility in combining the demands of work and family. Among self-employed workers, for instance, half of women are employed part-time compared to only a third of men (Hipple 2010, 28). Finally, some women may start new businesses to circumvent the glass-ceiling effects often encountered in wage employment.

Although self-employment is often seen as a vehicle of upward social mobility for ethnic minorities, whites have higher rates of self-employment than these groups. In 2009 for instance, whites were about twice as likely to be self-employed as blacks, with white self-employment at 7.4 percent compared to 4.5 percent for blacks (Hipple 2010, 21). Some of this difference may be attributed to reluctance among white customers to patronize black-owned businesses and whites' assumption that black-owned businesses produce inferior products or services (Feagin and Sikes 1994; Parker 2004). Blacks, who have less wealth than whites, also have less capital to start businesses and more difficulty securing business loans (Parker 2004; Shapiro 2004). Finally, blacks have encountered difficulty in locating their businesses in "white" areas. For similar reasons, the rate of self-employment for Hispanic Americans at 6.1 percent in 2009 (Hipple 2010, 21) was only slightly higher than the rate for African Americans. Some Asian minorities, with cultural norms that encourage the pooling of familial capital among extended-kin networks, had rates of self-employment at 6.6 percent in 2009 (Hipple 2010, 21), approaching that of whites.

Some studies suggest that the self-employed tend to have different psychological characteristics than wage workers (cf. Thornton 1999 and Parker 2004 for systematic reviews). These studies suggest, for instance, that need for achievement, internal locus of control, risk-taking propensity, and independence are associated with the likelihood of self-employment. Other studies suggest that self-employment disproportionately attracts workers with low productivity who might otherwise have difficulty finding suitable employment in the wage sector. Such "trait" studies, however, are plagued by methodological problems, especially the basic issue of separating cause and effect. In short, do certain psychological characteristics or predispositions lead to self-employment, or does self-employment create such characteristics in individuals? Also, such traits are not unique to the self-employed, creating problems of demarcation. Not surprisingly, the results of these studies have been very mixed. Regardless of specification and the direction of causality, the idea that individual characteristics alone account for self-employment or entrepreneurship has largely been abandoned in favor of more multidimensional models that take into consideration the influence of organizational, market, and environmental influences.

At least some self-employment, for instance, occurs not as a matter of individual choice or personal preference but as the result of unemployment (e.g., a downsized white-collar executive who freelances as a self-employed "consultant"), subemployment (the laid-off factory worker who works as a self-employed "handyman"), or outsourced employment (a former wage employee who contracts with an employer to perform the same services as a contract laborer, often for less pay and little or no benefits) (Wright 1997, 139–42).

In addition, some employment in the "irregular" economy is involuntary; that is, individuals may resort to working "off the books," often in illegal activities, when stable wage employment is not available or is difficult to secure (Fusfeld 1973; Naylor 2002; Venkatesh 2006). The full extent of nonvoluntary self-employment is difficult to estimate. Most studies, however, show that self-employment tends to decline during periods of economic expansion and increase during periods of economic decline (Hipple 2010, 19), further indicating that at least some self-employment is reluctantly entered into when wage employment is otherwise not available or is difficult to secure.

The income of self-employed workers is also difficult to assess. According to the U.S. Census Bureau's Current Population Survey (U.S. Census Bureau 2010), the mean (mathematical average) annual earnings of self-employed workers in 2009 was $50,133, compared to the mean of $41,928 for all workers. Mathematical averages, however, are sensitive to extreme scores. A few high values can greatly increase the overall average. In cases where distributions are highly skewed in this manner, median scores (which divide the population into two equal halves) are generally understood to be better measures of central tendency. Using median scores, the annual income difference between self-employed workers ($30,245) and all workers ($30,899) is essentially reduced to parity. The greater difference between the mean and median earnings of the self-employed compared to the mean and median of all workers reflects the more highly skewed distribution of earnings among self-employed workers. A few do extremely well (driving up mathematical averages), but many more struggle (lowering the median). Self-employed hedge-fund managers, for instance, may make millions, but there are relatively few of them compared to hundreds of thousands of self-employed child-care workers and hairdressers, most of whom earn very little.

Assessing the real income of self-employed workers is further complicated because self-employed workers, in an attempt to reduce tax liability, are more likely to underreport income than are wage workers (Aronson 1991). Or, as in the case of the illegal irregular segment of the economy, self-employment earnings may be disguised or not reported at all. What is more, self-employed workers who own their own businesses tend to work many more hours than wage laborers, which effectively reduces the hourly rate of return among the self-employed. In addition, income alone does not tell the whole story, since self-employed workers must fund their own retirements, medical insurance, and vacation time, the effective value of which further exacerbates the annual median-income disadvantage (−$654) in self-employed earnings. The recent inflationary surge in the costs of private medical insurance and the lack of pooled risks for self-employed people have especially eroded effective wage benefits for the self-employed.

Another characteristic of self-employment is that it is associated with very high risks for workplace injury and death. Self-employed workers, for instance, are 2.7 times more likely to be victims of fatal work injuries than wage and salary workers (Pegula 2004, 31). This higher rate of on-the-job fatalities among the self-employed is primarily associated with the disproportionate tendency for self-employed workers to work in industries with higher injury and fatality rates, especially agriculture, forestry, fishing, and construction. However, the self-employed are also more likely to have higher fatality rates even when working in the same occupations as their wage and salary counterparts (Pegula 2004, 33). This difference may be related to several factors associated with the conditions of work among self-employed workers, including fewer workplace safety measures (self-employed workers may ignore safety concerns to try to stay competitive or have fewer resources to spend on safety education and equipment), longer hours worked among self-employed (increasing the risk of fatigue while operating hazardous machinery), and the older ages among self-employed workers (increasing risks of more strenuous physical activities) (Pegula 2004, 35–36). Self-employed workers are not only at greater risk for fatal on-the-job injuries but also are more likely to be murdered on the job. The higher risk for homicide among self-employed workers is primarily in retail sales. Small mom-and-pop retail and lodging establishments are often located in marginal or low-income areas and may be more attractive targets for robberies than larger stores or national retail chains (Pegula 2004, 34), which are also more likely to be located in suburban malls and use electronic surveillance, private police, and other more elaborate security measures.

Another type of risk for self-employed workers is the high risk of business failure, especially for those striking out alone to start a new business. Rates of survival for new businesses are notoriously low. According to a recent U.S. Small Business Administration (2010) study, data from the U.S. Census Bureau's Business Information Tracking Series show that only 69 percent of new businesses survive for two years, half close within five years, and only about one-third make it ten years or more.

This is nothing new; self-employment and new business starts have always been very high-risk ventures. But the presence of large corporations makes such ventures even more risky. Small businesses that take on established corporations for market share are at a distinct disadvantage. Small-business starts that have the best chance of success are those that find new, localized, or unique market niches. Even then, such establishments run the risk of being swallowed up by larger concerns seeking entry into niche markets, especially if these niches yield high returns and offer opportunities for national or global expansion. We now turn our attention to the flip side of declining self-employment: the growth of corporate production and employment.

SWIMMING WITH THE SHARKS: THE ASCENT OF THE MODERN CORPORATION

At the time of the American Revolution, corporations did not exist. During colonial times, a handful of joint stock companies, such as the East India Company, the Massachusetts Bay Company, and the Hudson Bay Company, were chartered by the British Crown to reap the bounty of the New World (Derber 1998). With the establishment of American independence, a few establishments were granted corporate charters by states and sometimes the federal government to provide specific public services, such as roads, bridges, colleges, or canals. In exchange for these expressly public services, such private entities were granted powers normally delegated to governments, such as the power to collect tolls.

At first, corporate charters were granted only under strictly delimited conditions. In addition to requiring that corporations explicitly serve the public interest, corporate charters were granted for limited periods and restricted the amount of assets corporations could accumulate (Derber 1998, 122). These restrictions were consistent with the distrust that early legislators had of all large organizations, including the new corporate entities (Perrow 2002, 33–35). Individual states, however, competed with one another for corporate revenue by offering increasingly lenient statutes for incorporation. One small state, Delaware, host to a particularly large and important corporation, DuPont, ultimately offered the most lenient statutes for incorporation and became the darling of large corporations everywhere. Roughly half of today's Fortune 500 companies, regardless of where they conduct business, are incorporated in the state of Delaware. With most government restrictions lifted, the modern corporate form emerged (Derber 1998; Miller 1977; Perrow 2002; Roy 1997). By 2008, corporations accounted for 81.3 percent of all business revenue, while partnerships accounted for only 14.8 percent and proprietorships only 3.9 percent (U.S. Census Bureau 2012a).

Crucial to the establishment of the modern corporation was a series of legal decisions that redefined the essence of the corporation. These decisions allowed corporations to operate for private gain without explicitly serving the public interest, established the principle of limited liability, and extended the legal rights of individuals to corporations. The elimination of the requirement for public service enabled an unrestricted profit motive. Under the principle of limited liability, investors would risk only the amount of money they invested in a corporation and would not be liable for whatever other debts the corporation acquired. Especially critical to these court rulings was the extension of the legal rights of individuals to corporations. These rulings allowed the pooling of enormous amounts of capital from multiple investors in single companies, a phenomenon that has been described as the "socializing of capital" (Roy 1997).

When ratified in 1787, the Constitution of the United States did not contain the word "corporation"; nor does it today. It is understandable that its framers, otherwise concerned about concentrations of power not directly accountable to the public, overlooked corporations since the corporate-like entities of the day were neither numerous nor powerful. As corporations became more numerous and powerful, constitutional issues related to corporations arose. Since the Constitution recognizes only two legal entities, the government and the individual, the courts in essence had to decide which of these applied to corporations. In a series of key U.S. Supreme Court decisions in the early 1800s, corporations were interpreted legally as individuals under the provisions of the Constitution. As such, corporations were extended the legal rights of individuals, especially with regard to the Fourteenth Amendment, which provides for "equal protection" under the law.

Among the rights granted to corporations was the right to buy and sell property. With the legal ability to buy and sell property like individuals, corporations ferociously bought and sold each other. The history of corporations in America is the history of the big fish eating the little fish and eventually the big fish eating each other. Most major markets in the United States became dominated by a few big fish. The 1880s and 1890s marked an era of rapid consolidation. Through trade associations, pools, trusts, cartels, and other organizational devices, turn-of-the-century capitalists managed to consolidate economic power to an alarming degree. Widespread consolidation led to artificially inflated prices, which provoked organized efforts to reinstate more competitive conditions. Political agitation from farmers and small-business owners, who were caught in the grip of railroad combinations, prompted the establishment of the Interstate Commerce Commission in 1887, the government's first major attempt to regulate trade, and the Sherman Anti-Trust Act of 1890, the government's first organized effort to control monopolies.

Although monopolies were illegal, the major "smokestack" industries in the United States that made America an industrial giant—autos, steel, chemicals, and oil—became dominated by a few large corporations and settled into their current oligopolistic structure. Numerous other familiar manufacturing and food-production industries became similarly highly concentrated (see table 7.1). The beer industry is one example. Beer is big business in America. The U.S. beer industry directly employs approximately 1.8 million workers, with an annual payroll of $71.2 billion (Beer Institute 2011). In 2010, the largest five producers accounted for 88.8 percent of total market share (El-

Table 7.1. Examples of Highly Concentrated Industries, 2007

	Percent of Market Share of Four Largest Firms
Manufacturing industries	
Electric lightbulbs and parts	75
Petrochemicals	80
Aircraft manufacturing	81
Automobile manufacturing	68
Tire manufacturing	73
Household appliances	64
Ship and boat building	44
Paper mills	46
Construction machinery	54
Iron and steel mills	52
Audio and video equipment	41
Petroleum refineries	48
Cigarette manufacturing	98
Food production industries	
Breweries	90
Breakfast cereals	80
Cookies and crackers	69
Chocolate confectioneries	59
Snack food	53
Soft drinks	58
Coffee and tea	43
Ice cream and frozen desserts	52
Retail sales outlets	
Home centers	93
Variety stores	84
Office supply and stationary	80
Hobby, toy, and game stores	72
Department stores	73

Bookstores	71
Athletic footwear stores	68
Sewing, needlework, and piece goods	59
Cosmetics, beauty supplies, and perfume	54
Pet and pet supply stores	62
Computer and software stores	73
Pharmacies and drugstores	63
Paint and wallpaper stores	60
Family shoe stores	41
Electronics and appliance stores	46
Optical goods stores	51
Financial institutions	
Credit card issuing firms	79
Central banks	65
Consumer lending firms	61
National commercial banks	56
Federally chartered savings institutions	41

Sources: U.S. Census Bureau 2007a, 2007b, 2007c

zinga 2011, 220). Anheuser-Busch, the largest producer, alone accounts for nearly half (47.9 percent) of the total American market; the second-largest producer, MillerCoors, accounts for another 28.9 percent of market share, representing a combined 76.8 percent market share for just the two largest producers (Elzinga 2011, 220). Indicative of recent trends in the American economy in which foreign firms are increasingly merging with major U.S. companies, in 2008 Anheuser-Busch was acquired by InBev, a Belgian brewing company (producer of Stella Artois, Hoegaarden, Leffe, Beck's, Bass, Labatt, and Brahma), for $52 billion. The combined entity became the largest brewing company in the world. In the same year, Miller and Coors also combined in a joint venture, forming MillerCoors and further consolidating the industry. At the turn of the nineteenth century, there were thousands of brewing companies in the United States. Brewing was a classic family business in which products were produced and sold locally. With Prohibition, these companies were forced into other business ventures or out of business altogether. Once Prohibition was repealed in 1933, many of these breweries were reestablished, and other new companies were formed. By 1938, there were about seven hundred brewing companies in the United States. As companies went out of business or were bought by competitors, and as national distribution networks were established, the number of traditional lager breweries rapidly declined so that by 2001 only twenty-four remained (Tremblay and Tremblay 2005, 11). Since 1950, there have been over six hundred horizontal mergers and acquisitions of facilities and brand names (Tremblay and Tremblay 2005, 45). Companies often retain brand names of products from companies they acquire, giving the appearance of more competition than actually exists. For instance, Anheuser-Busch markets beer under several brand names, including Budweiser, Michelob, Busch, Rolling Rock, O'Doul's (nonalcoholic), and many others. This trend toward consolidation in the beer industry has been offset somewhat in the past few decades by an increase in imported beers as well as so-called microbreweries, domestic brew pubs, and "craft," or specialty, brewers. These domestic brewers are typically small, independent, on-site breweries that do not market nationally. Although these proportions are increasing somewhat, by 2012, imports accounted for 13.3 percent of market share, and craft brewers accounted for only 4.8 percent of total market share (Elzinga 2011, 224).

Overall, the largest one hundred manufacturing firms account for over one-third of the value of all manufactured products in America (U.S. Census Bureau 2007d). Retail outlets have followed the trend set initially in manufacturing and are now also rapidly becoming oligopolized (see examples in table 7.1). By 2007, the largest fifty retail firms were responsible for 33 percent of all retail sales (U.S. Census Bureau 2007b), a substantial sum considering that small-business establishments tend to be located in the retail sector of the economy.

At the top of the pyramid chain of corporate dominance in the U.S. economy are big banks and other major financial institutions, such as insurance, securities, credit, and mortgage companies. This is the "paper-tiger" sector of the economy involved not in the making of things but in moving money around, that is, in buying and selling money, credit, insurance, or financial risk. At over 20 percent of U.S. gross domestic product by 2005, the financial sector had become the largest sector of the U.S. economy, exceeding manufacturing, health care, and wholesale/retail trade (Phillips 2008). Like other sectors of the economy, the financial sector has become increasingly consolidated. In 1970, the largest five U.S. banks held 17 percent of total industry assets; by 2010, the largest five U.S. banks held 52 percent of total industry assets, or three times the earlier level of concentration (Rosenblum 2011). The rapid consolidation of U.S. industry in general and especially the financial sector has led to increasing concerns that these corporate entities are "too big to fail." That is, because of their sheer size and ripple effects if they should fail, they could drag the rest of the economy down with them and risk collapse of the economy as a whole, as was evident in the events leading to and precipitating the Great Recession.

The Great Recession

With rapidly mounting public and private debt, the paper tiger eventually became a house of cards. By late 2007, the financial sector was on the edge of economic collapse, reminiscent of the banking collapse that triggered the Great Depression in 1929. The full explanation of the causes of the subsequent Great Recession is still being debated (Davies 2010; Fligstein and Goldstein 2011), but there is widespread consensus that it was immediately triggered by a massive mortgage debt crisis. Following the structural shifts in the economy associated with globalization and deindustrialization, the U.S. economy was kept partially afloat by the dot-com bubble of the 1980s and 1990s, which crashed in 2000, driving stock market prices down sharply. To help stimulate the economy in the aftermath of this downturn, the Federal Reserve reduced interest rates (the costs of money to lenders) to practically zero. This meant that banks could borrow money cheaply and get good returns by loaning it back out, even at reduced rates. The availability of low-interest mortgage loans along with increased housing demand inflated housing prices, fueling a rapid housing bubble. Rising housing prices and reduced interest rates encouraged existing homeowners to refinance, giving them access to credit that helped offset otherwise flat or falling wage income.

In the 1960s and 1970s, the federal government had set up programs to help low-income families become home owners. These programs insured mortgage loans against default under relaxed rules for eligibility. These "subprime" loans were "packaged" with conventional loans and resold to investors. Once the conventional mortgage market was saturated, banks—anxious to earn fees and turn quick profits—increasingly turned to the subprime market (Fligstein and Goldstein 2011). By 2007, 70 percent of all loans made were unconventional mortgages (Fligstein and Goldstein 2011). The buying and selling of these so-called "ninja" loans in the subprime market occurred in an economic climate of both deregulation and corporate consolidation. Commercial banks previously restricted from investments of this type entered the frenzy with zeal. The largest of these soon dominated the mortgage-backed securities market. Market confidence in these securities eventually eroded, and the credit supply dried up. Housing prices fell sharply, and large numbers of American home owners defaulted on mortgages. Investment companies were then stuck with large amounts of "toxic assets" in loans that exceeded the value of homes and the capacity of home owners to make payments, and the economy as a whole went into free fall. Several of the large investment firms that had entered the frenzy were now in trouble. Lehman Brothers and AIG quickly collapsed under downward market pressures. Several other big banks and financial concerns were on the brink of failing. To try to avoid further erosion of the credit market and at the urging of federal officials, the four largest central banks—Bank of America, Citigroup, JPMorgan Chase, and Wells Fargo—quickly moved to absorb other large ailing banks, leaving these remaining banks with virtually all of the remaining central banking assets. In the midst of the crisis and in a matter of weeks, JPMorgan Chase acquired Washington Mutual, and Bank of America acquired both Countrywide and Merrill Lynch. Within a few months, Wells Fargo acquired Wachovia Bank. Even these acquisitions were not enough to shore up the ailing credit market. The federal government, itself deeply in debt, was reluctantly forced to step in and bail out the credit market at a staggering sum of over $700 billion.

All of these events had devastating effects, increasing job loss and unemployment, quite independent of the merit of discrete workers. The economy lost 8.5 million jobs from December 2007 to February 2010, and the unemployment rate more than doubled over that period from 5 percent to 10.4 percent (Hout, Levanon, and Cumberworth 2011). Construction and manufacturing were especially hard hit, and men were disproportionally affected, leading some to refer to the recession as the "man-cession." African Americans, Latinos, immigrants, and those with low levels of educational attainment experienced especially high rates of job loss (Hout, Levanon, and Cumberworth 2011). Also, compared to previous recessions, the duration of unemployment increased.

Moreover, job losses associated with the Great Recession concentrated in mid-pay and mid-skill range occupations—especially construction, manufacturing, and transportation—accelerating the long-term trend of hollowing out the middle and increasing overall wage inequality (Smeeding, Thompson, Levanon, and Burak 2011). Wealth has also become more unequal with the effects of the Great Recession (Wolff, Owens, and Burak 2011). While stock prices recovered, housing prices lagged behind. Since most of the value of assets of the nonrich is in home equity, the collapse of the housing market particularly affected them. With housing prices falling precipitously, many homeowners found themselves "underwater," owing more on their homes than they were worth. By the end of 2009, one in five home owners found themselves in that situation. Moreover, with many homeowners losing jobs and income, there has also been a sharp increase in both foreclosures and bankruptcies (Wolff, Owens, and Burak 2011).

Megamergers

The historically high level of market consolidation in all sectors of the economy has been fueled by a frenzy of megamergers occurring in recent decades (see table 7.2). Huge sums of money are taken out of the credit economy to finance such mergers without typically creating any new products or new jobs (as combined entities benefit from various economies of scale). Most of these are horizontal mergers in which large firms acquire other large firms in

Table 7.2. Examples of Recent Megamergers

Megamergers	Price ($ billions)	Date
AOL + Time Warner	165.0	2000
Exxon + Mobil	87.0	1998
Citicorp Bank + Travelers	84.0	1998
BellSouth + AT&T	67.0	2006
Bank of America + NationsBank	64.8	1998
JPMorgan + Bank One	58.0	2004
Procter & Gamble + Gillette	57.0	2005
InBev + Anheuser-Busch	52.0	2008
BP + Amoco	48.2	1998
Bank of America + FleetBoston	48.0	2004
Roche + Genentech	46.8	2009
Cingular Wireless + AT&T Wireless	41.0	2005
Merck + Schering-Plough	41.0	
Sprint + Nextel	35.0	2005
Express Scripts Inc. + Medco Health Solutions Inc.	34.3	2011
Duke + Progress Energy	32.0	2012
Bank of America + Merrill Lynch	19.4	2009
Time Warner + Adelphia	17.7	2006
Texaco + Unocal	16.8	2005
Bank of New York + Mellon Financial	16.5	2007
First Union + Wachovia	14.4	2003
McDonnell Douglas + Boeing	13.0	1997
Wells Fargo + Wachovia	12.7	2009
Sears + Kmart	11.0	2005
Microsoft Corporation + Skype	8.0	2011
Molson + Coors	4.0	2005
Adidas + Reebok	3.8	2006

the same industry group, resulting in even higher levels of market consolidation.

With name changes as well as acquisitions of new product lines, the average consumer simply cannot keep up with who owns what. In classical economics, the consumer is seen as "king," and every purchase is seen as a "vote" in the economic marketplace. As the story goes, if customers are dissatisfied with the products or policies of any particular company, they are free to take their business elsewhere (including using boycott as an organized form of protest). However, if choices are limited or nonexistent, or if the consumer does not know what the choices represent (who owns what), then this form of restraint on the marketplace is vastly compromised.

The largest corporation in America (and the world) is now Wal-Mart Stores, Inc., the largest retailer in the United States and emblematic of the postindustrial shift from goods production to retail and service industries. As measured by both total annual revenues ($419 billion) and total number of employees (2.1 million) (Wal-Mart Stores, Inc. 2011), Walmart Superstores and Walmart Sam's Clubs discount retail warehouses are a long way away from the mom-and-pop grocery stores of the 1950s.

Despite the expansion in size and power of corporate goliaths, small business is often heralded as the backbone of the American economy. Small businesses are often thought to be responsible for most employment, most business activity, and most innovation in the economy. However, the data indicate otherwise. While business establishments with no paid employees (most of which are self-employed businesses) represent about 74 percent of all business establishments, they account for only about 3 percent of total business receipts (U.S. Census Bureau 2012b). Among business establishments that have at least one paid employee, those with fewer than twenty employees account for 71 percent of such business establishments but employ only 18 percent of all paid employees and generate only 13 percent of total business receipts. At the other end of the continuum, business establishments with over five hundred employees account for only 4 percent of all business establishments but employ 50 percent of all paid employees and generate 62 percent of total business receipts (U.S. Census Bureau 2012b).

Even these numbers underestimate the dominance of large firms in the American economy. While separate business establishments are defined as single physical locations where business is conducted, these include branch offices and franchise sites for larger corporations. In addition, many smaller establishments are tied to the larger firms as suppliers or retailers of products and services provided by the megacorporations. Larger corporations often create "vertical networks" of smaller contractor firms under their control while at the same time downsizing their own labor forces (Harrison 1994, 47).

Not only are small businesses not dominant in the economy as a whole, but they are also not the major source of product innovation. In 1901, 80 percent of U.S. patents were issued to individuals (Caplow, Hicks, Wattenberg 2001, 258). By 2007, only 12.3 percent of all patents were issued to individuals (U.S. Patent and Trademark Office 2011). The remaining patents were issued to organizational entities, most of which are corporations. While some new technologies may originate with individuals and small businesses, most individuals or small companies do not have the capital to set up large-scale production facilities or market new technologies. As a result, larger established corporations often buy out small-time players. Buying out promising new technologies from individuals and smaller companies is often a way for large corporations to stay technologically competitive without heavily investing in expensive basic research programs that may not yield tangible results. Other major sources of technological innovation occur outside the private sector altogether through government- and university-sponsored research.

All of this is far removed from the self-employed entrepreneur. The ascendance of large-scale corporations affects self-employment in several ways. First, large corporations create barriers of entry for small businesses, especially sole proprietorships. Thus, neither do small businesses have the capital nor can they generate the volume of business to challenge large businesses operating in similar markets. In technologically advanced societies, some forms of production require large-scale operations that preclude self-employed or small-business operations. No one, for instance, would seriously consider establishing a self-employed sole proprietorship to produce automobiles. Second, compared to employment in large corporations, employment in the small-business sector is generally less stable, does not pay as well, and generally does not provide as good benefits. Third, the ascendance of large corporations has no doubt reduced opportunities for rapid social mobility. When sole proprietors had no corporations to compete against, it was more possible for individual entrepreneurs to establish new market niches and grow their businesses rapidly. Rags-to-riches scenarios, while never common, are now even less common. The decline of self-employment and the dominance of large bureaucratic corporations changes mobility in another way. Starting a new business requires different individual characteristics than maintaining an established one. The "entrepreneurial personality"—supposedly bold, visionary, risk taking, and ruggedly individualistic— while perhaps well suited for launching new business ventures, is probably not well suited for running large bureaucratic organizations. Once you are already ahead, the idea is to stay ahead, and the best way to do that is to play it safe.

Bureaucracies generally reward compliance, not defiance. In bureaucratic settings, one does not typically advance by being the defiant, rugged, and fiercely independent individualist of American folklore, but by going along to get along, being a team player, following rules and procedures, and slowly climbing the bureaucratic ladder one step at a time.

Clearly, some individual entrepreneurs who strike out on their own manage to defy the odds and do very well. Those who succeed do not necessarily work harder than those who fail; nor are they necessarily more inherently capable or meritorious. Having sufficient start-up capital to launch new enterprises (it takes money to make money) and being in the right place at the right time with the right idea (random-walk hypothesis) do, however, have a great deal to do with entrepreneurial success.

THE CASE OF MICROSOFT

In rare circumstances, such individuals may take advantage of temporary market imbalances and launch new enterprises that start out small but evolve into corporate giants. One particularly prominent example is the establishment of the Microsoft Corporation in 1975, now the forty-second largest corporation in the world (Forbes 2012a). Microsoft was cofounded by Bill Gates (now the richest American with wealth estimated at $66 billion) and Paul Allen (now the twentieth-richest American with wealth estimated at $15 billion) (Forbes 2012b). Gates and Allen were friends who in the late 1960s and early 1970s attended the same exclusive private prep school, Lakeside School in Seattle, Washington. Lakeside had a computer lab (which many universities did not have at the time) where Gates and Allen were first exposed to computing and initially honed their programming skills.

After graduating from Lakeside, Gates went on to Harvard University, and Allen went on to Washington State University. Allen dropped out of Washington State to take a job as a computer programmer for Honeywell. While Gates was still a student at Harvard, Gates and Allen read an article about a new personal computer, the Altair, which was being made in Albuquerque, New Mexico. Until then, most computers were large, expensive mainframes used by the military, corporations, and universities. The vision of Ed Roberts, the founder of Micro Instrumentation and Telemetry Systems (MITS) and the manufacturer of the Altair, was to build affordable, desktop computers for individual use. Gates and Allen contacted the company and offered to write software for the Altair. They secured the contract, and Allen became a full-time software director at MITS. Gates and Allen entered into a licensing agreement with MITS for their software program. Gates and Allen had formed a separate company, which they named Microsoft ("micro" for small personal computers and "soft" for software).

From there, Gates and Allen secured license contracts for their software with other companies just entering the field as well, including the National

Cash Register Company, NCR, General Electric, RadioShack, Texas Instruments, Commodore, Apple, and Intel (Wallace and Erickson 1992, 134). Microsoft expanded rapidly, adding additional programmers. Allen quit MITS to work full time at Microsoft, and Gates dropped out of Harvard to do the same. Although Microsoft was doing very well with its licensing contracts with these companies, the big prize was IBM, because IBM was coming out with a new line of personal computers and needed an operating system to run on a 16-bit Intel chip. Such an operating system called CP/M had been initially developed by Gary Kildall, a computer engineer, and it was then the fledgling industry standard.

The rest of the story is legend. Tim Paterson at Seattle Computer Products had developed an adapted version of Kildall's CP/M system, which came to be known as Quick and Dirty Operating System, or QDOS. Paterson leased his system to Microsoft. Gates and Allen ultimately bought the rights to Paterson's QDOS for a sum of $50,000 (Wallace and Erickson 1992, 202). They modified the program further and then leased it to IBM under the label Microsoft DOS. Interestingly, John Opel, then the CEO of IBM, knew Bill Gates' mother personally since both sat on the national board of the United Way, but it is not known if that personal connection had any bearing on the awarding of the contract with IBM. Instead of selling the program outright, Microsoft secured a royalty on DOS with every computer IBM sold, catapulting Microsoft and its young owners into computing history.

The Microsoft story serves to illustrate the presence of many factors that occasionally coalesce to bring about great entrepreneurial success. Bill Gates and Paul Allen exhibit many of the personal characteristics often associated with great entrepreneurs—intensity, intellect, vision, determination, brashness, and business savvy. But such individual traits alone do not create entrepreneurial success. Gates and Allen were poised to take advantage of these traits through inheritance of privilege and being in the right place at the right time. In other words, we do not know how many potential Bill Gates and Paul Allens are out there—people with similar individual abilities and character traits, who are just as capable, but whose life circumstances have not positioned them to take full advantage of such capabilities.

SUMMARY

Americans embrace the ideal of the self-made person. It is quintessentially American to "go your own way" and "do your own thing." In economic life, this ideal is best exemplified by self-employment. Since colonial times, however, the self-employed as a proportion of the total American labor force has steadily and drastically declined. Despite the entrepreneurial mystique surrounding the image of self-employment, the reality for many who are self-employed is often less than glamorous. The vast majority of jobs held by self-employed workers are either physically demanding blue-collar jobs, such as farmer or construction worker, or service jobs such as hairdresser, child-care worker, or retail shopkeeper. Such jobs carry high risks for workplace fatality, including becoming a victim of workplace homicide. Compared to their wage-worker counterparts, the self-employed tend to work longer hours, often for effectively lower earnings after having to fund their own health care, vacations, and retirement plans. Some reluctantly resort to involuntary forms of self-employment when wage or salaried jobs are unavailable, including self-employment in the irregular and often illegal "underground" economy. And while some do overcome the odds and do very well, striking out on one's own to start a new business is clearly an extremely high-risk pursuit.

The rapid historical decline in self-employment corresponds to the ascendance of large corporations in the American economy. The collective assets and associated economies of scale of the corporate behemoths tend to undercut competition from smaller companies and discourage new entrants. Despite the reality of an economy dominated by increasingly large corporations, many Americans cling to the imagery of the go-it-alone entrepreneurial spirit as the backbone of the American economy. Such language, however, no longer accurately describes an economy dominated by goliath corporate entities and a labor force composed of individuals who mostly work for somebody else.

REFERENCES

Aronson, Robert L. 1991. *Self-Employment: A Labor Market Perspective.* New York: ILR Press.

Arum, Richard. 1997. "Trends in Male and Female Self-Employment: Growth in a New Middle Class or Increasing Marginalization of the Labor Force?" In *Research in Stratification and Mobility*, vol. 15, ed. Michael Wallace, 209–38. Greenwich, CT: JAI Press.

Beer Institute. 2011. "Economic Impact." http://www.beerservesamerica.org/economic/default.aspx (accessed October 12, 2012).

Berle, Adolf A., and Gardiner C. Means. 1932. *The Modern Corporation and Private Property.* New York: Macmillan.

Bills, David B. 1998. "A Community of Interests: Understanding the Relationships between Franchisees and Franchisors." In *Research in Stratification and Mobility*, vol. 16, ed. Kevin T. Leicht, 351–69. Greenwich, CT: JAI Press.

Blair, Roger, and Francine Lafontaine. 2005. *The Economics of Franchising.* New York: Cambridge University Press.

Caplow, Theodore, Louis Hicks, and Ben J. Wattenberg. 2001. *The First Measured Century: An Illustrated Guide to Trends in America, 1900–2000.* Washington, DC: AEI Press.

Dallago, Bruno. 1990. *The Irregular Economy: The "Underground Economy" and the "Black" Labour Market.* Hants, UK: Dartmouth Publishing.

Davies, Howard. 2010. *The Financial Crisis: Who Is to Blame?* Cambridge, UK: Polity Press.

Derber, Charles. 1998. *Corporation Nation: How Corporations Are Taking Over Our Lives and What We Can Do about It.* New York: St. Martin's Griffin.

Elzinga, Kenneth. 2011. "The U.S. Beer Industry: Concentration, Fragmentation and a Nexus with Wine." *Journal of Wine Economics* 6, no. 2: 217–30.

Everett, Wallace C. 2006. "Using State and Local Programs to Fuel Franchise Growth." *Franchising World* 38, no. 12: 63–64.

Fairlie, Robert W. 2002. "Drug Dealing and Legitimate Self-Employment." *Journal of Labor Economics* 20, no. 3: 538–76.

Feagin, Joe R., and Melvin P. Sikes. 1994. *Living with Racism*. Boston: Beacon Press.

Fligstein, Neil, and Adam Goldstein. 2011. "The Roots of the Great Recession." In *The Great Recession*, ed. David B. Grusky, Bruce Western, and Christopher Wimer, 21–55. New York: Sage.

Forbes. 2012a. "The World's Biggest Public Companies." *Forbes*, April. http://www.forbes.com/global2000/list (accessed November 26, 2012).

———. 2012b. "The Forbes 400: The Richest People in America." *Forbes*, September. http://www.forbes.com/forbes-400 (accessed November 26, 2012).

Fusfeld, Daniel. 1973. *The Basic Economics of the Urban Racial Crisis*. New York: Holt, Rinehart & Winston.

Greenfield, Harry I. 1993. *Invisible, Outlawed, and Untaxed: America's Underground Economy*. Westport, CT: Praeger.

Harrison, Bennett. 1994. *Lean and Mean: The Changing Landscape of Corporate Power in the Age of Flexibility*. New York: Guilford Press.

Hipple, Steven. 2004. "Self-Employment in the United States: An Update." *Monthly Labor Review*, July, 13–23.

———. 2010. "Self-Employment in the United States." *Monthly Labor Review*, September, 17–32.

Hout, Michael, Asaf Leanon, and Erin Cumberworth. 2011. "Job Loss and Unemployment." In *The Great Recession*, ed. David B. Grusky, Bruce Western, and Christopher Wimer, 59–81. New York: Sage.

Leonard, Madeleine. 1998. *Invisible Work, Invisible Workers: The Informal Economy in Europe and the US*. New York: St. Martin's.

Massey, Douglas S. 2007. *Categorically Unequal: The American Stratification System*. New York: Sage.

McCrary, Michael. 1998. "Same Song, Different Verse: Processes of Race-Sex Stratification and Self-Employment." In *Research in Social Stratification and Mobility*, vol. 16, ed. Kevin T. Leicht, 319–50. Greenwich, CT: JAI Press.

Miller, Arthur Selwyn. 1977. *The Modern Corporate State: Private Governments and the American Constitution*. Westport, CT: Greenwood Press.

Mills, C. Wright. 1951. *White Collar: The American Middle Class*. New York: Oxford University Press.

Mishel, Lawrence, Jared Bernstein, and Sylvia Allegretto. 2007. *The State of Working America, 2002–2003*. Ithaca, NY: Cornell University Press.

Muehlberger, Ulrike. 2007. *Dependent Self-Employment: Workers on the Border between Employment and Self-Employment*. New York: Palgrave Macmillan.

Naylor, R. T. 2002. *Wages of Crime: Black Markets, Illegal Finance, and the Underworld Economy*. Ithaca, NY: Cornell University Press.

Parker, Simon C. 2004. *The Economics of Self-Employment and Entrepreneurship*. New York: Cambridge University Press.

Pegula, Stephen M. 2004. "Occupational Fatalities: Self-Employed Workers and Wage and Salary Workers." *Monthly Labor Review*, March, 30–40.

Perrow, Charles. 2002. *Organizing America: Wealth, Power, and the Origins of Corporate Capitalism*. Princeton, NJ: Princeton University Press.

Phillips, Joseph D. 1958. *Little Business in the American Economy*. Urbana: University of Illinois Press.

Phillips, Kevin. 2008. *Bad Money: Reckless, Finance, Failed Politics and the Global Crisis of American Capitalism*. New York: Viking.

Rosenblum, Harvey. 2011. *Choosing the Road to Prosperity: Why We Must End Too Big to Fail Now*. 2011 Annual Report of the Federal Reserve Bank of Dallas.

Roy, William. 1997. *Socializing Capital: The Rise of the Large Industrial Corporation in America*. Princeton, NJ: Princeton University Press.

Schlosser, Eric. 2003. *Reefer Madness: Sex, Drugs, and Cheap Labor in the American Black Market*. Boston: Houghton Mifflin.

Shapiro, Thomas M. 2004. *The Hidden Cost of Being African American: How Wealth Perpetuates Inequality*. New York: Oxford University Press.

Smeeding, Timothy, Jeffrey P. Thompson, Asaf Levanon, and Esra Burak. 2011. "Poverty and Income Inequality in the Early Stages of the Great Recession." In *The Great Recession*, ed. David B. Grusky, Bruce Western, and Christopher Wimer, 82–126. New York: Sage.

Thornton, Patricia. 1999. "The Sociology of Entrepreneurship." In *Annual Review of Sociology*, vol. 25, ed. Karen S. Cook and John Hagan, 19–46. Palo Alto, CA: Annual Reviews.

Tremblay, Victor J., and Carol Horton Tremblay. 2005. *The U.S. Brewing Industry: Data and Economic Analysis*. Cambridge, MA: MIT Press.

U.S. Census Bureau. 2007a. *Finance and Insurance: Subject Series—Establishment and Firm Size: Summary Statistics by Concentration of Largest Firms for the United States: 2007 Economic Census*. Washington, DC: U.S. Government Printing Office.

———. 2007b. *Retail Trade: Subject Series—Establishment and Firm Size: Summary Statistics by Concentration of Largest Firms for the United States: 2007 Economic Census*. Washington, DC: U.S. Government Printing Office.

———. 2007c. *Manufacturing: Subject Series—Concentration Ratios: Share of Value of Shipments Accounted for by the 4, 8, 20 and 50 Largest Companies for Industries*. Washington, DC: U.S. Government Printing Office.

———. 2007d. *Manufacturing: Subject Series—Concentration Ratios: Share of Industry Statistics for Companies Ranked by Value Added: 2007*. Washington, DC: U.S. Government Printing Office.

———. 2010. "Table PINC-7, Class of Worker of Longest Job in 2009—People 15 Years Old and Over, by Total Money Earnings in 2009, Work Experience in 2009, Race, Hispanic Origin, and Sex." Current Population Survey: Annual Social and Economic Supplement. Washington, DC: U.S. Government Printing Office. http://www.census.gov/hhes/www/cpstables/032010/perinc/new07_001.htm (accessed October 10, 2012).

———. 2012a. "Table 744, Number of Tax Returns, Receipts, and Net Income by Type of Business: 1990 to 2008." *Statistical Abstract of the United States*. Washington, DC: U.S. Printing Office. http://www.census.gov/prod/2011pubs/12statab/business.pdf (accessed October 10, 2012).

———. 2012b. "Table 2b, Employment Size of Employer and Nonemployer Firms, 2007." *Statistics about Business Size (Including Small Business) from the U.S. Census Bureau*. Washington, DC: U.S. Government Printing Office. http://www.census.gov/econ/smallbus.html (accessed by January 20, 2013).

U.S. Department of Labor. 2002. "Self-Employed in 2000." *Editor's Desk*, January 28. www.bls.gov/opub/ted/2002/jan/wk4/art01.htm.

———. 2012a. "Occupational Employment." *Occupational Outlook Quarterly* 55, no. 4. www.bls.gov/opub/ooq/2011/winter/occupations_data18.htm (accessed January 21, 2013).

———. 2012b. "Projections Overview." In *Occupational Outlook Handbook, 2012–13 Edition*. Bureau of Labor Statistics. http://www.bls.gov/ooh/about/projections-overview.htm (accessed October 10, 2012).

U.S. Patent and Trademark Office. 2011. *Patent Trends Calendar Year 2011*. U.S. Patent and Trademark Office. http://www.uspto.gov/web/offices/ac/ido/oeip/taf/pat_tr11.htm (accessed November 26, 2012).

U.S. Small Business Association. 2010. Advocacy Small Business Statistics and Research. http://web.sba.gov/faqs/faqIndexAll.cfm?areaid=24 (accessed November 20, 2012).

Venkatesh, Sudhir Alladi. 2006. *Off the Books: The Underground Economy of the Urban Poor*. Cambridge, MA: Harvard University Press.

Wallace, James, and Jim Erickson. 1992. *Hard Drive: Bill Gates and the Making of the Microsoft Empire*. New York: Wiley.

Wal-Mart Stores, Inc. 2011. *Walmart 2011 Annual Report: Building the Next Generation.* http://www.walmartstores.com/sites/annualreport/2011/financials/Walmart_2011_Annual_Report.pdf (accessed November 26, 2012).

Williams, Colin. 2006. *The Hidden Enterprise Culture: Entrepreneurship in the Underground Economy.* Cheltenham, UK: Edward Elgar.

Williams, Colin, and Jan Windebank. 1998. *Informal Employment in the Advanced Economies: Implications for Work and Welfare.* New York: Routledge.

Wolff, Edward N., Lindsay A. Owens, and Esra Burak. 2011. "How Much Wealth Was Destroyed in the Great Recession?" In *The Great Recession*, ed. David B. Grusky, Bruce Western, and Christopher Wimer, 127–58. New York: Sage.

Wright, Erik Olin. 1997. *Class Counts: Comparative Studies in Class Analysis.* New York: Cambridge University Press.

Chapter Eight

An Unlevel Playing Field

Racism, Sexism, and Other Isms

The arc of the moral universe is long, but it bends toward justice.
—Martin Luther King Jr., Speech at Ebenezer Baptist Church in Atlanta, Georgia, March 30, 1967

According to the ideal of the American Dream, America is a land in which merit is the sole basis for vast and almost limitless opportunity. Discrimination, however, invalidates the American Dream. Discrimination not only interferes with, but is the antithesis of, merit. Discrimination allows some, who are not necessarily meritorious, to get ahead of others. In this way, discrimination creates a terrible irony—the very discrimination that invalidates the American Dream for many Americans creates conditions that appear to validate it for others and enables them to embrace it so fervently. By excluding entire segments of the American population from equal access to opportunity, discrimination reduces competition and increases the chances that members of some groups will get ahead on what they often presume to be exclusively their own merit.

DISCRIMINATION: INDIVIDUAL AND INSTITUTIONALIZED

Discrimination refers to exclusionary practices that create unequal access to valued social resources such as education, jobs, housing, income, wealth, and so on based on nonmerit characteristics (often ascribed) that would otherwise be irrelevant to the acquisition of those resources. Individuals may discriminate because they are openly bigoted toward others. Discrimination, however, can also occur unintentionally and without malice. Giving preference to people you know (social capital) or people who share your way of life (cultural capital), for instance, necessarily excludes others and is therefore discriminatory. Individuals may also discriminate because of perceived economic risk. An employer, for instance, may hesitate to hire a woman for a job for which on-the-job training is long and expensive based on a stereotypical assumption, however inaccurate, that she might later drop out of the labor force to raise a family.

Individuals can and do discriminate, but the most consequential discrimination occurs at the group, organizational, community, and institutional levels. This latter form, which is the consequence of cumulative individual acts of discrimination over time, sometimes called institutional discrimination, does not refer to isolated individual acts of discrimination but to actions, practices, and policies systematically embedded in the organization of society itself. Legalized slavery, Jim Crow laws, and voter suppression or disenfranchisement are examples of institutional discrimination.

Individual and institutional discrimination involves unequal treatment of individuals and groups on the basis of characteristics that have little, if any, relation to what could conventionally be considered individual merit. Further, discrimination can easily become reinforcing and self-perpetuating. Over time, individuals and groups affected by discrimination become as unequal as they have been treated. By depriving people of access to opportunities, for instance, discrimination often leads to lack of qualification for them. The involuntarily ascribed and negatively evaluated categorical status that emerges from discrimination not only takes precedence over any achieved status but reduces the probability of such achievement, thereby lowering all life chances. Put quite simply, discrimination makes it more difficult for the objects of discrimination to develop merit and reduces the likelihood that their merit will be recognized and rewarded.

RACIAL AND ETHNIC DISCRIMINATION IN AMERICA

The long history of deliberate discrimination against racial and ethnic groups in America belies the American ideology of individual freedom and equality of opportunity. From the near-genocide of Native Americans and the banishment of survivors to reservations, to the importation and enslavement of Africans, to the subsequent Jim Crow legislation that legalized racial segregation and unequal opportunity in the South, to exclusionary acts and discriminatory immigration quotas, to land displacement of Mexican Americans, to the internment of Japanese Americans during World War II, to current forms of residential, occupational, and educational discrimination against various minorities, the American experience has for many been more of an American *Nightmare* than an American *Dream*.

While most Americans acknowledge historical forms of discrimination, many insist that discrimination against racial and ethnic minorities is a thing of the past. Many assert that we have moved beyond this sordid past and that this is, in itself, a testimony to the American Dream. The election and reelection of America's first black president, Barack Obama, is often heralded as evidence that America has moved to a "postracial" era. Indeed, great strides to reduce discrimination have been made. Since World War II, the position of the federal and state governments has gradually changed from requiring, supporting, or tacitly accepting discriminatory practices to formally and actively opposing discrimination. These changes began in the late 1930s and culminated with the passage of the Civil Rights Acts of 1957, 1960, 1964, 1965, and 1968. For example, court rulings, legislation, and executive orders were designed to desegregate the military, end educational segregation and discrimination, protect voting rights, and require federal contractors to comply with nondiscrimination policies. The banning of overt discrimination and segregation in privately owned businesses came later in the form of legislation against employment and housing discrimination. Finally, at the local level, numerous antidiscrimination ordinances and laws were passed. Thus, by the late 1960s, the clear position of American law was against discrimination. This represents a near total reversal of the situation twenty-five to thirty years earlier, when the position of American law had been somewhere between tolerating and requiring such discrimination.

Unfortunately, it is also abundantly clear that these legal changes have not eliminated discrimination. Discrimination in America is down but not out. Since most forms of discrimination are now illegal and overt bigotry is no longer considered socially acceptable, today's discrimination is either more tacit or more elaborately cloaked and thus more difficult to detect. Instead, there is a "new racism" that is disguised through various codes and denials (Bonilla-Silva 2003). To put it another way, discrimination has been driven underground. Scratching just below the surface, however, reveals a continued pattern of political, occupational, educational, housing, and consumer discrimination.

Not only is there a continued pattern of discrimination, but the effects of past discrimination continue to have a long reach into the present. This is sometimes referred to as past-in-present discrimination (Feagin and Feagin 2007). For instance, if a person of color went to inferior, segregated schools in the South during the 1960s and was subjected to subsequent employment discrimination, that now middle-aged person is at current competitive disadvantage, even if the schools he or she went to are now equal and integrated and even if he or she is no longer being actively discriminated against. Prior discrimination not only likely hampered prospects for that person's own career advancement; it likely resulted in unequal starting points for his or her children.

ECONOMIC AND OCCUPATIONAL DISCRIMINATION

There are a variety of ways that social scientists measure ongoing occupational discrimination. One way is through self-report surveys indicating the percentage of workers who report having been discriminated against in employment. Another way is by keeping track of how many workers file official discrimination complaints. Yet another way is through the use of field audit studies in which researchers send out applicants of different race or sex with similar qualifications to answer job applications and see who gets callbacks or interviews. In addition, there is a variety of ways to measure outcomes that would imply the likely cumulative effects of discrimination such as systematic lower pay or how segregated jobs are by various social categories, controlling for strictly merit factors. Using these various methods, overwhelming evidence demonstrates that while there has been progress since the civil rights era, income and employment discrimination based on race in America lingers and is still pervasive (Stainback and Tomaskovic-Devey 2012; Massey 2007; Shapiro 2004; Feagin and Feagin 2007; Bonilla-Silva 2003; Farley 2005).

Lack of sustained progress is most clearly reflected in trends in income inequality. In 1970 the median income for blacks, for instance, was 74 percent that of whites, and in 2012 the median income for blacks had increased to only 78 percent of whites (U.S. Census Bureau 2012b). A similar lack of progress is evident with Hispanics. In 1995, the median income for Hispanics was 65 percent that of whites, and in 2012 the median income for Hispanics had increased to only 72 percent of whites (U.S. Census Bureau 2012b). Although all races have experienced some rising income since the civil rights era, very little progress has been made in closing the racial income gaps. The gaps in wealth accumulation are even more unequal and in many ways even more consequential. In 2010, blacks had only 5 percent of the net worth of whites, and Hispanics had only 1.3 percent of the net worth of whites (Mishel, Bivens, Gould, and Shierholz 2012, 385). Moreover, blacks and Hispanics on average have rates of unemployment and poverty that are about double that of whites. Some of these differences reflect the current effects of past discrimination, including unequal access to educational opportunity due to unequal access to asset-building opportunities, which in turn produced housing discrimination and unequal access to housing in areas with quality schools (Shapiro 2004). But current discrimination also continues to contribute to these huge economic deficits.

Discrimination has been found in recruitment, hiring, promotion, layoff, and discharge practices. It may take the form of selective placement of job advertisements, the use of word of mouth and informal recruitment networks, or recruitment limited to local areas. Exclusive union referral systems exclude nonunion workers and permit nepotism. Discrimination has also been found in screening practices, where it may take the form of discriminatory hiring standards and procedures. Credential requirements, including educational and physical requirements, can be discriminatory when, for instance, such requirements are irrelevant to the demands of a particular job. Nonvalidated credentials—those that cannot be demonstrated to measure what they purport to measure or cannot be demonstrated to be necessary for satisfactory job performance—continue to be used to the disadvantage of minorities and women.

Employment interviews may be used to screen out candidates who have unwanted characteristics unrelated to merit. Presumptions of inferiority and use of negative stereotypes that lead to constant scrutiny and overly close supervision are discriminatory. Promotion practices that give high consideration to subjective evaluations and supervisors' recommendations can be discriminatory. Various forms of tracking can be discriminatory. Segregative tracking into "job ghettos"—dead-end jobs in departments or units with short mobility ladders, as well as organizational rules that do not permit movement out of such units—can be discriminatory. Assignments to "fast-track" jobs are often based on nonmerit criteria. Discriminatory informal workplace relations can create a "hostile workplace environment." Selective mentoring, sponsorship, and exclusion from "old boy" networks can be discriminatory.

Beyond these forms of discrimination, basic characteristics of the American industrial structure produce differentiated occupational opportunities that are allocated in discriminatory ways. As discussed in chapter 6, wages and benefits received for doing essentially the same job vary by the type of organization, industry, and region in which the job is performed. Large, capital-intensive, high-profit firms with large market shares in the "core" economic sector pay employees the most. Small, labor-intensive, low-profit businesses with small market shares in the "periphery" sector pay employees the least. Being a janitor at the NBC office building in New York, for instance, pays better and has better benefits than doing essentially the same job in an elementary school in Thomasville, North Carolina.

Research shows that minorities and women are underrepresented in core employment, and when they do obtain employment in the core, they are paid less than white males (Massey 2007). Research also reveals that a set of individual characteristics that could be taken as measures of merit actually explain little of the core-periphery differences in wages and little of the race and gender differences in wages found *within* the industrial sector. Finally, research suggests that individual characteristics that could be taken as measures of merit are more highly rewarded in the core than in the periphery. In short, controlling for what people do for a living, rewards for merit are contingent upon characteristics of the employing organization, race, and gender.

DISCRIMINATION IN THE POLITICAL AND LEGAL SYSTEMS

Until the mid-1950s, the American political and legal systems enforced and even required discrimination against minorities. Today, government at all levels, at least formally, has taken an antidiscrimination position; yet problem areas remain. Past discrimination by government policy has led to minority disadvantage, and current government inaction and unwillingness to undo the effects of past discrimination perpetuate minority disadvantage.

Several sources of evidence verify this pattern. The higher a person's socioeconomic status, for instance, the greater the number and availability of government services and benefits (Kerbo 2012). Thus, many patterns of government spending differentially harm minorities simply because large proportions remain poor. Public preoccupation with the welfare system and its purported benefits to the minority poor diverts attention from the "wealthfare" system, a purposefully hidden but larger and more lucrative system that benefits the privileged. Essentially, wealthfare is revenue forgone through a variety of tax breaks and subsidies for which only the privileged qualify (Phillips 2003; Domhoff 2009; Kerbo 2012).

Despite the election of Barack Obama as the first black president in 2008 and his reelection in 2012, discrimination continues in voting and other forms of political participation, including office holding. For instance, even though Barack Obama was reelected in 2012, there were allegations of systematic efforts to suppress minority voting in some key swing states. This took the form of proposals to require state-approved forms of voter identification to supposedly reduce the potential for voter fraud even in the absence of evidence that such fraud was actually taking place. These proposals were potentially discriminatory since such requirements placed a much more severe burden on poor and minority populations to secure such identification. In addition, several states reduced the days and hours available for citizens to vote, especially in areas with heavy concentrations of minority voters.

Minorities are underrepresented in major elected and appointed offices at the state and federal levels. Historically, voting and political participation have been directly correlated with socioeconomic status. Minority overrepresentation among the less privileged partially explains minorities' lower political participation. Thus, the political power of minorities is limited by their numbers, geographical concentrations, residential segregation, and overrepresentation among the less privileged, as well as by continuing individual and institutional discrimination.

Abundant research documents a continuing pattern of racial discrimination throughout the American legal system. From the definition of crime itself, to decisions concerning the severity of penalties for behavior defined as criminal, to the various stages of the criminal-justice process, to the lack of protection of the rights of law-abiding minority citizens, there is evidence of discrimination against racial minorities. Crime in America is highly racialized. The focus is on violent street crime. Hate crime and corporate crime, including employee and white-collar crime, get much less attention.

Discrimination is well documented at each step in the criminal-justice process, from police scrutiny and detection of crime to the severity of sentencing (Reiman and Leighton 2013). If one's criminal activity is not detected, then one is not arrested. Most would agree that the detection of crime is a good thing. But police stereotypes and negative expectations about blacks lead to elevated police scrutiny and racial profiling, which in turn lead to racial discrimination in crime detection. Varying degrees of racial discrimination have been documented in all of the following: police decisions to follow up on observations of possible violations, to apprehend, and to arrest suspects; decisions about whether to prosecute, to refer a case to the court system, and, if so, to what type of court; the setting and administration of bail for the accused; decisions made by judges, judicial panels, or juries about whether an accused is guilty or innocent (conviction decisions); and decisions regarding the nature and severity of penalties for crimes (sentencing decisions). Minorities receive longer and more severe sentences (controlling for criminal record and severity of crime).

At any given step of the criminal-justice process, the bias may be large, small, or even nonexistent, but enough bias exists in enough places at each step that, even though the effect at any one step may be small, the cumulative effect over the entire course of the criminal-justice process can be substantial. At the point of arrest, the population of the accused is quite racially mixed, but the proportion of racial minorities rises substantially as one moves through the criminal-justice process to the endpoint of the imprisoned population. The consequences of the criminal label can be severe. Former convicts (and sometimes those merely arrested but not convicted) often face reduced employment and credit opportunities. Denial of legitimate opportunities can increase chances of recidivism and entrapment in a vicious circle (Western 2006). Douglas S. Massey (2007) and several others have described what has come to be called the prison-industrial complex and its large and varying discriminatory impacts.

Blacks and other minorities have long complained of various forms of inadequate police protection—from inadequate patrol of their neighborhoods to inadequate response to calls for assistance. Minorities have also complained, sometimes bitterly, of police brutality, of the lack of respect shown them by police, and of the inability of police to distinguish law-abiding minorities from minority criminals. Again, while complaints have at times been exaggerated for political purposes, it is clear that minorities experience more police violence and receive less respect from police than apologists for the police can explain away. Finally, there is abundant evidence that the historical failure of the American court system to protect the legal rights of minorities continues. For example, the courts have failed to protect minorities against police brutality and other abuses by the state. Further, because civil courts make no presumption of the right to an attorney, racial minorities have less ability to make use of civil courts to protect or pursue their economic interests. We conclude that as custodians of the American Dream, the political and legal systems have constructed and are administering an unfair game.

DISCRIMINATION IN EDUCATIONAL SYSTEMS

Chapter 5 is devoted to a discussion of the relationship between education and the American Dream. Briefly, the American education system is viewed as the basic mechanism through which the American Dream can be achieved. Thus, the education system is seen as a means to produce, measure, and certify merit. Discrimination in educational systems, however, erodes the very foundation of the American Dream because it invalidates this basic assumption of meritocracy.

Throughout American history, access to education has varied by class, race, and gender. In colonial times, education was reserved for privileged white males. Since then, the history of American education has been one of increasing access to education for previously excluded groups. While access has been expanded, discrimination continues.

One form of educational discrimination is continuing segregation of schools by race and socioeconomic status. Although *Brown vs. Topeka Kansas Board of Education* (1954) signaled the end of blatant de jure segregation, de facto segregation continues, and America's public schools remain highly segregated. Public schools in America became less segregated in the 1960s and 1970s, but since the 1980s, in a process that has been referred to as resegregation, these trends are being reversed. By the 2003–2004 school year, for instance, 73 percent of black students attended schools with a student body made up primarily of minority students (Orfield and Lee 2006). Much of the resegregation that exists today is between school districts and is due to the abandonment of integration measures such as school busing. In addition, the rise of charter schools, magnet schools, and other alternate school choice settings have accelerated the trend toward resegregation as white families seek alternatives to sending their children to school districts with high minority enrollments. Finally, official segregation figures often underestimate the actual amount of segregation because calculations are typically based only on public school data. Private schools, except for some inclusive Catholic schools in large cities in the Northeast, are overwhelmingly white.

Thomas Shapiro (2004), Douglas Massey (2007), and others have explained that unequal access to educational opportunity is partially due to the fact that at every class level, however social class is measured, blacks and Hispanics have only a small fraction of the wealth of whites. The repercussions of these staggering levels of wealth inequality are clear: economically disadvantaged blacks and Hispanics cannot provide what Shapiro has called "transformative assets" to their offspring for crucial financial support for higher education, down payments for a first house in a good neighborhood, or other opportunities at crucial junctures in their children's lives. This lack of financial assistance in turn requires minorities to come up with their own resources. This often limits them to the purchase of houses in neighborhoods with low-quality schools. In turn, these lower-quality schools enroll larger proportions of students from minority and other lower-income groups, reducing the possibility of equality of educational opportunity.

Some of the racial differences in educational opportunity are partially explained by the fact that school revenues come from local property taxes, which tend to produce less revenue in the racially segregated areas in which the schools that minorities attend are located. Schools with high minority enrollments are more likely to have "poor reputations" (Shapiro 2004); to be older or run down; to have inadequate facilities, programs, and technology; to be overcrowded; to have larger classes; to have less experienced and qualified teachers; to have student bodies that are disproportionately lower in socioeconomic status; and to have a host of other characteristics that hinder academic achievement (Kozol 1991, 2006).

Racial segregation is not the only form of discrimination in education. Minorities may be excluded or reduced to stereotypes in curricula, texts, and other teaching materials. Blacks, Hispanics, and other minorities need to see real, complete, and unbiased images of themselves. Teachers and administrators may discriminate against minority students in a variety of indirect ways. For example, teacher expectations can be discriminatory. Low teacher expectations of minorities create self-fulfilling prophecies and lower achievement.

Tracking or ability grouping is almost universal in secondary schools. When based on valid measures of ability and performance, tracking seems to have a positive effect on achievement. However, studies have revealed that placement into tracks is correlated with factors other than ability, aptitude, performance, and other nonmerit factors such as race and socioeconomic status. Placement in a lower track could result from initial cultural disadvantage upon entering schools for children from disadvantaged backgrounds independent of their inherent capacities. On the other hand, wealthy and highly educated parents may be especially aggressive in securing higher track placements for their children independent of ability level or aptitude. Once placed in higher or lower tracks, students experience cumulative advantages or disadvantages that result in self-fulfilling prophecies of higher or lower aspirations and achievement. Another problem has been an inability to recruit and keep minority teachers. Racial minorities are underrepresented in the teaching profession and in positions of authority within education. As we move from elementary school to secondary school to higher education, the underrepresentation increases. Thus, blacks and other minority students have few role models and must learn in an authority structure and culture that is largely white.

According to the American Dream, there is a strong correlation between educational achievement and occupational success; doing well in school is seen as the ticket to a good job. But educational discrimination against minorities reduces their chances for academic achievement, and occupational discrimination reduces their chances for occupational success. Even if minorities manage to transcend educational discrimination and become academically successful, research consistently shows that minorities receive much lower income and occupational returns on equivalent amounts of educational attainment than whites.

SEGREGATION IN HOUSING AND EVIDENCE OF CONTINUING DISCRIMINATION

The federal government, through weak enforcement of fair housing laws, as well as Federal Housing Administration (FHA) and Department of Housing and Urban Development (HUD) practices, continues to be implicated in housing discrimination. Additionally, local governments continue to use exclusionary, or "snob," zoning and control of the location of publicly subsidized housing to discriminate and perpetuate racial segregation of housing.

The impacts of housing discrimination are severe. Minorities, especially African and Mexican Americans, pay more and get less for their housing dollar and are underrepresented as home owners at every income level. They are thus disproportionately denied a major means of wealth accumulation, and this jeopardizes their ability to transmit wealth to their children. Minorities end up living in neighborhoods with fewer resources, services, and amenities, poorer schools, and higher rates of poverty than whites of similar socioeconomic status. Stores in poor and minority areas tend to have poorer selection, lower quality, and higher prices (Walker, Keane, and Burke 2010). Further, residential segregation contributes to school segregation, which as we have seen tends to perpetuate existing inequalities across generations. Residential segregation of groups with high proportions of poverty leads to concentrated poverty and the additional problems it creates (Massey 2007; Massey and Denton 1989; Wilson 1987). Residential segregation often limits its victims to areas of declining job opportunities. Finally, the racial residential segregation produced by housing discrimination isolates and marginalizes people, denying them full and equal participation in American society. In short, this egregious form of discrimination most certainly violates the American Dream.

A major component of the American Dream is home ownership. Equity in a home is the major form of asset accumulation for the large majority of Americans (Shapiro 2004). A home is a nest egg that can be sold in one's later years to help fund retirement or be bequeathed to the next generation. One's home and the neighborhood in which it is located represent materially one's achievements and social class. Finally, homes have a psychological value. One's home is a safe haven, a place of refuge from the realities of the harshly competitive and increasingly graceless world in which we live.

Home ownership and socioeconomic status are positively related; almost all of the privileged are home owners, while much less than half of the poor own their own homes. This is reflected in highly unequal rates of home ownership by race. In 2011, the rate of home ownership for whites was 73.8 percent, but the corresponding figures for blacks and Hispanics were 44.9 and 46.9 percent, respectively (Mishel, Bivens, Gould, and Shierholz 2012, 396). Yet the issue is not simply owning or not owning a home. Inequalities in home ownership are much greater if one considers the value of homes. For example, both an upper-middle-class and a working-class family may own homes. However, the home of the former may be worth from several hundred thousand dollars to more than a million dollars, while the home of the latter may be worth one hundred thousand dollars or less. What is more, many of the privileged own second, "vacation" homes that sit empty most of the year or are rented to pay a mortgage and build equity for the owner. Many of the poor, on the other hand, settle for housing that is not only inadequate but is worth less than the second homes of many of the privileged. The differences in both rates of home ownership and the value of homes owned further contribute to the staggering wealth differences by race.

There continues to be considerable racial and ethnic segregation of housing. Residential segregation by race is one of the legacies of a long history of racial discrimination with effects that reach into the present. That is, even if further housing discrimination ceased altogether, most people would continue to live in already highly segregated neighborhoods and communities. The simplest and most commonly reported measure of residential segregation is the index of dissimilarity. Ranging from 0 (no segregation) to 1 (complete segregation), it indicates the proportion of one group that would have to move to a different census tract to reproduce the residential pattern of the other group. Although the current percentages may differ slightly, the following are illustrative: In 1980, there were 220 metropolitan areas (of the 330 total) with 3 percent, or twenty thousand, or more blacks. The average index of black-white residential segregation for these 220 metropolitan areas declined from 0.73 in 1980, to 0.66 in 1990, to 0.64 in 2000 (Iceland, Weinberg, and Steinmetz 2002, 60). Although this represents a clear reduction, 64 percent of blacks (or whites) would have to move to a different census tract to reproduce the residential pattern of the other group. This is considered to be substantial segregation.

Discrimination in the sale and rental of housing became illegal with the Civil Rights Act of 1968 and subsequent fair housing laws. But this has not stopped such discrimination. Discrimination persists in the post–civil rights era, but it is expressed in more subtle and clandestine ways that are not readily observable and are unlikely to trigger legal action or invite public disapproval. Government officials and social scientists nevertheless have developed powerful and convincing techniques to measure discrimination unobtrusively. Using field audit studies, units being marketed for sale or rent are randomly selected, and separate teams of white and nonwhite auditors posing as home seekers are sent to inquire about the availability of the advertised unit, the number of other units available, and the terms under which units might be obtained. Auditors are assigned similar personal, social, and economic characteristics by the researcher and carefully trained to present themselves in a neutral fashion and to ask standard questions about the housing being marketed. Afterward, each auditor fills out a form describing the nature and outcome of the encounter without knowing what happened to the other auditor. These forms are then collated across white and nonwhite auditors and tabulated to see whether there were discernible differences in treatment by race. HUD has conducted three major nationwide housing audits (in 1979, 1989, and 2000). These studies and others continue to find significant discrimination against minorities in the rental and sale of housing (Massey 2007, 76–100).

Minorities are also subjected to discrimination in securing loans and property insurance. Blacks and Hispanics, for instance, are more likely to be turned down for mortgage loans and more likely to pay higher rates when they are approved than can be accounted for by black-white differences in income and other relevant characteristics (Bocian, Li, and Ernst 2010). In 2011, the U.S. Justice Department announced that Bank of America had agreed to pay $335 million in the largest residential fair-lending settlement in history to resolve allegations that its Countrywide unit engaged in a widespread pattern of discrimination against qualified African American and Hispanic borrowers. Countrywide is alleged to have engaged in these practices prior to the height of the housing boom from 2004 to 2008 and prior to Bank of America's acquisition of Countrywide in 2008. Countrywide is alleged to have charged African American and Hispanic applicants higher loan fees and to steer applicants who qualified for regular mortgages into riskier and more expensive subprime loans (Savage 2011).

Finally, there has been much recent research on a related phenomenon of voice discrimination (Feagin and Sikes 1994). Segregation itself makes linguistic profiling possible. One consequence of historical segregation in the United States is that a large proportion of African Americans speak a distinctive version of English, with different rules for pronunciation, diction, grammar, and syntax from that ordinarily spoken by whites. Research has shown that white Americans are capable of making accurate racial attributions on the basis of very short speech fragments (Feagin and Sikes 1994; Massey 2007). Not only are whites quick to identify the race of someone speaking black English, but they are able to identify the race of a *code-switching* black—one who speaks mainstream English but with a "black" pronunciation of certain words (Doss and Gross 1994).

A WORD ON THE INTERCONNECTEDNESS OF INSTITUTIONAL DISCRIMINATION

Despite angry protests to the contrary, institutionalized political, legal, educational, and economic (job, housing, and consumer) discrimination are facts of life in America, providing advantages for some and excluding others for reasons that have nothing to do with merit.

All forms of institutional discrimination have important negative effects, and each reinforces disadvantages in other areas because all forms tend to have important negative side effects. For example, discrimination in the political system reduces the power and influence of its victims, which in turn reduces access to all forms of economic opportunity. Educational discrimination is so damaging because it reduces chances of getting a good job and all the things that depend on the income from a good job, like wealth accumulation, housing, and quality education for one's children. In itself, job discrimination can be psychologically damaging, but it also leads to reduced earnings, which limits housing opportunity and educational opportunity for one's children. Housing discrimination, in turn, may reduce access to areas in which good jobs, good schools, and good shopping are located. Discrimination by the police and criminal-justice system increases chances for criminal victimization, as well as for arrest and conviction, lowering subsequent employment opportunity.

SEX DISCRIMINATION

Women experience all the forms of employment discrimination discussed above for racial and ethnic minorities, as well as several that are unique to women. But unlike racial and ethnic minorities, women as a whole are not as systematically disadvantaged by social class background. As a result, since the civil rights era of the 1960s and the resurgence of the women's movement in the 1970s, women have more quickly closed gaps between themselves and men than nonwhites have closed gaps with whites. Once artificial barriers to achievement were lifted, women from privileged social backgrounds were poised to take immediate advantage, especially in educational attainment. For instance, once Ivy League universities opened admissions to women beginning in the 1970s, women from privileged backgrounds with high-quality preparatory education and abundant parental resources could immediately take advantage of these new admission policies. Following the civil rights struggles of the 1960s, by contrast, racial and ethnic minorities generally did not have the social, economic, or cultural capital available to take as much advantage of expanding opportunities.

The closing of the gender gap is most apparent in educational attainment, where women as a group have caught up to, and largely surpassed, men. As recently as the 1970s, men substantially exceeded women in almost all areas of educational attainment. By 2009, however, women earned 58 percent of all bachelor's degrees, 60 percent of all master's degrees, and 52 percent of all doctoral degrees (U.S. Department of Education 2012). Women have also achieved parity or near parity in professional degrees in law (46 percent), medicine (49 percent), osteopathic medicine (51 percent), dentistry (46 percent), and podiatry (42 percent), and they have far exceeded men in earning degrees in optometry (65 percent), pharmacy (64 percent), and veterinary medicine (78 percent). Among major professional degree areas, women lag behind men in chiropractic (37 percent) and theology (33 percent), but those remaining gaps are also steadily closing (U.S. Department of Education 2010). Likewise, women are rapidly closing gaps in degrees in the male-dominated field of engineering, increasing representation from 0.07 percent in 1970 to 18.4 percent by 2011 (Yoder 2011).

Despite the women's movement, rapidly increased educational achievement and labor-force participation, and continuing social, economic, and cultural change, the power structure of the United States remains heavily male dominated. In both the public and private sectors, nearly all of the positions at the top, such as those held by corporate officers, members of boards of directors, top professionals, and high elected officials, are held by males. Men continue to dominate socially, politically, and economically. In short, gender, a factor with no demonstrable independent effect on individual merit, conditions access to opportunity, and women have been denied full participation in the American Dream. Indeed, women's continued subordinate status is visible in practically every aspect of American life.

THE PINK-COLLAR GHETTO

Historically and cross-culturally, the degree of male dominance in society is directly related to the kind and extent of female participation in economic production. That is, the more women participate in economic production, and the more equally they participate in economic production, the less the degree of male dominance. Since the 1970s, female labor-force participation has steadily increased. In 1970, women made up 38 percent of the U.S. labor force; by 2010, women made up 47 percent of the total labor force, about parity with men (U.S. Department of Labor 2011). Although the level of female participation in the labor force is now almost equivalent to that of men, women are not equally spread out within the labor force. In particular, women are highly concentrated in the mostly low-wage service sector of the economy. While there has been a steady decline in occupational segregation, there is still a substantial amount of sex-based occupational segregation in the labor force (Stainback and Tomaskovic-Devey 2012). For instance, in 2010, women comprised 96 percent of secretaries and administrative assist- ants, 97 percent of preschool and kindergarten teachers, 91 percent of regis- tered nurses, 95 percent of dental hygienists, 95 percent of child-care work- ers, 93 percent of receptionists and information clerks, and 91 percent of booking, accounting, and auditing clerks, just to name a few (U.S. Depart- ment of Labor 2011). Although there has been some sex desegregation in the labor force, the movement of men and women into and out of job categories has been uneven. Women, for instance, have been rapidly moving into tradi- tionally male-dominated professions, especially as lawyers, doctors, profes- sors, veterinarians, and pharmacists. Men, however, have not been moving as quickly into traditionally female-dominated professions, such as social work, nursing, and elementary school teaching. Likewise, there is very little move- ment of women into traditionally male-dominated blue-collar trades such as construction, and there has not been much movement of men into the lower- white-collar service jobs such as secretary. Collectively, the jobs in which women remain highly concentrated have come to be called the pink-collar ghetto.

Some jobs in which women are concentrated, such as nursing and teach- ing, pay moderately well and carry moderate prestige. Nevertheless, they are often lower in pay and prestige than "men's jobs" that require equivalent levels of skill and training. These jobs also tend to be "order-taker" rather than "order-giver" positions and are often located in direct relation to an occupationally defined chain of command: nurses take orders from doctors, secretaries take orders from bosses, and so on. Often these are "dead-end" jobs because promotion opportunities are limited or nonexistent; that is, they have short mobility ladders with few rungs available for advancement. A nurse, for instance, may aspire to be head nurse, but there are few rungs on the advancement ladder beyond that. Even if one is an especially skilled and competent nurse, the head nurse on the floor may also be competent, forty years old, and going nowhere.

Many pink-collar jobs are disproportionately located in the low-wage service sector of the economy. The jobs themselves are insecure, and those who hold them face higher-than-average risks of irregular employment, involuntary part-time work, and layoffs or firing. These jobs typically carry limited fringe benefits, and some require shift work. Pink-collar jobs and the industries in which they are located are typically not unionized; therefore, workers do not benefit from protections won by the collective power of unions. Change has occurred in a few of the female-dominated professions, such as social work, teaching, and nursing, which have formed more powerful professional associations. But most pink-collar jobs are in the low-wage service sector of the economy, which is grossly unrepresented by either unions or professional associations. Finally, pink-collar jobs are often extensions of traditional domestic female sex roles: nurses and nursing aides taking care of the sick and the elderly, teachers and day-care workers taking care of children, and so on. These nurturing tasks are critical to any civilized society, but as paid labor they are grossly underappreciated, undervalued, and underrewarded.

THE GENDER INCOME AND WEALTH GAPS

In 2010, the median earnings of full-time, year-round female workers were 81 percent of the median hourly wage of their male counterparts, whereas in 1979 they were only 62 percent (U.S. Department of Labor 2011). However, the *rate* at which the male-female wage gap has declined has slowed in recent decades, perhaps indicating that while the most blatant forms of wage discrimination have been largely eliminated, remaining more subtle forms may be more difficult to overcome. In addition, much of the recent wage-gap reduction is due to the falling wages of men rather than increasing wages of women. Also, most of the gains relative to male incomes have been experienced by upper-class women, whereas incomes for lower-class women have remained stagnant (Massey 2007, 240; Mishel, Bivens, Gould, and Shierholz 2012, 236).

Differences in the occupational distributions of men and women—occupational segregation of women into "women's jobs," which are lower paying and low-wage industries—explains the largest portion of the aggregate male-female wage gap (Blau and Kahn 2006; Blau 2012). Other factors include interrupted careers due to marriage and childbearing, lower rates of unionization for women, differences in hours worked, and interactions of race and gender. However, even when these factors are taken into account, women earn less than men in almost every field. Even among recent college graduates working in the same field, men typically earn more than women (Corbett and Hill 2012).

While pay gaps have narrowed and discrimination has been reduced, efforts to eliminate employment discrimination against women have not been entirely successful. The federal Equal Pay Act of 1963, which mandates equal pay for equal work, applies to a relatively small proportion of female workers: those who perform the same job as male workers for the same employer. Although these women's wages have increased as a result of the Equal Pay Act, as we noted above, many women remain segregated in a small set of occupations in which few or no men work. The 1964 Civil Rights Act and its enforcement arm, the Equal Employment Opportunity Commission, address cases of sex discrimination. But neither this nor subsequent federal legislation has removed all employment discrimination against women.

Since men and women tend to do different kinds of work, the call for "equal pay for equal work" did not fully address pay equity issues for women. During the 1980s, pay equity, or comparable worth, was proposed as a means to address the tendency for the paid work that women perform in the labor force to be undervalued. Comparable worth calls for equal pay for different types of work that are judged to be comparable in value by measuring such factors as employee knowledge, skills, effort, responsibility, and working conditions. In terms of the actual skills needed to do the job, for instance, the female office secretary might score higher than the male truck driver working in the same firm who earns more. Except for some local initiatives mostly in government employment, comparable-worth programs have not been widely implemented.

Although such proposals make sense from an equity and merit standpoint, one of the problems with implementing them is that people do not ordinarily get paid on the basis of merit in the first place. According to market principles, people get paid on the basis of whatever the market will bear, which may not be directly affected by the demands of the job, the qualifications of employees, or the contribution of employees to their employing organization or to society as a whole.

In addition to having less income than men, women also typically have less wealth. Men and women have an equal chance of being born into wealth or poverty, and married couples at least nominally share assets. Single women, however, have only 36 percent of the median wealth of single men, and never-married women have only 6 percent of the median wealth of never-married men (Chang 2010). Although married couples nominally share assets, research shows that men tend to have greater control of those assets. Furthermore, divorced women have 31 percent less median wealth than divorced men (Chang 2010). Finally, at the very top of wealth echelons, women are especially underrepresented. Among the 2011 Forbes list of the wealthiest Americans, only 10 percent were women, and 90 percent of them inherited their wealth (United for a Fair Economy 2012).

THE GLASS CEILING

The phrase *glass ceiling*, another form of employment discrimination, refers to discriminatory policies that limit the upward mobility of qualified women and minorities, keeping them out of top management positions. As previously noted, many of the jobs in which women are concentrated have short mobility ladders. Secretaries rarely become bosses. Even though many secretaries *could* do the work of their bosses—and, indeed, they often do—they do not get the credit, the salary, or the opportunity to move up, regardless of their level of competence. The glass ceiling operates so that although all applicants may be welcomed by a firm at entry levels, when it comes to powerful managerial and executive positions, there are limits, generally unstated, on the number of women and nonwhites welcomed or even tolerated. Women may be doing better at getting top management positions than minorities, but they still lag well behind men.

Part of this overall differential is due to lag effects of women's more recent entry into the professions in particular and into the labor force in general. It often takes twenty or thirty years in a company or a profession to ascend to the highest levels of management. For example, though women now are graduating from law schools at rates comparable to men, for instance, few women occupy judgeships or senior partnerships in major law firms, in part because few women graduated from law schools twenty or thirty years ago, and those who did were often subjected to much more severe discrimination than occurs now, derailing their prospects for advancement. The same pattern is reflected in other professions in which women have more recently approached parity with males at the entry level, including medicine and the professoriate. On top of these lag effects, however, discrimination continues. Even among younger cohorts, research shows that women do not ascend as often or as quickly as men.

OLD BOY NETWORKS

Regardless of where women are located in the labor force (i.e., be they doctors or secretaries), women as a group face unique nonmerit impediments that make it more difficult to compete evenly with men. One of these impediments is lack of sponsorship—one form of social capital. Since the most powerful and influential positions are usually held by men, women are at a critical disadvantage. Mentor–protégé relationships are crucial for advancement, especially in the professions. After all, it is the senior partners in the law firm, the full professors in the department, and the top-level executives in the corporation who have the most experience and the most knowledge to impart to aspiring protégés. Mentors take their protégés under their wings, show them the ropes, and when the time comes, go to bat for them.

Women are less likely to receive these benefits: they receive far less informal support, inclusion in networks, mentoring, and sponsorship than men (McDonald, Lin, and Ao 2009). Men seem to be less willing to mentor and sponsor women than other men, partially because climates of sexual tension or appearances of sexual harassment may make cross-gender mentorship and sponsorship seem dangerous or uncomfortable for both men and women. In the business world, for example, women have been denied equal access to male-dominated "inner sanctums": many deals are cut on the golf course, on the racquetball court, over drinks at the men's club, "at the game," or at sites not fully open to women.

FAMILY VERSUS CAREER

Women experience a greater degree of perceived role conflict between family and career than men do. Role conflict occurs when the expectations and requirements associated with one position that an individual occupies interfere or conflict with those of another position. Although males can act as homemakers and caretakers for children, women have customarily performed these roles. Men are far less likely to feel that they must make an either-or choice (homemaker or caretaker versus paid employment) or to attempt to "burn the candle at both ends." It has been said that we will know that the women's liberation movement has fully arrived when men routinely ask themselves if they can combine family and career.

Research further shows that even though fertility has declined *and* having children no longer keeps most women out of the labor force *and* it is illegal to discriminate on the basis of marital or family status, some employers still assume that women are temporary workers in the labor force whose careers will be derailed by childbirth. As a result, such employers may be reluctant to hire women in the first place and, if they hire them, will invest less in their training and career development. This precludes eligibility for top-level positions and forces women into a career trajectory with lower chances for advancement.

Related to the issue of child care is the issue of reproductive freedom. A rapid decline in fertility has coincided with the increased participation of women in the labor force. As women have fewer children, they are freer to participate in the labor force. And as women participate in the labor force, they choose to have fewer children. By increasing control over their reproductive lives, women are more able to compete as equals in the public domains from which they were previously excluded. In concrete terms, reproductive freedom means freedom to pursue educational and occupational goals, unconstrained by unplanned or unwanted pregnancies. In more abstract terms, it means freedom to construct and pursue a dream of one's own making.

Another type of role conflict for women has sometimes been referred to as the "fear of success syndrome." This is actually a misnomer because women do not fear success. Instead, some women are understandably leery of being stigmatized for exhibiting behaviors associated with a formula for success defined in male terms. The formula for success for the successful business*man*, for instance, includes being assertive and aggressive. Business talk often mimics athletic or military jargon: "beating the enemy at his own game," "hitting a home run," "coming on board," and the like. Men who exhibit these behaviors and orientations are perceived as "self-starters" and "go-getters" on the fast track to success. Women who exhibit these same behaviors, however, risk being labeled as "pushy," "bitchy," or "cold." Such double standards and stigmatizing labels are clearly discriminatory against women.

THE SECOND SHIFT

When men and women in the same household are both working, men and women spend about equal time in paid and unpaid work combined, although a larger share of unpaid work typically is done by women (Offer and Schneider 2011). Although differences are narrowing, there continues to be an inequitable division of domestic labor. Women are much more involved in labor-intensive routine chores than men and in the invisible mental labor associated with taking care of children and planning for their activities (Offer and Schneider 2011). Women also do the bulk of the "emotional work" that sustains relationships—between husband and wife, between parents and children, and between the immediate and extended families and friends (Hochschild 1989, 1990). For instance, women typically make the phone calls, send birthday and anniversary cards, buy and send gifts, plan special family events, and the like. Moreover, women are more likely than men to multitask in performing paid and unpaid labor. Multitasking, in turn, produces higher levels of stress and work–family conflict (Offer and Schneider 2011).

Sociologist Arlie Hochschild (1989, 1990) has used the term *second shift* to describe this double burden—work outside the home followed by child care and housework. These extra duties off the job may affect performance on the job. Despite the image of the "24/7" woman who can have it all and do it all, the reality is that any one person has only a finite amount of time, energy, and attention available. To the extent that women carry these additional burdens more than men, they are at a collective nonmerit disadvantage in the labor force competing with men. Young professionals, especially, work long hours and are often called upon for additional work duties on short notice. It is the fast-track professional on the make who "goes the extra mile" who gets the promotion—not the one who has to rush home immediately after work to take care of the kids, is chronically sleep deprived, or is unavailable to fly off to London over the weekend to seal a deal. In this way, unequal division of household labor creates severe handicaps for women who bear these responsibilities and a distinct nonmerit advantage for men who do not.

SEXUAL HARASSMENT

Prior to women's recent surge into the labor force, men and women mostly operated in separate social worlds: the home was women's domain, and the workplace was men's domain. As women have entered the labor force in larger numbers, and as they have become less concentrated in a limited number of jobs, non-family-related men and women are working in the same social space more often. This, along with heightened sensitivity to the issue, has increased the incidence, as well as the awareness, of sexual harassment in the workplace. Sexual harassment is another nonmerit impediment that women face in the labor force in far greater proportion than men. Social scientists know that opposite-sex social interaction is different from same-sex social interaction. Opposite-sex interaction is more sexually charged, often resulting in an element of flirtation that is missing in same-sex interaction. Most of this casually flirtatious behavior is innocent enough and falls outside the realm of sexual harassment. The line is crossed when flirtatious behavior turns into unwelcome sexual advances that interfere with a person's ability to perform a job and enjoy its benefits. Sexual harassment may include everything from blatant demands for sex, to subtler pressures regarding sexual activity, to a panoply of behaviors that create a hostile workplace environment. Depending on how sexual harassment is defined, as many as one-quarter to one-third of all working women report having been sexually harassed in the workplace—an alarming rate of victimization.

In the 1986 decision in *Meritor Savings Bank v. Vinson*, the Supreme Court declared that sexual harassment is a form of discrimination and therefore violates Title VII of the 1964 Civil Rights Act. Since then, the courts have typically used thirty-one pages of guidelines from the Equal Employment Opportunity Commission to protect employees from conduct considered illegal under that act. Nevertheless, sexual harassment has continued in the military, and numerous women have filed suits against government agencies, private-sector companies, and universities. Sexual harassment is not only an indicator of the continuing dominance of men in the workplace but a form of discrimination that jeopardizes women's chances for occupational success and impinges upon their pursuit of the American Dream.

POLITICAL ACTIVITY AND OFFICE HOLDING

Women constitute over half of the voting population and about half of the labor force but only a small percentage of those holding high governmental positions. Since 1789, for instance, women have made up only 2 percent of all members of the House of Representatives (Carr 2008, 58). Nevertheless, the numbers of women holding elected office has been increasing rapidly. The number of women in the House increased from ten (out of 435 members) in 1969 to eighty-one in 2012, and the number of women in the Senate increased from one (out of 100) in 1969 to a record twenty in 2012. What is more, the number of women in state legislatures has increased even more rapidly. The percentage of women in state legislatures has increased from 4.4 percent in 1971 to 21.7 percent of state senate seats and 24 percent of state house or assembly seats (Carr 2008, 58; Center for American Women and Politics 2012). Similarly, the percentage of women occupying statewide elective executive offices (such as governor, lieutenant governor, and attorney general) has also steadily increased. In 1969, women held just 6.6 percent of all such statewide elective executive offices, but in 2012 they held 23.4 percent (Carr 2008, 58; Center for American Women and Politics 2012).

In 2008, Hillary Clinton ran for the Democratic nomination for president of the United States in a very close primary race against Barack Obama, receiving over eighteen million votes (which she referred to as "eighteen million cracks in the glass ceiling") and winning many state primaries. Also in 2008, Sarah Palin was selected to be the first Republican vice presidential nominee and only the second woman to run for that office (the first was Democrat Geraldine Ferraro in 1984).

As sociologist Deborah Carr (2008) has pointed out, there are several possible explanations for the continuing underrepresentation of women in political office, including perceived familial role conflict; fewer available economic resources; the power of incumbency and name recognition, which favor males already holding office; and voter stereotypes regarding women as less suited to positions of power. Also, most political careers evolve out of training, experience, and leadership in law, the military, and business, areas from which women were largely excluded until the last few decades.

To summarize, while women's political office holding is increasing, women remain severely underrepresented in major elected and appointed offices at the state and federal levels, and the more powerful the office, the greater the underrepresentation. In short, gender inequality continues in the political system. The continued denial of full and equal political participation also denies women equal access to the American Dream and deprives women of the full potential for political clout to reduce gender inequalities in other spheres of social life.

OTHER ISMS

When we discuss discrimination and its victims, we are not talking about a few people. More than half of the population is female, at least a third of the population is the member of a racial or ethnic minority, and a sizable proportion is both. Although race and gender discrimination are most prevalent, ranking first and second in number of charges filed with the Equal Employment Opportunity Commission (EEOC) from 1992 to 2011 (U.S. EEOC 2012), they are not the only forms of discrimination. Other, less visible forms of discrimination continue to operate in ways that deny equal opportunity to their victims.

SEXUAL ORIENTATION AND IDENTITY: DISCRIMINATION AGAINST LESBIANS, GAYS, BISEXUALS, AND TRANSGENDERED

Today, homophobia and heterosexism—individual and institutionalized prejudice and discrimination against gays and lesbians—are present in every facet of life: the family, organized religion, the workplace, official policies, and the mass media. While there are anecdotal accounts of public recognition of homosexuality throughout American history, it was not until the 1920s and 1930s that it became visible. Before then, most gays and lesbians, apparently fearing hostility and discrimination, hid their sexual orientation from public view, remaining "in the closet." Whatever fears they may have had were justified because, as homosexuality became more visible, efforts to suppress it grew and became institutionalized. As recently as 1960, no cities or states protected the rights of gays and lesbians, sodomy was outlawed in every state, and no openly gay or lesbian individuals held elected office. Well into the 1960s, discrimination against gays and lesbians was common and legal. Psychiatrists thought homosexuality was a disease, and efforts were made to prevent, control, and "correct" it. The American Psychiatric Association declassified homosexuality as a mental disorder in 1973 although discrimination and prejudice continued.

Most recently, the issues of institutional discrimination regarding sexual orientation have focused on military service and marriage. The military has often been seen as a vanguard institution in overcoming discrimination. The military was largely racially segregated until 1948 when President Harry Truman signed an executive order to desegregate the military, long before the height of the civil rights movement and desegregation of other major social institutions. The U.S. military, however, did not permit homosexuals to openly serve. President Bill Clinton's attempt in 1993 to end this discriminatory policy met with severe opposition in Congress and from some segments of the general population. In the end, the discriminatory law was retained, modified by the "don't ask, don't tell" compromise. Under this compromise policy, military recruits no longer had to state their sexual orientation and the military was not supposed to inquire about it, but the policy still permitted investigations and dismissals of military personnel if evidence was found that they had engaged in homosexual acts. Ironically, according to a 2000 report, more gay and lesbian troops were discharged from the military under this policy than were under the old, supposedly harsher rules (Schaefer 2004). Finally in 2011, with increasingly public tolerance toward homosexuality although with still strong pockets of resistance, a new policy was put into effect allowing homosexuals to serve openly in the military.

Another form of discrimination against gay and lesbian couples is the withholding of legal recognition of their relationships. Legal recognition of what has come to be called domestic partnerships provides numerous benefits and protections for gay and lesbian couples with respect to inheritance, parenting, pensions, taxation, housing, immigration, workplace fringe benefits, and health care. Several dozen cities now recognize domestic partnerships. But anticipating that some states might allow gay and lesbian couples to marry legally, Congress enacted the Defense of Marriage Act (DOMA) in 1996, which denies federal recognition of same-sex marriages. Nevertheless, as of 2012, nine states as well as the District of Columbia permit same-sex marriages.

Public sentiment is quickly shifting in favor of more tolerant attitudes regarding homosexuality, especially among younger cohorts. After thirty failed state public referenda to allow same-sex marriage, for the first time in 2012 public referenda in Maine, Maryland, and Washington passed allowing same-sex marriages to take place. Using General Social Survey data from 1973 to 2010, Tom W. Smith (2011) found that the American public clearly makes a distinction between whether homosexuality is morally wrong and whether homosexuals should be allowed certain civil rights. Americans' attitudes regarding the *morality* of homosexuality became more liberal; less than half of Americans (43.5 percent in 2010) view homosexuality as "always wrong." Over the same time period, self-reported willingness to restrict the civil liberties of homosexuals steadily declined. In 2010, 46 percent of Americans supported gay marriage, 14 percent neither agreed nor disagreed with gay marriage, and 40 percent disagreed. However, current law still largely excludes gays from forming legal marriages, and the federal DOMA law remains in effect, although the Obama administration directed the Justice Department in 2011 to stop defending the law in court.

In short, despite these gains, gays and lesbians still face discrimination in most areas of life, including employment, which severely jeopardizes their access to opportunity and their pursuit of the American Dream. For instance, there is especially strong resistance to hiring those known to be gay or lesbian in certain occupations, such as teaching and the clergy. Open avoidance, stereotyping, name-calling, physical threats, and assaults against gays and lesbians remain commonplace, and antigay hate crimes, including physical attacks, continue to occur. Finally, it has become clear that the transgendered—individuals whose gender identity does not "match" their sexual identity in conventional ways—face much of the same stereotyping, hostility, discrimination, and outright exclusion as that encountered by gays and lesbians.

WHERE THE HANDICAPPED GET PARKED: DISCRIMINATION AGAINST THE DISABLED

Americans with disabilities have long been the victims of prejudice and stereotypes and the objects of various forms of discrimination, which have denied them equal opportunity to pursue the American Dream. Disabilities may result from congenital defects, injury, or disease and include a wide range of impairments and limitations (Thomason, Burton, and Hyatt 1998).

Nearly 19 percent of the population have some level of disability, and 12.6 percent have a severe disability (Brault 2012). The most common types of disability include hearing, vision, and cognitive impairments, arthritis, back or spine problems, and heart trouble. All told, over fifty-six million Americans report some level of disability. The proportion of people with disabilities continues to increase. Because of advances in medicine, many people who once would have died from an accident or illness now survive. Disabilities are found in all segments of the population, but racial and ethnic minorities are disproportionately more likely to experience them and have less access to assistance.

Employers have been reluctant to hire people with disabilities even when the disabilities do not keep them from doing the job. Only about 41 percent of working-age people with a disability in the United States are employed, compared to 79 percent of the nondisabled (Brault 2012). Marjorie L. Baldwin and William G. Johnson (1998) found that after controlling for differences in productivity, large wage differentials between disabled and nondisabled people constitute evidence of labor-market discrimination. They also note a number of misconceptions. For example, contrary to the stereotype of the disabled person as someone forced into a wheelchair due to a traumatic accident or birth defect, most disabled people suffer from musculoskeletal or cardiovascular conditions caused by chronic degenerative processes. Further, the onset of disability typically occurs in middle age, so most disabled people were not subject to discrimination upon their initial entry into the labor market.

In addition to employment discrimination, design characteristics of public buildings and transportation facilities have made it difficult for people with disabilities to gain access to education, work, shopping, and entertainment, even when their disabilities do not impair their actual ability to study, work, shop, or enjoy entertainment facilities.

Stigmas attached to many forms of disability have become the basis of stereotypes and discriminatory treatment. For example, individuals with physical disabilities must deal with those who assume that they have mental limitations as well. People with disabilities are often viewed unidimensionally as disabled so that the single characteristic of their disability comes to define their identity. For example, they are seen only as blind, rather than as complex human beings with individual strengths and weaknesses whose blindness is but one aspect of their lives.

The media have contributed to the stereotyping of people with disabilities, often treating them with a mixture of pity and fear. For example, some nationwide charity telethons have unwittingly contributed to negative images of the disabled as being childlike, dependent, and nonproductive. In literature and film, evil characters with disabilities—Captain Hook, Dr. Strangelove, and Freddy Krueger—sometimes imply that disability is a punishment for evil. In short, the stigmas attached to disability and the discrimination imposed on people with disabilities are widely institutionalized and often become a greater handicap than the disability itself.

World War II and the Korean, Vietnam, Gulf, Iraq, and Afghanistan wars have produced thousands of disabled veterans. Increases in the number of disabled Americans have produced a growing effort to ensure people with disabilities the same rights as enjoyed by others. By the early 1970s, a strong social movement for disability rights had emerged in the United States, and legislation and labor–management contracts have forbidden discrimination on the basis of disabilities not related to job performance. Discrimination against the disabled was forbidden by the Rehabilitation Act of 1973, but only for federal employment and private employers with federal contracts. In 1992, the Americans with Disabilities Act (ADA) went into effect and greatly extended these protections. This law broadens protections for people with disabilities against discrimination, requires that employers accommodate them, and requires that public facilities be accessible. Among the specific provisions is a ban on discrimination against people with physical and mental disabilities in hiring and promotion. This ban applies to all employers with more than twenty-five employees and allows people to directly sue the organizations that discriminate. It also outlaws tests that have the effect of screening out job applicants with disabilities unless it can be shown that the tests relate to a worker's ability to perform the job. In addition to strengthening the ban on discrimination, the ADA requires that workplaces and public accommodations be made accessible to people with disabilities. Restaurants, colleges and universities, transportation systems, theaters, retail stores, and government offices are among the kinds of public facilities that must now be accessible. Finally, employers are required to make "reasonable accommodations" for employees with disabilities. The word *reasonable*, however, is subject to various, often self-serving interpretations.

It is difficult to quantify gains that those with disabilities may have made because of this legislation. From the time the EEOC began enforcing the ADA in July 1992, formal complaints of violations have fluctuated from a high of 25,742 in 2011 to a low of 14,893 in 2005 and averaged around 18,000 per year since then (U.S. EEOC 2012). While these figures suggest considerable discrimination, studies also reveal that people with disabilities do feel empowered and perceive increased access to employment opportunities. More recently, in December of 2012 the U.S. Senate failed to ratify an international treaty which would in essence make the provisions of the ADA apply to international signatories, making work and travel abroad, for instance, easier for the disabled. Despite support from U.S. veterans groups, ratification of the treaty failed because of concerns raised by Republican senators regarding perceived threats to U.S. sovereignty in signing on to such international treaties.

OLD DOGS AND NEW TRICKS: AGE DISCRIMINATION

Older Americans are the victims of stereotypes, prejudice, and various forms of discrimination that jeopardize their chances to fulfill important parts of the American Dream. While older Americans constitute a significant segment of the population—about 13 percent of the population was over sixty-five in 2010 (U.S. Census Bureau 2012a)—one does not become the object of age discrimination until one grows old. In short, one does not suffer a lifetime of age discrimination, and many who die young never face age discrimination at all. However, everyone hopes to grow old, and those who do eventually face age discrimination. Further, the population is aging—an increasing proportion of the population is composed of older people. In fact, this group will constitute an estimated one-fifth of the U.S. population by 2050 (U.S. Census Bureau 2004); therefore, more people will suffer age discrimination. Finally, since people are now living longer, they are the objects of age discrimination for more years and a larger proportion of their lives.

According to the American Dream, after a lifetime of employment, one has earned the right to a comfortable and secure retirement. Pensions, savings, Social Security, and other programs to which one has contributed during one's working years are now "paid back," so that one may live the remainder of one's life as a financially secure and respected member of one's community. If one's resources prove inadequate, society will provide any needed assistance.

It is clear, however, that the American Dream is not fulfilled for many because of various forms of discrimination. Negative stereotypes of old age are strongly entrenched in our youth-oriented society. Age discrimination has been increasingly evident in the disproportionate firing of older employees during layoffs, and older employees in long-term jobs lose work at a higher rate than their younger counterparts. It is often difficult for older workers to find work after being displaced by layoffs, automation, or downsizing. Once conditions improve, employers often prefer to hire younger workers at less pay who might be available for continued employment over longer periods, independent of the ability of applicants to do the job. As a result, the number of age-discrimination complaints received by the EEOC typically increase when layoffs increase.

According to the EEOC, since 1992, age-discrimination complaints have ranked third or fourth. While they fell during the 1990s, they have turned upward recently. For example, for fiscal year 2006, there were 16,548 cases of age discrimination. At the height of the Great Recession in fiscal year 2008, complaints peaked at 24,582 such cases, an increase of 48 percent and the largest annual increase since fiscal year 2002 (U.S. EEOC 2012). Age discrimination has led to protective and advocacy efforts by groups who are the objects of such discrimination. Although the AARP, founded in 1958, is the best known of such organizations, numerous other organizations have developed in response to age discrimination.

GETTING STUNG BY THE WASP: RELIGIOUS DISCRIMINATION

One might argue that an important component of the American Dream is freedom of religious belief and practice. However, even during colonial times, instances of religious intolerance and discrimination were not uncommon. Throughout the eighteenth, nineteenth, and early twentieth centuries, religious minorities—Catholics, Jews, and Mormons, for example—were victims of severe discrimination, persecution, and even violence.[1]

Catholics were not welcomed to America (Cullen 2001; Varacalli 2006). By the mid-seventeenth century, all the colonies had passed laws designed to thwart Catholic immigration, most of them denying Catholics citizenship, voting rights, and office-holding rights. Large-scale Catholic immigration began in the 1830s, and as it increased throughout the remainder of the century, anti-Catholic hostility grew. American Catholics became the objects of severe discrimination, including vicious literature of all sorts, hostile political-party platforms, Know Nothing and Ku Klux Klan demonstrations and violence, and American Protective Association activities. Catholic beliefs and practices were misrepresented and stereotyped. Harsh attempts at religious assimilation in the public schools, as well as discrimination in higher education, led to the development of Catholic K–12 schools, colleges, and universities. Catholics faced job and housing discrimination, as well as various other forms of social exclusion. Jews who migrated to America encountered many of the same problems as Catholics and were often victimized by the same nativist groups.

Members of the Church of Jesus Christ of Latter-Day Saints (Mormons) were another persecuted religious minority. The westward movement of Mormons from New York to Utah involved violence and a series of expulsions from several states, including Ohio, Missouri, and Illinois. Joseph Smith, founder of the faith, was lynched by a mob that broke into a jail to get him. In some circles, Mormons are still stereotyped as polygamists, racists, and sexists, whose beliefs and practices are not "truly" Christian. Finally, in contemporary American society, "religious outsiders," most notably Middle Easterners of all nationalities, "Arabs," and "Muslims," are stereotyped and face various forms of discrimination and exclusion.

Even today, severe competition, intolerance, and hostility among various religious groups surface sporadically. For instance, anti-Muslim stereotypes and hostility surfaced following the terrorist attacks of September 11, 2001, subsequent U.S. military intervention in the Muslim countries of Afghanistan and Iraq, and ongoing international tensions in much of the Middle East. Islam has been stereotyped as a fundamentally flawed and intolerant faith that sanctions violence and terrorism. Sikhs have also been victimized by religious ignorance and bigotry.

Notwithstanding these and similar occurrences, religious pluralism, the privatization of religion, and other aspects of continuing secularization have largely eliminated institutionalized forms of religious discrimination in America. Individual-level religious bigotry where it occurs, however, continues to deny full participation in the American Dream to the unchurched and those of nondominant faiths. For example, Pentecostal and Holiness groups, Jehovah's Witnesses, Seventh-Day Adventists, and other nondominant Christian groups, as well as non-Christian groups like Jews, Muslims, Hindus, Rastafarians, and Sikhs continue to suffer hostility, discrimination, and exclusion at the hands of individual religious bigots. Finally, the merely *non*religious (agnostics and atheists) have also been subject to individual acts of prejudice and exclusion.

Compared to other forms of discrimination today, religious discrimination appears to be less common, although there is evidence of recent increases. In 2002, for instance, there were more than eleven times as many race-discrimination charges and ten times as many sex-discrimination charges filed with the EEOC. However, since 2006, the number of charges of religious discrimination filed has increased each year. In fact, the number of such charges filed in 2011 was a record high—almost triple that of 1992. In fiscal year 2010, there were 3,790 charges of religious discrimination; in fiscal year 2011, there was a 9.5 percent increase to 4,151 (U.S. EEOC 2012).

SURVIVAL OF THE PRETTIEST: THE ADVANTAGES OF ATTRACTIVENESS

Physical attractiveness is another nonmerit factor that affects getting ahead in America. Lookism—favoritism for the attractive and discrimination against the unattractive—creates a structure of unequal opportunity, providing unearned advantages to the attractive and disadvantages to the unattractive. While it is often claimed that "beauty is in the eye of the beholder"—that the assessment of attractiveness is a highly subjective matter—in fact there are high levels of agreement about attractiveness that are largely unaffected by the "beholder's" sex, age, or socioeconomic status. There is even substantial cross-cultural agreement.

"Good looks" for both men and women provide decided advantages in almost every aspect of life. For nearly twenty years, University of Texas at Austin economist Daniel S. Hamermesh has studied the effects of physical appearance on economic outcomes. His conclusions are summarized in his book, *Beauty Pays: Why Attractive People Are Successful* (2011). Hamermesh estimates that, apart from other factors, attractive people earn on average about 5 percent more in income than average-looking people and as much as 10 percent more compared to below-average-looking people. Consistent with American poet Dorothy Parker's observation that "beauty is only skin deep but ugly goes clean to the bone," Hamermesh's research shows that the penalty for being below average looking is greater than the premium for being above average looking. Although the income premium for being above average looking is greater for women than men, somewhat surprisingly, the income penalty for being below average looking is substantially greater for men than women. Hamermesh estimates that for the average paid worker the economic premium for being above average looking compared to below average looking is about $230,000 over a lifetime of earnings.

Hamermesh notes that the effect of physical attractiveness may be greater for some occupations, such as politicians, athletes, salespersons, and, interestingly, professors. Hamermesh, for instance, cites research showing that better-looking professors, apart from other factors, get higher teaching evaluations from students and receive higher income. Attractiveness matters not just for income but for other economic outcomes as well. Research shows that above-average-looking people are more likely to obtain loans even with the same demographic characteristics and credit histories as less attractive applicants. Moreover better-looking borrowers get lower interest rates on loans than other borrowers. The ability to secure loans as investment capital, in turn, is a critical factor in starting a business and establishing equity for wealth accumulation.

In another thorough examination of the effects of attractiveness, in her book *Survival of the Prettiest* (1999), Nancy Etcoff concludes, "Beauty is howlingly unfair. It is a genetic given. And physical appearance tells us little about a person's intelligence, kindness, pluck, sense of humor, or steadfastness, although we think it does" (1999, 242). Americans seem to know that the link between beauty and goodness is spurious; yet attractive people tend to be the beneficiaries of positive stereotypes and unearned opportunities. Beautiful is good, and the good get all sorts of advantages. Unattractive people, on the other hand, receive no such benefits but are instead victimized by negative stereotypes and discrimination.

Etcoff shows that preferential treatment of beautiful people is extremely easy to demonstrate, as is discrimination against the unattractive. From infancy to adulthood, beautiful people are treated preferentially and viewed more positively. This is true for men as well as women. Beautiful people find sexual partners more easily, and beautiful individuals are more likely to receive leniency in the courts and to elicit cooperation from strangers. Beauty conveys modest but real social and economic advantages, and equally importantly, ugliness leads to major social disadvantages and discrimination (1999, 25).

Etcoff reviewed a large body of research and catalogued the numerous advantages of attractiveness. Lookism affects us all from an early age: Parents respond more affectionately to physically attractive newborns. Attractive schoolchildren differentially benefit from positive teacher expectations. People are more likely to help attractive individuals, and this holds even if they don't like them. People are less likely to ask good-looking people for help. Efforts to please good-looking people with no expectation of immediate reward or reciprocity are clear evidence of the unearned rewards of beauty, which are not unlike those of being born into the nobility or inheriting wealth. Etcoff also reports research showing that good-looking people are given more "personal space" than unattractive people and are more likely to win arguments and persuade others of their opinions. People divulge secrets to them and disclose personal information. "Basically people want to please the good-looking person, making conciliatory gestures, letting themselves be persuaded . . . and backing off from them, literally, as they walk down the street" (Etcoff 1999, 47).

Attractive people are expected to be better at everything, and such expectations at school and work can be self-fulfilling. Despite the "dumb-blonde" stereotype, people presume that attractive people of both sexes are more, not less, intelligent than unattractive people. Better-looking women are more likely to marry than unattractive women, and they are more likely to "marry up"—to marry men with more education and income than they have. The better one looks, the better looking one's partner is likely to be, and having a good-looking partner increases men's status. Good-looking people are more likely to get away with anything from shoplifting, to cheating on exams, to committing serious crimes.

Etcoff reports research findings that good looks are an advantage in the workplace: "Although it does not approach racism or sexism in magnitude, lookism appears to be a form of discrimination in the workplace. . . . Good-looking men are more likely to get hired, at a higher salary, and to be promoted faster than unattractive men" (1999, 83), which good looks may be related to both the higher confidence levels and greater social skills that more attractive individuals tend to develop (Mobius and Rosenblat 2006). Other research shows that men who are over six feet tall average $166,000 more income in a lifetime than men who are five feet five inches or less (Judge and Cable 2004).

The rhetoric of proponents of the American Dream is that the advantages that accrue to the attractive are legitimate because they are achieved. That is, meritocracy applies to considerations of beauty because it is argued that beauty is attainable through hard work and effort. But just *how* does one "achieve" attractiveness? A vast and complex multibillion-dollar beauty in-dustry (cosmetics, plastic surgery, diets, drugs, vitamins, herbs, potions, creams, ointments, food supplements, physical fitness and exercise, and fash-ion) supposedly levels the playing field, providing equal opportunity to achieve a socially constructed and mythical ideal of beauty (Wolff 1991). Hamermesh (2011) notes that in 2008, for instance, Americans spent roughly $400 billion in products and procedures attempting to enhance physical at-tractiveness, accounting for nearly 5 percent of consumer spending that year. Despite this expense, research suggests that only minor increments to others' perceptions of attractiveness occur as a result of these efforts (Hamermesh 2011). The "opportunities" to improve attractiveness offered by the beauty industry, however, are not equal. Natural variation in beauty creates different starting points and makes the most difference, but "working hard" to be attractive usually takes money, sometimes lots of it.

To sum things up, one can hardly doubt the considerable advantages that attractiveness provides in pursuit of the American Dream. What is more, there is no level playing field since attractiveness and the opportunities to "earn" it are distributed unequally. It is good to be pretty or handsome; it is not good to be homely. No sane person, offered a chance to be more attrac-tive, would turn it down. While attractiveness does not guarantee happiness any more than money does, having either is good, and having either helps in getting the other.

MULTIPLE JEOPARDY: A NOTE ON INTERSECTIONALITY AND THE MATRIX OF DOMINATION

It is harmful for any one individual to be subject to discrimination along any one of the various dimensions of discrimination discussed above. But it is exponentially harmful to be subject to discrimination along multiple dimensions simultaneously (Collins 1990; Weber 2001). For instance, on average there is a "cost" to being black in America in terms of the likely loss of opportunity and income; there is also a "cost" to being a woman in America. Social scientists have further identified an additional "cost" associated with the *combination* of factors such as being both black *and* a woman. The combination of sources of discrimination along multiple axes of inequality represents what sociologist Patricia Collins (1990) calls a matrix of domination. Within a matrix of domination, several axes of inequality can overlap for any one person, placing them at added risks at the points where those various axes intersect.

SUMMARY

Although race and sex discrimination are the most visible and damaging forms of discrimination in America, other forms of discrimination also interfere with the pursuit of the American Dream. Indeed, discrimination is not only inconsistent with meritocratic principles; it is the antithesis of merit. Although heterosexism, ageism, discrimination against the disabled, religious intolerance, and lookism may not victimize as many Americans as sex and race discrimination, they routinely operate in addition to sex and race discrimination and often in combination. We have seen that discrimination in most of its forms has declined in the sweeping history of American society, especially in recent decades. Although discrimination is down, it is not out. In most cases, the most public and overt forms of discrimination have become socially unacceptable, driving remaining discrimination underground in more tacit forms but with often equally devastating effects. Even as some forms of discrimination have been reduced, the effects of prior discrimination continue to reach into the present both in the form of permanent and cumulative costs of lost opportunity for its victims and in the creation of unequal starting points for successive generations.

REFERENCES

Baldwin, Marjorie L., and William G. Johnson. 1998. "Dispelling the Myths about Work Disability." In *New Approaches to Disability in the Workplace*, ed. Terry Thomason, John F. Burton, and Douglas E. Hyatt, chap. 2. Madison: University of Wisconsin, Industrial Relations Research Association.

Blau, Francine D. 2012. "The Sources of the Pay Gap." In *The New Gilded Age: The Critical Inequality Debates of Our Time*, ed. David B. Grusky and Tamar Kricheli-Katz, 189–208. Stanford, California: Stanford University Press.

Blau, Francine D., and Lawrence M. Kahn. 2006. "The Gender Pay Gap: Going, Going . . . but Not Gone." In *The Declining Significance of Gender?*, ed. Francine D. Blau, Mary C. Brinton, and David B. Grusky, 37–66. New York: Sage.

Bocian, Debbie Gruenstein, Wei Li, and Keith S. Ernst. 2010. *Foreclosures by Race and Ethnicity: The Demographics of a Crisis*. Durham, NC: Center for Responsible Lending.

Bonilla-Silva, Eduardo. 2003. *Racism without Racists: Color-Blind Racism and the Persistence of Racial Inequality in the United States*. Lanham, MD: Rowman & Littlefield.

Brault, Matthew W. 2012. "Americans with Disabilities: 2010." In *Current Population Reports*, 70–131. Washington, DC: U.S. Census Bureau.

Carr, Deborah. 2008. "Gender Politics." *Contexts* 7, no. 4 (Fall): 58–59.

Center for American Women and Politics. 2012. "Women in Elective Office 2012." http://www.cawp.rutgers.edu/fast_facts/levels_of_office/documents/elective.pdf (accessed November 6, 2012).

Chang, Mariko Lin. 2010. *Shortchanged: Why Women Have Less Wealth and What Can Be Done about It*. New York: Oxford.

Collins, Patricia. 1990. *Black Feminist Thought: Knowledge, Consciousness, and the Politics of Empowerment*. Boston: Unwin Hyman.

Conley, Dalton. 1999. *Being Black, Living in the Red: Race, Wealth, and Social Policy in America*. Berkeley: University of California Press.

Corbett, Christianne, and Catherine Hill. 2012. *Graduating to a Pay Gap: The Earnings of Women and Men One Year after College Graduation*. Washington, DC: American Association of University Women. http://www.aauw.org/GraduatetoaPayGap/upload/AAUWGraduatingtoaPayGapReport.pdf (accessed January 24, 2013).

Cullen, Jim. 2001. *Restless in the Promised Land: Catholics and the American Dream*. Chicago: Sheed and Ward.

Domhoff, G. William. 2009. *Who Rules America? Challenges to Corporate and Class Dominance*. New York: McGraw-Hill.

Doss, Richard C., and Alan M. Gross. 1994. "The Effects of Black English and Code-Switching on Intraracial Perceptions." *Journal of Black Psychology* 29:282–93.

Etcoff, Nancy. 1999. *Survival of the Prettiest: The Science of Beauty*. New York: Doubleday.

Farley, John E. 2005. *Majority-Minority Relations*. 5th ed. Upper Saddle River, NJ: Prentice Hall.

Feagin, Joe R., and Clairece Booher Feagin. 2007. *Racial and Ethnic Relations*. 8th ed. Englewood Cliffs, NJ: Prentice Hall.

Feagin, Joe R., and Karyn D. McKinney. 2003. *The Many Costs of Racism*. Lanham, MD: Rowman & Littlefield.

Feagin, Joe R., and Melvin P. Sikes. 1994. *Living with Racism: The Black Middle-Class Experience*. Boston: Beacon.

Hamermesh, Daniel S. 2011. *Beauty Pays: Why Attractive People Are More Successful*. Princeton, NJ: Princeton University Press.

Hochschild, Arlie. 1989. *The Second Shift: Working Parents and the Revolution at Home*. New York: Viking.

———. 1990. "The Second Shift: Employed Women Are Putting in Another Day of Work at Home." *Utne Reader* 38 (March–April): 66–73.

Iceland, John, Daniel H. Weinberg, and Erika Steinmetz. 2002. *Racial and Ethnic Residential Segregation in the United States: 1980–2000*. U.S. Census Bureau, Series CENSR-3. Washington, DC: U.S. Government Printing Office.

Judge, Timothy A., and Daniel M. Cable. 2004. "The Effect of Physical Height on Workplace Success and Income: Preliminary Test of a Theoretical Model." *Journal of Applied Psychology* 89, no. 3: 428–41.

Kerbo, Harold R. 2012. *Social Stratification and Inequality: Class Conflict in Historical, Comparative, and Global Perspective.* 8th ed. New York: McGraw-Hill.

Kozol, Jonathan. 1991. *Savage Inequalities: Children in America's Schools.* New York: Crown.

———. 2006. *The Shame of the Nation: The Restoration of Apartheid Schooling in America.* New York: Crown.

Massey, Douglas S. 2007. *Categorically Unequal: The American Stratification System.* New York: Sage.

Massey, Douglas S., and Nancy A. Denton. 1989. "Hypersegregation in the U.S. Metropolitan Areas: Black and Hispanic Segregation along Five Dimensions." *Demography* 26:373–91.

McDonald, Steve, Nan Lin, and Dan Ao. 2009. "Networks of Opportunity: Gender, Race, and Job Leads." *Social Problems* 56, no. 3: 385–402.

Mishel, Lawrence, Josh Bivens, Elise Gould, and Heidi Shierholz. 2012. *The State of Working America.* 12th ed. Ithaca, NY: Cornell University Press.

Mobius, Markus M., and Tany S. Rosenblat. 2006. "Why Beauty Matters." *American Economic Review* 96, no. 1: 222–35.

Offer, Shira, and Barbara Schneider. 2011. "Revisiting the Gender Gap in Time-Use Patterns: Multitasking and Well-Being among Mothers and Fathers in Dual-Earner Families." *American Sociological Review* 76, no. 6: 809–33.

Orfield, Gary, and Chungmei Lee. 2006. *Racial Transformation and the Changing Nature of Segregation.* The Civil Rights Project. Cambridge, MA: Harvard University Press.

Phillips, Kevin. 2003. *Wealth and Democracy: A Political History of the American Rich.* New York: Random House.

Reiman, Jeffrey, and Paul Leighton. 2013. *The Rich Get Richer and the Poor Get Prison: Ideology, Class, and Criminal Justice.* 10th ed. Upper Saddle River, NJ: Pearson.

Savage, Charlie. 2011. "Country Will Settle a Bias Suit." *New York Times*, December 21, 2011. http://www.nytimes.com/2011/12/22/business/us-settlement-reported-on-countrywide-lending.html?scp=1&sq=&st=nyt (accessed January 23, 2013).

Schaefer, Richard T. 2004. *Racial and Ethnic Groups.* 9th ed. Upper Saddle River, NJ: Pearson/Prentice Hall.

Shapiro, Thomas M. 2004. *The Hidden Cost of Being African American: How Wealth Perpetuates Inequality.* New York: Oxford University Press.

Smith, Tom W. 2011. "Public Attitudes towards Homosexuality." NORC, University of Chicago. http://www.norc.org/PDFs/2011%20GSS%20Reports/GSS_Public%20Attitudes%20Toward%20Homosexuality_Sept2011.pdf (accessed November 6, 2012).

Stainback, Kevin, and Donald Tomaskovic-Devey. 2012. *Documenting Desegregation: Racial and Gender Segregation in Private-Sector Employment since the Civil Rights Act.* New York: Sage.

Thomason, Terry, John F. Burton Jr., and Douglas E. Hyatt. 1998. "Disability and the Workplace." In *New Approaches to Disability in the Workplace*, ed. Terry Thomason, John F. Burton, and Douglas E. Hyatt, chap. 1. Madison: University of Wisconsin, Industrial Relations Research Association.

Tomaskovic-Devey, Donald. 1993. "The Gender and Race Composition of Jobs and the Male/Female, White/Black Pay Gaps." *Social Forces* 72:45–76.

United for a Fair Economy. 2012. *Born on Third Base: What the Forbes 400 Really Says about Economic Equality and Opportunity in America.* Boston, MA. http://faireconomy.org/sites/default/files/BornOnThirdBase_2012.pdf (accessed January 24, 2013).

U.S. Census Bureau. 2004. "Resident Population Projections by Sex and Age: 2010 to 2050." Washington, DC: U.S. Government Printing Office.

———. 2012a. "Profile America: Facts for Features." *Older Americans Month: May 2012.* http://www.census.gov/newsroom/releases/archives/facts_for_features_special_editions/cb12-ff07.html (accessed November 6, 2012).

———. 2012b. *Income, Poverty, and Health Insurance Coverage in the United States: 2011.* Washington, DC: U.S. Government Printing Office, table 1, figure 2, "Female-to-Male Earnings Ratio and Median Earnings of Full-Time, Year-Round Workers 15 Years and Older by Sex: 1960 to 2011."

U.S. Department of Education. 2010. *Digest of Education Statistics, 2010.* Table 291. http://nces.ed.gov/programs/digest/d10/tables/dt10_291.asp (accessed November 3, 2012).

———. 2012. *The Condition of Education 2012* (NCES 2012-045), indicator 47. National Center for Education Statistics. http://nces.ed.gov/fastfacts/display.asp?id=72 (accessed November 3, 2012).

U.S. Department of Labor. 2011. *Women in the Labor Force: A Databook.* Washington, DC: U.S. Government Printing Office. http://www.bls.gov/cps/wlf-databook-2011.pdf (accessed November 4, 2012).

U.S. Equal Employment Opportunity Commission (EEOC). 2012. "Charge Statistics FY 1997 through FT 2011." U.S. EEOC. http://www.eeoc.gov/eeoc/statistics/enforcement/charges.cfm (accessed November 6, 2012).

Varacalli, Joseph A. 2006. *The Catholic Experience in America.* The American Religious Experience. Westwood, CT: Greenwood Press.

Walker, Renee E., Christopher R. Keane, and Jessica G. Burke. 2010. "Disparities and Access to Healthy Food in the United States: A Review of Food Deserts Literature." *Health and Place* 16:876–84.

Weber, Lynn. 2001. *Understanding Race, Class, Gender and Sexuality: A Conceptual Framework.* Boston: McGraw-Hill.

Western, Bruce. 2006. *Punishment and Inequality in America.* New York: Russell Sage Foundation.

Wilson, William Julius. 1987. *The Truly Disadvantaged: The Inner City, the Underclass, and Public Policy.* Chicago: University of Chicago Press.

Wolff, Naomi. 1991. *The Beauty Myth: How Images of Beauty Are Used against Women.* New York: William and Morrow.

Yoder, Brian L. 2011. "Engineering by the Numbers." 2011 Profiles of Engineering and Engineering Technology Colleges. http://www.asee.org/papers-and-publications/publications/college-profiles/2011-profile-engineering-statistics.pdf (accessed November 3, 2012).

Chapter Nine

Growing Inequality in the Twenty-First Century

All animals are equal but some animals are more equal than others.
—George Orwell, *Animal Farm*

This book has challenged widely held assertions about meritocracy in America. According to the American ideology of meritocracy, individuals get out of the system what they put into it. The system is seen as fair because everyone is assumed to have an equal, or at least "fair," chance of getting ahead. Getting ahead is ostensibly based on merit—on being made of the right stuff. Being made of the right stuff means being talented, working hard, having the right attitude, and playing by the rules. Anyone made of the right stuff can seemingly overcome any obstacle or adversity and achieve success. In America, the land of opportunity, the sky is presumed to be the limit: you can go as far as your individual talents and abilities can take you.

But merit is only part of the story. We have not suggested that merit itself is irrelevant or that merit has no effect on who ends up with what. We have suggested that, despite the pervasive rhetoric of meritocracy in America, merit is in reality only one factor among many that influence who ends up with what. Nonmerit factors are also at work. These nonmerit factors not only coexist with merit, blunting its effects, but also act to suppress merit, preventing individuals from realizing their full potential based on merit alone.

Chief among the nonmerit factors is inheritance, broadly defined as the effect of where one starts on where one finishes in the race to get ahead. If we had a true merit system, everyone would start in the same place. The reality, however, is that the race to get and stay ahead is more like a relay race in which we inherit our starting positions from our parents. The passing of the baton between generations profoundly influences life outcomes. In-deed, the most important factor in getting and staying ahead in America is where one starts in the first place. Most parents wish to maximize the futures of their children by providing them with every possible advantage. To the extent that parents are successful in transferring these advantages to their children, their children's life outcomes are determined by inheritance and not merit.

Social capital (whom you know) and cultural capital (what you need to know to fit into the group) are also nonmerit factors that affect life outcomes. These factors, in turn, are related to inheritance. It helps to have friends in high places, and the higher up one starts in life, the greater the probability that one will travel in elite social circles. One must also have the cultural wherewithal to be fully accepted within these high-echelon social circles. Those who are born into these circles have a nonmerit cultural advantage over those not born into them, who have the difficult task of learning the ways of life of the group from the outside in.

We have shown that education is both a merit and a nonmerit factor. Education is widely perceived as the preeminent merit filter, sifting and sorting on the basis of demonstrated individual achievements. Although indi-viduals "earn" diplomas, certificates, and degrees based on demonstrated individual competencies, the nurturing of individual potential and opportu-nities to earn these credentials are unequally distributed. Parental social class markedly affects the amount and quality of education children are likely to acquire.

We have also shown that luck plays a part in where people end up in the system. Being in the right place at the right time matters. Nonmerit factors such as the year one is born, the number and types of jobs available, where one lives, where one works, and the vicissitudes of domestic economic cy-cles and the global economy profoundly factor into individual life chances—above and beyond individual merit or the lack of it. The imperfections and ultimate uncertainty of both the stock market on Wall Street and the labor market on Main Street add an undeniable element of luck into the mix of who "wins" and who "loses."

In many ways, the greatest expression of the ideals of rugged individual-ism, meritocracy, and the American Dream is starting your own business and becoming your own boss. We have seen, however, that rates of self-employ-ment in the United States have fallen sharply. The dominance of increasingly large corporations and national chains has severely compromised the entre-preneurial path to upward mobility.

Finally, we have reviewed the avalanche of evidence demonstrating the continuing effects of discrimination on life chances. Discrimination is not just a nonmerit factor; it is the antithesis of merit. In a pure merit system, the only thing that would matter would be the ability to do the job—irrespective of any non-performance-related criteria. To the extent that non-performance criteria affect life outcomes, meritocracy does not exist. At the beginning of the twenty-first century, race and sex discrimination are clearly on the decline and certainly less blatant than during earlier periods, especially the first half of the twentieth century. Nevertheless, the lingering effects of past discrimination persist into the present, and although less visible and more subtle, its remaining, contemporary forms continue to be damaging. The "underground" nature of modern forms of discrimination makes them especially damaging because it has enabled the emergence of an aggressive and popular denial of the persistence of discrimination and its continuing damaging effects. In addition to race and sex discrimination, we have shown how ageism, heterosexism, religious bigotry, "lookism," and discrimination against the disabled create differential access to opportunity and rewards that is quite independent of individual merit.

Americans desperately want to believe in the ultimate fairness of the system and its ability to deliver on its promises. To a great extent, this is the basis of the strength and durability of meritocratic notions and the American Dream. Opinion polls consistently show that Americans continue to embrace the American Dream. But as they strive to achieve it, they have found that it has become more difficult simply to keep up and make ends meet. Instead of "getting ahead," Americans often find themselves working harder just to stay in place, and despite their best efforts, many find themselves "falling behind"—worse off than they were earlier in their lives or compared to their parents at similar points in their lives.

INDIVIDUAL COPING STRATEGIES

Over the past several decades, there has been growing economic inequality in America. Those at the top of the system, deriving most of their income from investments, have done very well. Average wage earners, on the other hand, have experienced flat or declining wages in what amounts to a long wage recession extending as far back as the 1970s. During this period, rates of upward mobility have slowed. In response to growing economic pressures and the lack of opportunity, Americans have resorted to a variety of coping strategies to try to make ends meet or at least maintain a lifestyle to which they have become accustomed. Among these strategies are having multiple family wage earners and fewer children, working more hours, delaying retirement, and borrowing more.

Relying on Multiple Wage Earners

Between 1970 and 2010, the percentage of women aged sixteen and older in the labor force increased from 43 percent to 59 percent (U.S. Department of

Labor 2011, 1, 8). There are many reasons for the dramatic increase in female labor-force participation, including declining fertility; increasing divorce rates; growth of the service sector, in which women have been historically overrepresented; increasing levels of educational attainment among women; and the changing role of women in society. Another generally acknowledged factor is that women work for the same reason men do: to make ends meet. As prices have increased and wages have remained stagnant, more women have been drawn into the labor force to help make ends meet. Besides a sharp rise in female labor-force participation, there has also been a sharp increase in dual-income families. Among all married couples, those in which both husband and wife work increased from 44 percent of married couples in 1967 to 55 percent of married couples in 2009 (U.S. Department of Labor 2011, 75). Couples in which only the husband worked represented only 18 percent in 2009 compared with 36 percent in 1967 (U.S. Department of Labor 2011, 75). Related to the increase in dual-income families, working wives' contributions to median family income increased from 27 percent in 1970 to 37.1 percent in 2009 (U.S. Department of Labor 2011, 77). Having married couples both work as a strategy to offset increased costs of living, however, has an upper limit. That is, except in cases of bigamy, an already working husband or wife has only one spouse who can also enter the labor force.

The next line of defense would presumably be children, especially adult children working while going to school. This, too, is occurring as higher proportions of college students work while going to college and work longer hours. In 1970, among full-time college students, 33.8 percent were employed. By 2010, 40 percent of full-time college students were employed, representing an 18 percent increase over that period. Of full-time college students employed in 1970, 14 percent worked more than twenty hours per week, and 3.7 percent worked more than thirty-five hours per week. By 2010, 17 percent of employed full-time college students worked more than twenty hours, and 6 percent worked more than thirty-five hours (U.S. Department of Education 2012).

Having Fewer Children

Another potential strategy to offset increased costs of living is to reduce family size. For whatever combination of reasons, it is clearly the case that American women have sharply reduced rates of fertility in the past half century. A standard measure of fertility is the total fertility rate (TFR), which is an estimate of the average number of children that would be born to a woman over her lifetime. This rate has fallen from an average of 3.7 children born to American women in a lifetime at the height of the baby boom in 1957 (U.S. Census Bureau 2005) to 2.08 by 2008 (U.S. Census Bureau 2012a, 68), which is close to the replacement threshold of 2.1 that would be required to maintain current population size over time. According to the demographic transition theory, as countries industrialize, rates of fertility are reduced primarily because the economic incentives for higher fertility are reduced. That is, in agrarian societies it makes sense to have large families in order to have more potential workers available to work on the family farm. But as societies shift to industrial economies, children become net economic liabilities instead of potential economic assets. In a reinforcing pattern, reduced fertility is also associated with increased labor-force participation among women. That is, as more women work outside the home, they tend to have fewer children, and as women have fewer children, they tend to increase their rates of labor-force participation.

While reduced fertility rates have many potential causes, demographers generally agree that economic factors are paramount. According to the U.S. Department of Agriculture (2012, 23), the estimated cost of raising one child to age eighteen without college in 2011 for middle-income husband-wife families was $234,900.[1] Adding the average cost of a four-year public college education for in-state residents in the 2011–2012 academic year of $68,544[2] (College Board 2012) brings the total tab per child to slightly over $303,444. The extent to which parents or potential parents limit fertility in the face of such large potential expenditures is unknown but no doubt factors into reproductive decisions. Nevertheless, reduced fertility as a strategy to reduce total household expenses also has upper limits. Obviously a woman cannot reduce her fertility below zero. As noted above, the U.S. TFR, now about replacement level, has in recent years flattened, suggesting that fertility levels are approaching a probable effective ceiling below which couples who want children are unwilling to go despite the costs.

Working More Hours

Americans are working more. Between 1967 and 2010, the average number of annual hours worked per worker increased 5.8 percent from 1,716 hours to 1,815 (Mishel, Bivens, Gould, and Shierholz 2012, 179). The increase in the number of hours worked corresponds to the flat or declining wage income over the same period. This suggests that workers may be working more hours to offset losses in hourly wages or as a means to increase purchasing power in the absence of increases in wages. Working more outside the home, however, comes at a cost. Additional work-related costs such as transportation, child care, and clothing reduce net gains in discretionary income. Additional work hours also come at the cost of lost hours available for leisure, household maintenance, and time with children. New technologies such as iPhones, e-mail, and telecommuting are extending the reach of the employer outside the workplace—especially for mental labor—and further contributing to the blurring of public and private spheres. As with women working outside the home, increasing the number of hours worked per wage earner has upper limits.

Delaying Retirement

Not only are Americans working more, but they are also working longer over a lifetime. Demographer Murray Gendall (2008) documents that rates of labor-force participation for Americans over sixty-five have sharply increased since the mid-1980s, especially for women. Between 1985 and 2007, Gendall shows that rates of labor-force participation increased among men aged sixty-five to sixty-nine (25 to 34 percent), seventy to seventy-four (15 to 21 percent), and seventy-five and older (7 to 10 percent).[3] Labor-force participation increased among women aged sixty to sixty-four (33 to 48 percent), sixty-five to sixty-nine (14 to 26 percent), seventy to seventy-four (8 to 14 percent), and seventy-five and older (2 to 5 percent). In addition, since 1994, a higher proportion of workers sixty-five or older are working full time. The proportion of all older male workers working full time increased for men aged sixty-five to sixty-nine (53 to 70 percent) and aged seventy and older (48 to 55 percent). The proportion of all older female workers working full time also increased for women aged sixty-five to sixty-nine (39 to 53 percent) and aged seventy and older (37 to 41 percent).

Moreover, these trends are likely to continue into the future. Another Bureau of Labor Statistics study (Toossi 2009) projects that labor-force participation rates for workers sixty-five to seventy-four will likely increase between 2008 and 2018 from 25.1 to 30.5 percent. Similarly, labor-force participation rates are projected to increase over the same period for workers seventy-five and older from 7.3 to 10.3 percent.

Working at older ages and working more at older ages are due in part to longer life expectancies. As Americans live and attend school longer, the proportion of their total life spans spent working will also need to increase to be equivalent to prior generations. Many older workers choose to work to stay active as long as they remain in good health. However, older workers are also postponing retirement for financial reasons, for example, as full Social Security benefits have been made available only at older ages and as employers have cut back on health-care and pension benefits to retirees (Gendall 2008; Toossi 2009). During the Great Recession, the value of retirement securities and home values plummeted, which also contributed to delayed plans for retirement, especially for the "threshold generation" of baby boomers fifty to sixty-four years of age otherwise approaching traditional retirement age (Wolff, Owens, and Burak 2012). During the Great Recession, half of individuals in this age group reported that they might need to delay retirement (Morin 2009). Delaying retirement obviously leads to the loss of potential leisure time. In addition, like other individual coping strategies, delaying retirement in order to make ends meet has its upper limits, since most older workers will eventually reach a point at which they are physically or cognitively unable to continue working.

Going into Debt

Another strategy to make up for shortfalls in income is to go into debt (Massey 2007; Phillips 2008; Schor 1998; Sullivan, Warren, and Westbrook 2000; Warren and Warren Tyagi 2003; Wolff, Owens, and Burak 2012). During the long period of wage recession since the 1970s, Americans resorted to carrying record levels of debt. Household debt rose steadily into the beginning of the twenty-first century while savings rates steadily declined. More recently as a result of less credit availability, uncertainty about the future, and general belt-tightening associated with the Great Recession, household debt ticked down somewhat and savings rates have ticked up somewhat. Household debt as a percentage of disposable personal income more than doubled from 68 percent of disposable personal income in 1973 to a peak of 137.6 percent in 2007, then declining to 118.7 percent in 2011 (Mishel, Bivens, Gould, and Shierholz 2012, 404–5). Over roughly the same period, rates of personal savings sharply declined from 9.4 percent in 1970 to only 0.4 percent in 2005, then increased to 4.2 percent by 2011 (U.S. Department of Commerce 2012). Mounting debt without a reserve of savings ultimately leads to personal bankruptcy. In 2010 about seven in every one thousand adults declared personal bankruptcy, a rate over three times as high as in 1980 (Mishel, Bernstein, and Allegretto 2007, 275; Mishel, Bivens, Gould, and Shierholz 2012, 410). Despite the recent trend reversals, an overall pattern of high debt and low savings remains.

Job loss, divorce, or medical problems can trigger a free fall into debt that may ultimately lead to bankruptcy. Research has shown that these three factors combined account for 87 percent of the reasons for filing bankruptcy (Warren and Warren Tyagi 2003, 81). Bankruptcies steadily rose from the 1980s until 2005 when in an attempt to slow the rate of increase in bankruptcy filings, Congress passed the Bankruptcy Abuse Prevention and Consumer Protection Act. This act created new stipulations making it much more expensive and difficult for Americans even to file for bankruptcy. Bankruptcy filings increased from slightly less than 400,000 in 1983 to over 2 million in 2005 (Wolff, Owens, and Burak 2012). Filings dipped sharply with the passage of the new law to about 600,000 in 2006 but have since sharply increased again to 1.6 million in 2010 (Wolff, Owens, and Burak 2012). The increased filing despite the new law is a reflection of the depth of loss of wealth and assets associated with the Great Recession.

In addition to bankruptcies, by late 2008 rates of both delinquent mortgage payments and mortgage foreclosures reached the highest levels since the Mortgage Bankers Association, a trade group, began collecting data in 1979 (Mortgage Bankers Association 2008). In 2010, close to four million households were under foreclosure, representing slightly more than 2 percent of all homeowners and the highest level in thirty years (Wolff, Owens, and Burak 2012). Millions more American families were at risk for losing their homes. By 2010, about one in five homeowners were "underwater"; that is, they had mortgages in excess of the market value of their homes (Wolff, Owens, and Burak 2012). Obviously, debt as a means of making ends meet has its upper limits, which appear to have been reached in the American economy as a whole. Overextended, in debt, and without much of a safety net of savings and increasingly subject to being outsourced or outmoded, life in the middle class for many Americans has become increasingly precarious.

In short, in response to increased financial insecurity of the past several decades, Americans who have fallen behind have resorted to a variety of strategies in attempts to cling to at least the outward appearance of maintaining a middle-class lifestyle and living out the American Dream: increasingly relying on multiple wage earners, having fewer children, working longer hours, delaying retirement, and going into greater debt. Each of these individual coping strategies, however, obviously has its upper limits, which are quickly being realized: there are only two spouses who can work, fertility cannot be reduced below zero, there are only twenty-four hours in a day, retirement cannot be postponed indefinitely, and a spiral of borrowing and spending eventually results in financial collapse.

WHAT CAN BE DONE?

These individual coping strategies, though responses to societal-level imperatives, will not, in themselves, change social institutions, larger organizational forms, or the ways that resources are distributed. In short, they will not change America's social-class system, nor will they make America more equal, more meritocratic, or more just. Changes of this magnitude would require reductions in socially structured inequality, especially inequalities of wealth and power. How could such change be brought about? There are several policy options, all of which depend on the will of those in charge. In the final analysis, policy is determined by the outcome of political contests. These contests reflect competing visions regarding what kind of society people think we *ought* to have or what is desirable.

In the book *The Spirit Level: Why Greater Equality Makes Societies Stronger* (2009), epidemiologists Richard Wilkinson and Kate Pickett provide compelling cross-cultural evidence showing that countries with high levels of economic inequality are associated with a variety of what most would agree are undesirable outcomes such as poor physical health (including lower levels of life expectancy and higher rates of infant mortality), higher rates of stress and mental illness, higher rates of drug abuse, lower levels of overall childhood well-being (as well as higher rates of childhood obesity, lower levels of student math and literacy scores, and higher teenage rates of pregnancy), higher levels of violence (including homicide rates), higher rates of incarceration, and lower levels of social mobility.

Assuming that it is *desirable* to reduce levels of economic inequality and to make the system operate more like a meritocracy (an assumption we will examine at the end of this chapter), several policy options could be considered.

Tax Policy

One way to reduce the gap between the top and the bottom of the system is to impose a more heavily progressive system of taxation on income, wealth, or both. Progressive taxes are those in which the tax rate increases as taxable income increases. In other words, progressive taxation operates on an ability-to-pay principle; that is, those who have higher incomes and can presumably afford to pay more get taxed at higher rates. Progressive taxation does not necessarily result in simple redistribution of income or wealth from the rich to the poor. Revenue from more progressive taxation, for instance, rather than funding transfer payments to lower-income individuals (e.g., welfare payments) could be invested in public projects in ways that would provide more equal *access* to education, health care, public transportation, and other critical services, thereby reducing the nonmerit effects of cumulative advantages in these areas that higher incomes and wealth provide. In this way, the gap in *opportunities* between the rich and the poor would be reduced, and a more level playing field could be established.

Progressive taxation in itself, however, does not increase the prospects for equality of opportunity. Indeed, if income and wealth were entirely accrued based on individual merit, and if there were no advantages in opportunity to achieve based on one's current economic standing, then progressive taxation could create a disincentive for individuals to achieve. On the other hand, to the extent that income and wealth are acquired or augmented through non-merit advantage, then the progressive taxation of such nonmerit advantage would help to establish more equality of opportunity.

Two types of taxes aimed specifically at nonmerit forms of wealth accumulation are estate taxes and gift taxes. These are aimed at nonmerit forms of wealth accumulation since recipients of such largess do not technically "earn" them in the marketplace based on their individual merit (although one may argue that recipients could potentially "earn" these forms of largess informally through demonstration of familial loyalty or friendship, by rendering services such as caring for elderly parents, or as a return for prior favors). Resistance to wealth taxation has most recently coalesced around the push to eliminate federal estate taxes, renamed the "death tax" by opponents, because they seem to tax the dead. Of course, it is not possible to tax the dead. Instead, the estate itself is taxed, and its inheritors receive the remainder.

Federal estate taxes were used in the latter part of the nineteenth century and first part of the twentieth century to offset war costs (Johnson and Eller 1998). The federal estate tax was first enacted in 1862 to help fund the Civil War and was subsequently repealed in 1871. Federal estate taxes were reestablished in 1878 to provide additional revenue to offset the costs of the Spanish-American War and were also subsequently repealed in 1902. The modern form of federal estate tax was reenacted in 1916 with the advent of World War I.

Exclusions have historically been generous, so only the very largest estates have been subject to the tax. As part of the American Taxpayer Relief Act signed into law on January 1, 2013, an exemption of $5.12 million for individuals and $10 million for couples receiving estates was established which will subsequently be indexed to inflation. That means that only individuals receiving inheritances of more than $5.12 million and for couples $10 million (easily less than 1 percent of all estates) will be subject to an inheritance tax over that amount at a rate of 40 percent. Assets left to a surviving spouse or charitable organizations are not generally subject to estate taxation. In addition, estate taxation can be avoided or drastically reduced through inter vivos giving and careful estate planning. States can also level estate taxes independent of federal estate tax, but only about 20 percent of all states have any estate tax, often with complicated provisions for exemptions and exclusions. In short, existing estate taxes are currently not large enough and do not affect enough of the total amount of wealth transferred intergenerationally to make much difference in reducing the nonmerit effects of inheritance on who gets what and how much. Higher estate taxes could potentially help to "reshuffle the deck" between generations to create more equal starting points by both reducing the total amount of inequality and providing more resources for the government to allocate in ways to create more opportunity for those who start further behind.

Estate taxes are only one way of taxing wealth. Tax on wealth could also be based on its possession (assets tax), its use (consumption tax), or its exchange (transfer tax) (cf. Wolff 2002). Those who oppose such taxes often label them "confiscatory" and argue that they discourage work, savings, and investment. Supply-side advocates argue that taxing wealth in any form discourages investments that would otherwise create more jobs and a "trickle-down" effect of wealth creation. They contend that excessive taxation of wealth encourages the wealthy to flee to other countries that tax wealth less, thereby depriving American society of investment and spending that the wealthy would otherwise provide. Supply-siders argue that the sum of individual decisions with regard to the stewardship of resources is collectively more productive, efficient, and efficacious than collective decisions that emerge from the political process. Those who advance this position tend to view inheritance as a natural rather than a civil right, which should not be limited or abridged by the state.

The argument in favor of progressive wealth taxation suggests that unchecked accumulation of wealth increases social inequality to an unacceptable level. According to this view, taxes should be based on an ability-to-pay principle, with the wealthiest being taxed the most. The case in favor of estate taxation argues that inheritance rights are not natural but civil rights granted by the state, which has the power to both regulate and tax wealth in all its forms. According to this view, the state is coheir to claims of private property, the individual accumulation of which was made possible, protected, and promoted by the state.

Many forms of taxes tend to be regressive; that is, lower-income groups pay more as a proportion of total income than higher-income groups. Two such forms of regressive taxation, for instance, are Social Security and Medicare (known as FICA taxes). Employees and employers pay a percentage of employee income into each program. Unlike the Medicare tax, the tax base for Social Security taxes is capped. In 2012, the cap for the Social Security tax was a taxable income of $113,700; that is, income over that amount was not subject to the Social Security tax. As taxable income exceeds $113,700, the percentage of income paid in Social Security tax goes down. Thus, the higher the income above $113,700, the more the tax is regressive. Social Security taxes are capped because Social Security benefits are also capped at a maximum amount.

To the extent that Medicare and Social Security benefits exceed that which individuals pay in over a lifetime, additional benefits received are being subsidized by the general revenue, mostly through contributions of current workers. That is, both low-income and high-income individuals are eligible for these benefits, regardless of need. One proposal for reform is to means test the benefits (as in the case of Medicaid), which would make them essentially "welfare" programs based on need rather than "entitlement" programs available to all regardless of need. That is, everyone would pay into the system as a kind of destitution insurance, available only if you became destitute. A concern, however, is that this would create a disincentive to save or be frugal into old age and that the recipients would be stigmatized for receiving such benefits. Another form of federal regressive tax is based on the source of income. Unearned income from capital gains (income gained from selling stock at a higher price than it was originally purchased) is taxed in the United States for most Americans at about half the rate of earned income from salary and wages. The top tax rate for wages and salaries is 35 percent, but for most Americans income from capital gains is taxed at only 15 percent. Under the new provisions of the American Taxpayer Relief Act signed into law by President Obama in January 2013, the top rate for capital gains increased somewhat to 20 percent for individuals with incomes exceeding $400,000 and for married couples with incomes exceeding $450,000, still well below the equivalent rates for earned income. That is, income from investments is taxed at a much lower rate than income from labor. The higher one's total income, the more likely it is that a higher proportion of it comes from investments rather than wages or salary. This substantial difference in tax rates between earned and unearned income seems inconsistent with the work ethic associated with the American Dream. It is justified, however, on the assumption that capital gains taxes discourage investments, and investments stimulate the economy in ways that generate both jobs and total income. Increasingly, however, investments are used by companies to merge with other companies or invest in foreign markets, both of which typically result in loss of jobs and reductions of income for ordinary workers.

Government Spending

Like tax policy, government spending is determined by the outcome of political contests. And like tax policy, government spending has a major impact on both the extent of inequality and the prospects for mobility within society. As with all modern states, the United States has what economists refer to as a "mixed" economy. That is, part of the economy is produced by market forces, and part is administered by governments. There are no "pure" capitalist or socialist economies; instead, national economies are aligned on a continuum according to whether they are more or less capitalist (market driven) or socialist (government administered).

Even in highly capitalist societies such as the United States, segments of the economy are "set aside" from the marketplace because they are deemed either too important or too impractical to be left to the vicissitudes of market forces. One prominent example is public education. Public education is administered by governmental units (usually local municipalities or states). Public schools operate on essentially socialist principles; that is, they are not-for-sale, not-for-profit entities whose services are administered by government and are available to all citizens regardless of ability to pay. Since providing basic education to all of its citizens regardless of ability to pay is seen as in the public interest, this segment of the economy is set aside from the market. That is, in an ideal democracy in which everyone presumably has an equal say in what happens, it is in the best interest of society for citizens who are making decisions to make informed decisions. It is also seen as in the public interest to have a skilled labor force, which further justifies access to education regardless of the ability to pay. Likewise, it is considered in the interest of fostering democracy and an informed public to have access to information in the public domain. Most communities in the United States, for instance, have not-for-profit public libraries (as well as school libraries and government offices) in which individuals can "look it up" without payment or fees.

It is important to point out, however, that there are mixed entities even within education, such as private schools that are generally, but not always, not for profit, though they do operate on ability-to-pay principles, or public universities that are not for profit but are not available to all (most have competitive rather than open admissions policies) and not entirely free (although usually subsidized). Other sectors of the economy such as police and fire protection, waste disposal, public parks, and so on are similarly set aside from the market. And still others operate on modified market principles, such as for-profit utility companies, which typically operate as government-sanctioned but regulated monopolies, or private defense contractors, which often have no competitors (e.g., only the Electric Boat company builds submarines for the U.S. Navy) or operate for security reasons on no-bid, cost-plus contracts.

Economies vary, then, by the extent to which, and the reasons that, segments of them are, for various reasons, set aside from market forces. These are ultimately political decisions regarding what aspects of an economy should be set aside from the market and to what extent. In Western European democracies (especially the Nordic states), for instance, a much greater portion of their economies are set aside from market forces compared to the United States. In most Western European democracies, medical care and public transportation, for instance, are heavily subsidized. Other segments of the economy may also be, to varying degrees, wholly or partially government administered such as energy and munitions. Among advanced industrialized democracies, the United States until recently was unique in not having some form of government-guaranteed health care. With the passage of the Affordable Health Care Act in 2010, a step was made in that direction with a model for government-guaranteed access to health insurance for most Americans but one that is still mostly market driven and organized through private insurance companies. The passage of this act was intensely contested not only in its particulars but in the role of government in providing access to health care and essentially to what extent, if any, health care should be set aside from ability-to-pay market principles.

There are a variety of ways in which government spending could result in a society that operates on more strictly meritocratic principles. To the extent that access to opportunity to achieve is based on ability to pay, meritocracy is compromised. The most obvious case is education. As we noted in chapter 5, to the extent that access to opportunity is mediated through education, and to the extent that educational opportunities are unequally distributed, meritocracy is compromised. More centralized funding and standards of quality for public schools set by states and the federal government instead of local governments could reduce inequities in educational opportunity. To the extent that government-funded schools were as "good" as private alternatives, the incentive for private retreats from the public school system would be reduced. However, there is great resistance to such proposals because parents want to retain "local control of local schools," and wealthier families often have a vested interest in retaining the advantage of "better" schools located in "better" neighborhoods.

Government could also extend "free" public education beyond secondary schools to include university and professional education. Likewise, opportunities for vocational or trade schools could be publicly funded. The government could also more aggressively fund preschool and after-school programs aimed at making up cultural or social capital deficits among low-income or at-risk children. All of these measures would reduce the nonmerit access to opportunity predicated on ability to pay and thereby foster a more genuinely meritocratic society.

Beyond education, government could provide or improve infrastructure (roads, bridges, sewer and water supply, electrical grids, telecommunication systems, airports, and so on) and other basic services such as health care available to the general public. This would reduce the expenses of lower-income groups in particular who would otherwise have to expend limited resources to gain market access to such services and would detract time and resources that could be directed toward investment in their own human-capital potential. This principle is illustrated by Abraham Maslow's well-known "hierarchy-of-needs" concept. According to Maslow, individuals have a hierarchy of needs that begins with basic subsistence such as food, clothing, and shelter. Maslow further notes that individuals cannot attend to higher-order needs, much less "self-actualization," the highest-order need, until the more basic needs are met. Poor people are essentially "stuck" at lower-order needs and are therefore at a personal-development disadvantage regardless of their individual capacities or potential. Government could intervene in the market by providing such critical basic needs, which would allow lower-income groups to compete with others based more on individual capacities than individual circumstance.

While some forms of government spending could promote meritocracy, other forms violate meritocratic principles. A purely meritocratic society would operate on strict survival-of-the-fittest social Darwinist principles. In such a society, individuals who, for whatever reasons, were "unfit" would not get ahead and in many cases would not even survive. Children, the disabled, the infirm, the elderly, and others with no viable means of support would be on their own. Most modern industrial countries, however, furnish some form of "safety net" to provide for the basic necessities of citizens if they cannot provide for themselves. Such individuals are often referred to as "the deserving poor" since their inability to provide for themselves is beyond their control.

What about individuals who are willing and able to work but are poor nevertheless because they do not have jobs or do not have jobs that provide a living wage? Individuals may be unemployed or underemployed because they are less fit than others (assuming that "fitness" can be determined), or they may be unemployed or underemployed simply as the result of market forces. If the market itself does not provide enough jobs that pay at least a subsistence wage for all those who are able and willing to work, governments could intervene in the market by providing direct financial assistance to such individuals or by becoming "the employer of last resort," putting people to work, presumably on public works projects that could benefit society as a whole.

Government's spending is limited by the amount of revenue it can raise or borrow. In this way, government tax and spending policies are inextricably linked. How government revenue is expended affects both the extent of inequality in society and prospects for mobility. In general, societies with more progressive tax systems, along with more extensive welfare programs, have lower levels of inequality and higher rates of social mobility, while those with more regressive tax systems, along with less extensive welfare programs, have higher levels of inequality and less social mobility (Dreier 2007).

Affirmative Action

Discrimination remains a major source of nonmerit inequality. For America to extend true equality of opportunity to all, discrimination would have to be eliminated, or at least significantly reduced. Several specific reform strategies could be pursued to this end. Antidiscrimination laws could be strengthened and more effectively enforced. Additional resources could be made available for individuals to pursue complaints. Punishments for demonstrated acts of discrimination could be made more certain and consequential. Beyond mere passive nondiscrimination, more proactive measures designed to reduce the effects of past discrimination and prevent future discrimination could be more aggressively pursued. Such proactive measures generally fall under the label of what has become known as affirmative action.

Like antidiscrimination laws, the goal of affirmative action policies is to make equal opportunity a reality for members of groups that have historically been the objects of discrimination. Unlike antidiscrimination laws, which provide remedies to which individuals can appeal after they have suffered discrimination, affirmative action policies aim to keep discrimination from occurring and compensate for injustices incurred in the past. Affirmative action can prevent discrimination by replacing practices that are discriminatory, either by intent or default, with practices that safeguard against discrimination. Rather than a single policy that involves the same procedures, affirmative action comprises a complex set of policies and practices, including admission standards for schools and universities, guidelines for hiring practices, and procedures for the granting of government contracts. Affirmative action grew out of civil rights laws, presidential executive orders, court cases, federal implementation efforts, and voluntary human resource practices implemented by employers. Each has its own characteristics and complex history (Reskin 1998; Waters 2012).

In a series of affirmative action cases, the U.S. Supreme Court has progressively limited affirmative action policies and practices. The most extreme and controversial form of affirmative action, using quotas or set-asides as a means to increase diversity in schools and workplaces, was ruled unconstitutional in 1978 by the U.S. Supreme Court in the landmark *Regents of the University of California v. Bakke* case regarding admission practices at the UC Davis Medical School. Quotas or set-asides were in practice rarely used. More typically, affirmative action programs have sought to promote efforts to include members of groups that have been historically excluded from consideration for school admissions, jobs, and promotions. With such efforts, there are no requirements or quotas to hire members of certain "protected classes" or disadvantaged groups. Instead, in the context of proactive affirmative action, efforts are made to make the admission, hiring, or promotion processes as open as possible to encourage members of disadvantaged groups to apply. For instance, many jobs were formerly filled without public advertisement through word-of-mouth networks, which favor the already privileged and reproduce the demographic and social profile of existing occupants of such positions (social capital). To counter these exclusionary tendencies, the Equal Employment Opportunity Commission put requirements in place for some jobs that job notices be posted in widely publicly accessible outlets before positions can be filled. Job listings may specifically invite members of disadvantaged groups to apply (using language such as "women and minorities are encouraged to apply"), and other extra recruitment efforts (e.g., advertising in outlets targeted to such groups) may be used to encourage such applicants to apply. Human resources departments may demographically analyze applicant pools to ensure that female and minority representation in those pools is reasonably in proportion to the pool of potential applicants in the local or general population. Once such pools are established, hiring decisions are then based exclusively on merit. If a nonminority is recommended for hire in a unit or organization in which minorities are proportionally underrepresented, under affirmative action policies, hiring agents may be required to indicate how that candidate's qualifications are superior to the highest-ranked minority candidate in the pool.

In 2003, in an important test case involving admission procedures in use at the University of Michigan, the U.S. Supreme Court reasserted the ban against quotas but condoned the use of race as a factor in admission decisions. Specifically, race may be used to pursue a legitimate institutional goal of diversity of access, not in any across-the-board fashion but in conjunction with other factors. That is, race can be one consideration for admission to promote diverse student populations but cannot be used as the single determinative factor. All of these efforts are intended to ensure that members of formerly excluded groups are given full consideration for educational and occupational positions, but there is no requirement to hire and no quota to fill.

Opponents of affirmative action argue that such programs constitute "reverse discrimination." Affirmative action has been characterized as a set of highly discriminatory policies and practices in hiring and promotion decisions, resulting in the selection of less-qualified minorities over more-qualified white males. Empirical evidence, however, shows that there is not now nor has there ever been a widespread pattern of reverse discrimination and that white males continue to be advantaged in gaining access to most good jobs (Stainback and Tomaskovic-Devey 2012).

Such reverse discrimination, if and when it occurs, does indeed violate strict meritocratic principles. In order to have a strictly meritocratic society, *all* forms of discrimination and nonmerit preference "reversal" would need to be eliminated. In addition to those forms discussed above, for instance, commonly used nonmerit preferences for such categories as seniority, legacy status, or veteran preference would also be disallowed. Preference based on seniority is not in itself a measure of merit, although organizations may consider such privileges of rank as reward for prior service. Similarly, legacy preference in admissions often used in elite universities (preference given to those whose relatives previously attended) is nonmerit based and indeed tends to reproduce existing social and demographic profiles. Although a grateful nation may want to extend preference in hiring to veterans for prior service rendered, veteran status in itself does not qualify as a merit consideration.

Although Americans are generally in favor of the ideal of equality of opportunity, they are often opposed to affirmative action attempts to achieve that outcome. The objection is not so much against affirmative action in principle but against specific provisions of some forms of affirmative action, especially those that target minorities and women. As a result, race- or sex-based affirmative action programs are a "hard sell" to the American public, especially during periods of economic slowdown or decline (Wilson 1987; Conley 1999). This is further complicated in the case of race-based programs by increasing rates of racial intermarriage, increasingly blurred racial boundaries, and increasing multiracial identities (Winant 2012). One potential for reform, then, is to develop affirmative action programs for the economically underprivileged, regardless of race or sex. Such an essentially class-based affirmative action program may be more politically palatable and overcome many of the objections related to charges of reverse discrimination. An economically means-tested affirmative action policy using net worth as a criterion of eligibility would promote asset accumulation, which would clearly improve children's chances for educational and occupational success, as well as for intergenerational wealth transfers, which we have argued provide a nonmerit basis for opportunity. Racial minorities, disproportionately represented among the economically underprivileged, would therefore disproportionately, but not exclusively, benefit from such arrangements. Such programs, however, would not fully take into account the uniquely damaging effects of the cumulative *combination* of class *and* racial disadvantage.

Asset Accumulation

To lack capital in a capitalist society is to be at a distinct economic and social disadvantage. As we have seen, compared to income inequality, the extent of wealth inequality in the United States is much greater, involves much higher total sums, persists much more both intra- and intergenerationally, and is ultimately more consequential for economic well-being. Because so much wealth is transferred intergenerationally either through bequests or inter vivos gifts, the distribution of wealth in American society compared to income is also much more related to inheritance and much less related to merit.

Sociologists Dalton Conley (1999) and Thomas Shapiro (2004) have presented persuasive evidence that the basic and persisting economic problem for minorities especially is their continuing inability to accumulate wealth. They point out that African Americans may have improving educational and occupational opportunities but have not made much economic progress because at every educational, income, and occupational level, they have fewer assets than white Americans. And, as we have seen, those gaps have increased in the wake of the Great Recession. As Shapiro puts it, "Family wealth and inheritance cancel gains in classrooms, workplaces, and paychecks, worsening racial equality" (2004, 183).

Asset-building policies, such as government assistance for home purchases or starting and expanding businesses as well as tax incentives targeted at those of modest means to encourage savings and investments, could help stimulate wealth creation. Shapiro, for instance, proposes government-subsidized children's savings accounts, individual-development accounts, and down-payment accounts as means to build assets for low-income populations. Shapiro proposes the establishment of an initial $1,000 savings account for every child born in the United States provided by government funds. Additional payments into these accounts by families could be matched by government funds. Account holders could use accumulated funds to defray college costs, make down payments for first-time home buyers, start businesses, or, if still active, supplement retirement or pass on to the next generation. Similar accounts could be set up for low-income adults as individual-development accounts aided by tax credits or matching public or private funds. Shapiro further suggests programs to stimulate home ownership, the major form of wealth equity for most Americans. For asset-poor families, savings from tax credits on rate payments could be set aside along with personal savings to be used for down payments for first-time home buyers.

Shapiro notes that such government-sponsored programs would be available to all Americans but would disproportionately benefit minorities, who are currently disproportionately asset poor. Shapiro notes that government-sponsored policies that stimulate asset accumulation for asset building are not new. He points to policies and programs such as the Homestead Act, the GI Bill and Veterans Administration home loans, mortgage deductions, tax deductions for IRA accounts, and other policies that previously helped middle-class families accumulate assets but were largely unavailable to the poor and especially poor minorities. Finally, Shapiro notes that such asset-building initiatives are helping to build up the idea of a "stakeholder society" in which individuals and families feel economically vested in all aspects of society. For instance, research shows that families with more assets also have greater marital stability, less domestic abuse, and better school performance for children.

Asset-building programs could therefore be seen as investments in the future that could in the long run realize net savings to society as a whole by avoiding costs associated with a variety of social problems now closely linked to poverty. As with other government-sponsored programs, however, funding would need to come from public sources, and resistance to such support is likely. Alternatively, funds for such programs could also come from private philanthropic sources, to which we now turn our attention.

Noblesse Oblige

Noblesse oblige has its roots in feudal Europe, where it referred to the sense of obligation that the nobility had toward the peasantry. The difference between slave societies and estate societies is that slaves had no rights, but peasants did. Although the peasantry did not own land in its own name and had to forfeit to the nobility all but a meager portion of their crops, the nobility, in exchange for the loyalty of its subjects, was expected to provide the peasants with land to work, protection from thieves and invaders, and occasional collective celebrations, especially at harvest. These expectations were implicit rather than explicit—a set of moral obligations embedded in the culture of the group. These felt obligations of the rich toward the poor became known as noblesse oblige, a term that has its modern-day equivalent in the view that "to whom much is given, much is expected."

In modern times, noblesse oblige essentially means a combination of philanthropy and a desire to "give something back" through public service or service to humanity. Both philanthropy and progressive taxation are possible ways to reduce levels of inequality and restore more equity to the system, that is, to reduce the nonmerit effects of inheritance across generations. The primary difference between the two is that the former is voluntary, and those who benefit are selected by the giver, whereas the latter is nonvoluntary, and the objects of beneficence are not chosen by the giver. Through charitable giving, the wealthy can control who receives their largesse, the purposes for which they might receive it, the amounts given, and the pace at which amounts are given.

Conservatives tend to favor this type of giving. The control that it affords can be seen as an extension of individual property rights—the right to dispose of one's property as one sees fit. Private donations at the local level as a means of addressing social problems are preferred by conservatives to public taxation at the national level. President George Herbert Walker Bush, for instance, emphasized the importance of an array of private charitable organizations, which he characterized as "a thousand points of light," as the preferred alternative to government programs. Later, his son, President George Walker Bush, emphasized faith-based organizations, in particular, as means to address social needs in the community.

Liberals, on the other hand, are less inclined to rely on private charities to address social needs. They contend that much of this "charity" is directed toward the rich themselves in the form of support for the arts and "highbrow" culture, exclusive boarding school and Ivy League alma maters, and other upper-class institutions, thereby extending rather than reducing the degree of inequality. Liberals further contend that the piecemeal approach of local charities is woefully inadequate to deal with large-scale systemic problems affecting the nation as a whole.

Compared to other industrialized nations, Americans are relatively generous in donating money to charitable causes (Brooks 2005). Almost nine out of ten Americans report making contributions to charity, and this level of giving appears steady overtime (Hodgkinson 2004, 259). In 2009, for instance, Americans gave $303.8 billion to charities, with 75 percent coming from individuals and the remainder from foundations (13 percent), charitable bequests (8 percent), and corporations (5 percent) (U.S. Census Bureau 2012b). Among funds allocated, religious causes received 50 percent, education 20 percent, human services 4 percent, public/societal benefits 11 percent, health 11 percent, arts and culture 6 percent, international charities 4 percent, and environmental projects 3 percent (U.S. Census Bureau 2012b).

It is difficult to assess the total impact of such giving on assisting the poorest segments of society, reducing inequality, and increasing the prospects for equality of opportunity. Many charitable dollars are given to very worthy causes but are not targeted to the poor. For instance, the vast portion of donations to religious organizations—by far the largest recipient of charitable funds—goes to support the internal operations of such organizations. Religious groups vary in the degree to which their resources are otherwise directed toward social services and "outreach" ministries, with traditional conservative churches and denominations providing the least and more liberal churches and denominations the most (Hall 2005).

Despite the apprehensions of liberals, at least some of this largesse eventually makes its way to the truly needy. Robber barons of the Gilded Age, feeling pressure to justify growing accumulations of wealth, extended charitable giving to the poor to the national level, often creating charitable foundations in their names dedicated to helping those less fortunate than themselves. More recently, billionaires Bill Gates (Microsoft), Warren Buffett (Berkshire Hathway), and Mark Zuckerberg (Facebook) have pledged to eventually give the bulk of their fortunes to charity. However, with some such notable exceptions, there appears to have been a general historical decline in the ethos of noblesse oblige among those who have amassed new fortunes since the end of World War II (Hall and Marcus 1998).

We argue that diversity of access to opportunity is a legitimate institutional goal. Thus, if philanthropy is directed to the poor in significant amounts, then it does have at least the potential to reduce both the distance from the top to the bottom and the nonmerit advantages of inheritance. For instance, if those who inherit great fortunes were to feel greater social pressure to voluntarily donate large amounts of those fortunes in ways that increased *opportunity* for the less fortunate (not direct transfers or handouts), then such philanthropy would indeed produce such effects. One potential "solution" to the problem of inequality, then, is to encourage a greater sense of noblesse oblige among the wealthy in ways that would help level the playing field (e.g., providing scholarships to needy students), simultaneously increasing the potential for meritocracy while decreasing the nonmerit intergenerational advantages of inheritance.

Labor Unions and Poor People's Movement

The United States has a long and noteworthy history of social reform movements. The country itself was born in "revolution" as a movement against a dominant colonial power. Since then, other reform movements have helped to bring about more equality of opportunity, including the labor movement of the 1930s, the civil rights movement, the women's liberation movement, and the gay liberation movement. Each of these movements, with varying degrees of success, has reduced discrimination and exclusion and has made the system more meritocratic than it was previously. Reform movements tend to draw their power from a combination of withholding services (e.g., strikes or boycotts) and mobilizing voting support for their cause (Piven 2008).

While minority movements in the United States have been ascendant in the past several decades, the labor movement has been in decline. Union membership as a proportion of the labor force has fallen off sharply from a high of 35 percent during the mid-1950s to 11.3 percent in 2012, representing a ninety-seven-year low (Greenhouse 2013). This is significant because the labor movement has been responsible for a variety of reforms that have reduced inequality and enhanced the quality of life for workers that we now take for granted, such as the eight-hour workday, the two-day weekend, paid holidays, minimum wage, and restrictions on child labor. During the height of industrialization in America in the middle of the twentieth century, labor unions in the United States helped check the power of corporations over workers in what was sometimes described as a "countervailing" force. Without strong worker unions, it is much easier for employing organizations to "divide and conquer" individual workers and take a larger portion of productivity in the form of profits, dividends, and management salaries. Several factors have accelerated the decline of unions in the United States, especially deindustrialization and globalization. In the United States, unions have not represented workers as a whole as much as workers in specific industries and trades. The most heavily unionized segment of the labor force was manufacturing, and as manufacturing declined, so did unions. Globalization also has weakened unions, giving corporations alternative sources of cheap and unorganized labor overseas. Finally, corporations have aggressively resisted unions, forcing concessions and givebacks and systematically discouraging the formation of unions in the workplace. More recently, unions have increased representation in arenas of the labor force not traditionally highly unionized, such as public workers and service workers. Public-sector workers, for instance, now have a rate of union membership (35.9 percent) more than five times higher than that of private-sector workers (6.6 percent) (Greenhouse 2013). However, it is illegal for most public workers to strike, and the right of public unions even to collectively bargain has been challenged and is an especially contentious issue.

Reversing the decline of unions and restoring more balance to management–labor negotiations could potentially help to make the system more equal and more equitable than it is. Another version of strengthening the relative power of workers is to establish more worker owned and controlled businesses. This is a challenge since most unions and workers do not have the resources to buy businesses outright; indeed, most employee-owned business are acquired as high-risk rescues when businesses are failing and workers would otherwise lose their jobs. Unions could also be strengthened by organizing across industries and work settings and contributing to global rules and guidelines for fair labor and market practices.

Other social movements in America have confronted issues of race, gender, and sexual orientation with varying degrees of success. While not fully resolved, they are nevertheless on the political radar screen and are now part of the mainstream political discourse. The primary justification for reform that gives these movements both their energy and their moral purpose is that discrimination unrelated to ability to do the job violates deeply held American values of fair play, equality of opportunity, and meritocracy.

What has not been fully confronted as yet and has not generally been part of mainstream political discourse is the issue of class. Whether the inherent contradiction between inheritance and meritocracy can be addressed politically in America through a people's reform movement remains to be seen. America appeared to be on the edge of directly confronting class issues during the buildup to the Great Depression, but ameliorative reforms of the New Deal era seemed to ease these concerns. As with the Great Depression, the Great Recession reached deeply into the middle class, and class issues began to surface. This was most evident with the rise of the Occupy Wall Street (OWS) movement. Starting in September 2011, protesters convened in Zuccotti Park located in the Wall Street financial district, drawing attention to economic inequality and specifically banks and investors that had triggered the recession. The OWS slogan, "We are the 99 percent," referred to the top 1 percent of the population in which wealth is highly concentrated compared to everyone else. OWS groups sprung up in many other cities in the United States and around the world. The initial occupation of Zuccotti Park ended in December 2011 when the New York City Police forced occupiers to leave the park, presumably because of health and sanitation concerns. The movement itself has been intentionally nonhierarchal, depriving the movement of formal leadership and hindering its long-term effectiveness. Since the closing of the park, the movement has dissipated, and it remains to be seen if it can be sustained. It did have the effect, however, of bringing national attention to class issues in a public forum. If inequality continues to increase, a crisis of legitimacy could spark new class movements and create additional grassroots pressure for reform.

A Note on Other Economic and Political Reforms

In addition to the options discussed above as possible ways to decrease inequality in general and create more equitable conditions in society, other reforms in the organization of economic and political institutions themselves might also be considered. Corporations could be reformed in such a way to make them more publically accountable and more socially responsible. This could include changes in corporate governance that foster greater public transparency, accountability, and inclusiveness; more aggressive antitrust enforcement; more scrutiny of foreign investments; more oversight of public health and safety issues and the long-term integrity of the environment; and greater restrictions on risk taking where the public interest or tax dollars are involved. Political institutions could also be reformed in ways that would make them more genuinely democratic. Chief among such reforms would be reducing the influence of money in politics. Measures could also be taken to make elections more genuinely competitive by eliminating political gerrymandering and by making it easier rather than harder to vote. The intent of such reforms would be to make economic and political institutions more responsive to the general public and less captive to the narrow interests of the wealthiest segments of society.

IS A MERITOCRATIC SOCIETY NECESSARILY A FAIR AND JUST SOCIETY?

For all the reasons discussed in this book, true equality of opportunity is highly unlikely. The system, however, could be made much fairer, much more open, and much more meritocratic than it is. Most Americans, sometimes grudgingly, acknowledge that because of discrimination on the bases of sex, race, creed, or other characteristics irrelevant to individual ability, the system has not always been entirely fair or just. The assumption is, however, that these forms of discrimination are rapidly being eliminated and that their ultimate elimination will finally bring about true equality of opportunity. But, as we have demonstrated in this book, even if all such forms of discrimination and their residual effects were somehow miraculously eliminated, we would still not have genuine equality of opportunity or a system entirely based on merit. Other nonmerit factors, including inheritance and patterns of social and economic organization that are external yet constraining to individuals, operate to modify and reduce the effects of individual merit on life chances.

In the abstract at least, Americans enthusiastically embrace the principle of proportional contribution; that is, one should get out of the system what one puts into it. According to this formulation, individuals should have an equal opportunity to get ahead, and getting ahead should be exclusively based on individual merit. But what does this mean in practice? As political scientist Richard Longoria has pointed out,

> As long as the family and class background have an influence on a person's outcome, the distribution of social goods are not distributed entirely on merit. In its ideal, it is only after these factors are eliminated that the distribution of

goods and positions can be based on merit. In short, the correlation between one's social origins and one's outcome in life is zero in a meritocracy. (2009, 4)

In a purely meritocratic system, therefore, parents would not be able to engage in any practice that would give advantage to any of their children not available to all others. Parents, for instance, could not use their personal resources to send children to private schools, take children on vacations that may have educational benefit, pay for private tutors, or rescue children who falter because of their own incompetence or inadequacies. Parents would not be permitted to bequeath an inheritance to children or indeed to provide them with any resource not equally available to all other children. As political philosopher Adam Swift (2005, 269) has pointed out, perhaps this could only be accomplished through the establishment of universal state-sponsored orphanages that all children would be required to attend. Since it is unlikely that parents would voluntarily surrender their children to such institutions or submit to restrictions that would prevent them from naturally trying to do everything they could to provide their children with every assistance possible, it is unlikely that a pure merit system could ever be established. And herein lies the great American contradiction. Americans desperately want to believe that the system is fair and that everyone has an equal chance to get ahead. At the same time, we also emphatically endorse the right of individuals, with minimal state intervention, to dispose freely of their property as they personally see fit. But we simply cannot have it both ways. Inheritance and meritocracy are zero-sum principles of distribution; the more there is of one, the less there is of the other.

Furthermore, for a truly meritocratic system to operate, the influence of all other nonmerit factors identified in previous chapters would also need to be reduced to zero, including luck. To the extent that valued resources are distributed by random chance, they are not distributed by merit. As we have seen, luck comes in many forms, including being in the right place at the right time. As Swift correctly points out, "Taking equality of opportunity seriously means that people should not have better or worse prospects in life than one another because of things for which they are not responsible" (2005, 263). Luck could also refer to the genetic dice roll that provides individuals with whatever innate capacities they have over which they have no personal control. Even allowing genetic endowment as part of "merit," the extent to which forces beyond one's control influence life outcomes is substantial. While genuine equality of opportunity and achievement based only on merit are probably not possible, what is less well acknowledged by both the Left and the Right is that they may be neither entirely just nor desirable. British sociologist Michael Young, in his fictional satire *The Rise of the Meritocracy* (1961), envisions a society based truly on merit. In this futuristic society, individuals are assigned their place in society exclusively based on a system of rigid tests. Those who score highest on the tests fill the most important positions and get the most rewards. A strict hierarchy of merit is created and maintained. What at first seems like an eminently fair and just system in practice degenerates into a ruthless regime. The meritocratic elite feels righteously superior to all those below it and holds those at the bottom of the system in utter contempt. The meritocratic elite, secure in its lofty status, exercises complete and total domination of society. Those at the bottom of the system are incapable of challenging the elite and are permanently deprived of the capacity to rise up against their oppressors.

One possible advantage of a nonmeritocratic society is that at any time, for whatever combination of reasons, at least some of those at the top of the system are less capable and competent than at least some of those at the bottom. Such discrepancies should inspire humility in those at the top and hope and dignity in those at the bottom. But this can only happen if it is widely acknowledged that inheritance, luck, and a variety of other circumstances beyond the merit of individuals are important in affecting where one ends up in the system. This is why the *myth* of meritocracy is harmful: it provides an incomplete explanation for success and failure, mistakenly exalting the rich and unjustly condemning the poor. We may always have the rich and the poor among us, but we need neither exalt the former nor condemn the latter.

REFERENCES

Brooks, Arthur C. 2005. Introduction to *Gifts of Time and Money: The Role of Charity in America's Communities*, ed. Arthur C. Brooks, 1–9. Lanham, MD: Rowman & Littlefield.

College Board. 2012. *Trends in College Pricing: 2012*. College Board. http://trends. collegeboard.org/sites/default/files/college-pricing-2012-full-report_0.pdf (accessed November 13, 2012).

Conley, Dalton. 1999. *Being Black, Living in the Red: Race, Wealth, and Social Policy in America*. Berkeley: University of California Press.

Dreier, Peter. 2007. "The United States in a Comparative Perspective." *Contexts*, Summer, 38–46.

Gendall, Murray. 2008. "Older Workers: Increasing Their Labor Force Participation and Hours of Work." *Monthly Labor Review*, January, 41–54.

Greenhouse, Steven. 2013. "Share of the Work Force in a Union Falls to a 97-Year Low, 11.3%." *New York Times*, January 23, 2013. http://www.nytimes.com/2013/01/24/business/union-membership-drops-despite-job-growth.html?pagewanted=print (accessed January 24, 2013).

Hall, Peter Dobkin. 2005. "Religion, Philanthropy, Service, and Civic Engagement in Twentieth-Century America." In *Gifts of Time and Money: The Role of Charity in America's Communities*, ed. Arthur C. Brooks, 159–83. Lanham, MD: Rowman & Littlefield.

Hall, Peter Dobkin, and George E. Marcus. 1998. "Why Should Men Leave Great Fortunes to Their Children? Dynasty and Inheritance in America." In *Inheritance and Wealth in America*, ed. Robert K. Miller Jr. and Stephen J. McNamee, 139–71. New York: Plenum Press.

Hodgkinson, Virginia A. 2004. "Individual Giving by Household." In *Philanthropy in America: A Comprehensive Historical Encyclopedia*, vol. 2, ed. Dwight F. Burlingame, 256–59. Santa Barbara, CA: ABC-CLIO.

Johnson, Barry W., and Martha Britton Eller. 1998. "Federal Taxation of Inheritance and Wealth Transfers." In *Inheritance and Wealth in America*, ed. Robert K. Miller Jr. and Stephen J. McNamee, 61–90. New York: Plenum Press.

Longoria, Richard T. 2009. *Meritocracy and Americans' Views on Distributive Justice*. Lanham, MD: Lexington Books.

Massey, Douglas S. 2007. *Categorically Unequal: The American Stratification System*. New York: Sage.

Mishel, Lawrence, Jared Bernstein, and Sylvia Allegretto. 2007. *The State of Working America: 2006–2007*. Ithaca, NY: Cornell University Press.

Mishel, Lawrence, Josh Bivens, Elise Gould, and Heidi Shierholz. 2012. *The State of Working America*. 12th ed. Ithaca, NY: Cornell University Press.

Morin, Rich. 2009. "Most Middle-Aged Adults Are Rethinking Retirement Plans: The Threshold Generation." Pew Research Center Publication No. 1234, May 28. Washington, DC: Pew Research Center.

Mortgage Bankers Association. 2008. "Delinquencies and Foreclosures Increase in Latest MBA Delinquency Survey." Mortgage Bankers Association, September 5. http://www.mortgagebankers.org/NewsandMedia/PressCenter/64769.htm (accessed February 23, 2009).

Phillips, Kevin. 2008. *Bad Money: Reckless Finance, Failed Politics and the Global Crisis of American Capitalism*. New York: Viking.

Piven, Frances Fox. 2008. "Can Power from Below Change the World?" *American Sociological Review* 73 (February): 1–14.

Reskin, Barbara F. 1998. *The Realities of Affirmative Action in Employment*. Washington, DC: American Sociological Association.

Schor, Juliet. 1998. *The Overspent American: Why We Want What We Don't Need*. New York: Basic Books.

Shapiro, Thomas M. 2004. *The Hidden Cost of Being African American: How Wealth Perpetuates Inequality*. New York: Oxford.

Stainback, Kevin, and Donald Tomaskovic-Devey. 2012. *Documenting Desegregation: Racial and Gender Segregation in Private-Sector Employment since the Civil Rights Act*. New York: Sage.

Sullivan, Theresa, Elizabeth Warren, and Jay Lawrence Westbrook. 2000. *The Fragile Middle Class: Americans in Debt*. New Haven, CT: Yale University Press.

Swift, Adam. 2005. "Justice, Luck, and the Family: Intergenerational Transmission of Economic Advantage from a Normative Perspective." In *Unequal Chances: Family Background and Economic Success*, ed. Samuel Bowles, Herbert Gintis, and Melissa Osborne Groves, 256–76. New York: Sage.

Toossi, Mitra. 2009. "Labor Force Projections to 2018: Older Workers Staying More Active." *Monthly Labor Review*, November, 30–51. http://www.bls.gov/opub/mlr/2009/11/mlr200911.pdf (accessed November 13, 2012).

U.S. Census Bureau. 2005. "Fertility of American Women: June 2004." *Current Population Reports*, December. Washington, DC: U.S. Government Printing Office.

———. 2012a. *Statistical Abstract of the United States*. Washington, DC: U.S. Government Printing Office, table 83.

———. 2012b. *Statistical Abstract of the United States*. Washington, DC: U.S. Government Printing Office, table 580.

U.S. Department of Agriculture. 2012. *Expenditures on Children by Families, 2011*. Center for Nutrition Policy and Promotion, Miscellaneous Publication No. 1528-2011. http://www.cnpp.usda.gov/Publications/CRC/crc2011.pdf (accessed November 13, 2012).

U.S. Department of Commerce. 2012. "Table 2.1, Personal Income and Its Disposition. National Income and Product Accounts Table." Bureau of Economic Analysis. http://bea.gov/scb/pdf/2012/08%20August/NIPA%20Tables/0812_income_outlays.pdf (accessed January 8, 2013).

U.S. Department of Education. 2012. *College Student Employment (Indicator 37-2012)*. http://nces.ed.gov/programs/coe/indicator_csw.asp (accessed November 10, 2012).

U.S. Department of Labor. 2011. *Women in the Labor Force: A Databook*. Washington, DC: U.S. Government Printing Office. http://www.bls.gov/cps/wlf-databook-2011.pdf (accessed November 4, 2012).

Warren, Elizabeth, and Amelia Warren Tyagi. 2003. *The Two-Income Trap: Why Middle-Class Mothers and Fathers Are Going Broke*. New York: Basic Books.

Waters, Mary C. 2012. "Racial and Ethnic Diversity and Public Policy." In *The New Guilded Age: The Critical Inequality Debates of Our Time*, ed. David B. Grusky and Tamar Kricheli-Katz, 230–46. Stanford, CA: Stanford University Press.

Wilkinson, Richard, and Kate Pickett. 2009. *The Spirit Level: Why Greater Equality Makes Societies Stronger*. New York: Bloomsbury Press.

Wilson, William Julius. 1987. *The Truly Disadvantaged: The Inner City, the Underclass, and Public Policy*. Chicago: University of Chicago Press.

Winant, Howard. 2012. "A Dream Deferred: Toward a U.S. Racial Future." In *The New Gilded Age: The Critical Inequality Debates of Our Time*, ed. David B. Grusky and Tamar Kricheli-Katz, 211–29. Stanford, California: Stanford University Press.

Wolff, Edward C. 2002. *Top Heavy: Increasing Inequality of Wealth in America and What Can Be Done about It*. New York: New Press.

Wolff, Edward N., Lindsay A. Owens, and Esra Burak. 2012. "How Much Wealth Was Destroyed in the Great Recession?" In *The Great Recession*, ed. David B. Grusky, Bruce Western, and Christopher Wimer, 127–58. New York: Sage.

Young, Michael. 1961. *The Rise of the Meritocracy, 1870–2033: An Essay on Education and Equality*. Baltimore: Penguin.

Notes

2. ON BEING MADE OF THE RIGHT STUFF

1. Between 1961 and 1969, NASA conducted a similar, but much less publicized, program for women pilots. Thirteen of these women were selected after two rounds of the same testing that the male Mercury astronauts had passed earlier. The men were put through a third round of testing, but NASA prevented the women from taking the third round of tests, and the program was suddenly dropped, essentially negating any prospect that any of the women would be included in NASA's space program regardless of their individual abilities (Ackmann 2003).

2. The phrase "the right stuff" was used by Tom Wolfe in a 1979 book of the same title in reference to flight pioneers and the selection of NASA's first American astronauts. The book became the basis of a popular 1983 movie also of the same title.

3. Human IQ is distributed normally only by definition. The standard distribution of IQ scores is, by definition, "normal." We don't really know how intelligence is distributed in "nature"—it is only distributed this way because the tests are constructed to produce normal distributions.

4. In American sociology, for instance, three of the most famous such individuals are George Herbert Mead (1863–1931) at the University of Chicago, whose work was seen as the inspiration for the symbolic interactionist perspective in sociology; George Casper Homans (1910–1989) at Harvard University, who was a pioneer in the development of social-exchange theory; and David Riesman (1909–2002), also of Harvard, who wrote the best-selling book of all time in the history of American sociology, *The Lonely Crowd*. Not only did Mead and Riesman not have PhDs, but neither was trained as a sociologist. Mead was a philosopher whose ideas attracted the attention of sociologists. Riesman was trained as a lawyer but became interested in social issues. Homans was trained as a sociologist but never earned a PhD, which he considered nothing more than a "status symbol." Despite the lack of this journeyman's credential, Homans became an important sociologist at America's most elite university and even served a term as president of the American Sociological Association.

6. BEING IN THE RIGHT PLACE AT THE RIGHT TIME

1. States coded "Northeast" include Connecticut, Maine, Massachusetts, New Hampshire, New Jersey, New York, Pennsylvania, Rhode Island, and Vermont. States coded "South"

include Alabama, Arkansas, Delaware, Florida, Georgia, Kentucky, Louisiana, Maryland, Mississippi, North Carolina, Oklahoma, South Carolina, Tennessee, Texas, Virginia, and West Virginia, and the District of Columbia. States coded "Midwest" include Illinois, Indiana, Iowa, Kansas, Michigan, Minnesota, Missouri, Nebraska, North Dakota, Ohio, South Dakota, and Wisconsin. States coded "West" include Alaska, Arizona, California, Colorado, Hawaii, Idaho, Montana, Nevada, New Mexico, Oregon, Utah, Washington, and Wyoming.

8. AN UNLEVEL PLAYING FIELD

1. It is sometimes difficult to distinguish discrimination based on religious identity from that based on ethnicity because of the considerable overlap of religion and ethnicity. However, it should be clear that Mormons are not an ethnic group. Those who converted to Mormonism included immigrants from several European nations, especially England and the Scandinavian countries. Similarly, Catholics have never represented a single ethnic group but include Germans, Irish, Italians, and other Europeans, who, while enormously different in national and cultural backgrounds, all shared one important characteristic in the eyes of the Protestant majority—they were Catholics. Jews are not really a religious group but are best considered an ethnic group. Jews migrated from several different regions and nations of Europe. But to dominant-group Christians, it mattered little that a Jew might be a German, or a Pole, or a Ukrainian—what mattered was that Jews were not Christians. Finally, "Middle Easterners" are a diverse aggregate of numerous nationalities and religions. In Iraq alone, for example, there are Muslim Shiites, Muslim Sunnis, and Kurds, to name only the three largest groups. Of course, in Israel, there are Jews, Palestinians (Muslims), and Christians.

9. GROWING INEQUALITY IN THE TWENTY-FIRST CENTURY

1. Middle income is defined as a before-tax income of between $45,800 and $77,100.
2. This includes average costs of tuition, fees, and room and board.
3. Percentages are rounded to the nearest whole percent.

Index

Adams, James Truslow, 2
affirmative action, 38, 115–116, 229–232
Affordable Health Care Act, 61, 227
African Americans: culture-of-poverty
    theory, 29; discrimination experiences,
    188, 190, 211; education issues, 81,
    186–188, 232; Great Recession,
    affecting, 168, 232; income inequality,
    182; inner-city neighborhoods, moving
    out of, 81, 142; IQ tests and, 24, 25;
    language pronunciation, 191; police
    interaction, 185; segregation, 189–190;
    self-employment among, 159; social
    mobility traps, 28; in the South, 141
ageism, 205–206, 217
Alger, Horatio, 5, 129, 148
Allen, Paul, 172–173
American Dream: achievement of, 1, 11,
    13, 129, 222; avenues frowned upon,
    68, 92, 93, 157; continued belief in,
    217; cultural origins, 9; defined, 2, 4;
    discrimination and, 18–19, 179,
    180–181, 186, 192, 200, 201, 203,
    205–207, 210, 211; education as key,
    101, 105–107, 114, 120, 186, 188;
    home ownership as major component,
    189; lottery winning, achieving
    through, 146; Obama election as
    reaffirmation of, 95; retirement as
    culmination, 14, 205; self-employment
    epitomizing, 153, 216; self-made men

as component, 102–103; taxes and, 226
The American Occupational Structure
    (Blau and Duncan), 107
attitude. *See* right attitude

baby boomers, 15, 56, 63, 140, 220
Baltzell, E. Digby, 64, 68
Bank of America, 168, 190
bankruptcies, 12, 113, 168, 221–222
banks and financial institutions, 12,
    166–167, 237
Beauty Pays: Why Attractive People Are
    Successful (Hamermesh), 208–209
beer and brewing companies, 163–166
Bell, Daniel, 134–135
The Bell Curve: Intelligence and Class
    Structure in American Life (Herrnstein
    and Murray), 24–25, 32
Bellow, Adam, 83–85
Bernhardt, Annette, 139–140
Blau, Peter, 107
Bourdieu, Pierre, 78, 86, 88, 109
bourgeoisie, 157–158
Buffet, Warren, 70, 235
Building Wealth (Thurow), 145
Bush, George H. W., 94, 234
Bush, George W., 94, 95, 234

Calvinism, 3, 5
capitalism: as a continuum, 226;
    entrepreneurial capitalists, 157, 158;

free-market expression, 8, 9; hard work and self-denial as aspects of, 5; human capital, 107; risk, 57, 147, 148; turn-of-the-century capitalists, 36, 163; venture capitalists, 31; wealth inequality in capitalist societies, 232

Carnegie, Andrew, 103, 153

Catholics and Catholicism, 5, 186, 206–207, 244n1

Chambliss, William, 26

charitable giving, 57, 70, 91, 224, 234–235

children: American Dreams for, 11, 13; cost of raising, 219; cultural capital and, 17, 58–59, 86–88, 90, 97, 109, 112, 121; in culture-of-poverty theory, 29–30; discrimination and, 181, 186–187, 188, 191; downward mobility, insulation from, 60–61; education and parental influence, 101–102, 105, 106, 109, 109–113, 114, 116, 216; health issues, 61, 223; as heirs, 16, 49, 51, 55, 56, 57, 59–60, 65, 71, 105, 216; of immigrants, 24; numbers, declining, 197, 217, 218–219, 222; parental occupation, effects on, 51; of the privileged, 58, 66, 68, 89, 110, 113, 121; proposed reforms benefiting, 232, 232–233; in a pure meritocratic system, 239; social class, education affected by, 216; social mobility and, 91, 94

Clinton, Hillary, 95, 200

cognitive elite, 24, 32

Coleman, James S., 78, 113

college: American dream, as part of, 11, 13; aptitude tests, 115, 117; cognitive elect sorted out by, 32; credentialism, 118–120, 136; employment during attendance, 218; enrollment, 103–104, 105; funding accounts, 233; hiring practices, 38–43; income, effects on completion, 114–115; job prospects, 132–134; legacy admissions, 115–116, 231; student debt, 13, 116–117; tracking, effects of, 111–112; types of colleges and social standing, 101–102, 114; the wealthy and, 64, 66, 89

Collins, Randall, 118, 136

Coming Apart: The State of White America, 1960–2010 (Murray), 31–32

competition: capitalism and, 8, 154; destructive vs. constructive forms, 44; discrimination reducing, 18, 179, 181; at elite colleges, 116, 227; foot race metaphor, 49; foreign business competition, 127–128; large corporations discouraging, 18, 163, 166, 171, 174; reforms enhancing, 228, 238; women and, 68, 196, 197, 198

The Competition Paradigm (Rosenau), 44

conflict theory of inequality, 10, 11

corporations, large: American economy, dominating, 154, 174; ascent of, 162–163; competition, discouraging, 18, 163, 166, 171, 174; highly concentrated industries, 163, 164, 165; labor unions and, 128, 236; megamergers, 168–170, 169; reform suggestions, 238; restructuring, 127–129, 148; self-employment affected by, 14, 18, 126; small businesses, vs., 161–162, 171, 216

Countrywide financial corporation, 168, 190

Creating a Class: College Admissions and the Education of Elites (Stevens), 116

credentials: credential underemployment, 134; cultural credentials, 77, 87, 94, 96, 109, 117; importance of, 105–106, 108, 117; inflation of, 14, 118–120, 136; nonvalidated, 183; opportunities to earn, 216

cultural capital: acquisition of, 86–89; defined, 17, 58, 77; discrimination and, 180, 192; educational inequalities, 109, 109–111, 112, 115, 117, 121; elite circles, acceptance into, 64; employers impressed with, 119–120; government programs leveling field, 228; information access, 147; inheritance and, 71, 216; media portrayals, 85; nouveau riche, 90; right attitude, 33; social climbing, 90–94, 97; transmission settings, 89–90; U.S. presidents, exemplifying, 94–96

culture-of-poverty theory, 29–30, 33

debt: as a coping strategy, 221–222; Great Recession, during, 167, 168, 221; housing/mortgage debt, 12, 113; as a liability, 52; student loans, 13, 116–117

democracy, 6, 7–8, 8, 9, 70, 106, 226–227

Democracy in America (de Tocqueville), 7–8

disabled Americans, 203–205, 211, 217

discrimination: affirmative action as a remedy, 229–232; ageism, 205–206, 211; American Dream, affecting, 18–19, 179, 180–181, 186, 192, 200, 201, 203, 205–207, 210, 211; continuing effects of, 216–217, 238; the disabled, experiences of, 203–205, 211, 217; in education, 179, 180–181, 182, 186–188, 191, 207; expansion of opportunity and, 11; heterosexist prejudices, 201–203, 211, 217; in-group solidarity, 81; institutional favoritism, 180, 184, 191; legal and political injustice, 184–186, 191, 200–201; occupational unfairness, 180, 181, 182–183, 188, 191, 195, 200, 203; the physically attractive as favored, 208–210; racial bigotry, 18, 140–141, 180–181, 189, 190–191, 211, 217, 238; reform movements combating, 235–236, 237; religious intolerance, 206–208, 211, 217, 244n1; residential inequity, 188–191; women, experiences of, 9, 18, 180, 183, 191–192, 194–195, 196, 197–198, 199–200

Domhoff, William, 70, 89

Duncan, Otis Dudley, 107

education: affirmative action and, 231, 232; African Americans, educational issues of, 81, 186–188, 232; American Dream, as part of, 101, 105–107, 114, 120, 186, 188; cognitive elite and educational attainment, 24; credentials, importance of, 105–106, 108, 109, 117–120; discrimination affecting, 179, 180–181, 182, 186–188, 191, 207; educational endogamy, 67; government spending on, 226–227, 228; human capital theory, 38, 107; income affected by, 102; individualism, aiding in, 8;

inequalities and, 17, 101–102, 106–107, 109, 111, 112, 114, 117, 121; occupational opportunities, linked to, 17, 101–102, 106, 108, 111, 112–113, 118–120, 132–134, 137, 138, 148–149, 188, 227–228; parental circumstances affecting, 51, 55, 60, 187, 216; school completion, 104; school quality and school funding, 112–113; social/cultural capital and, 77, 79, 85, 91, 94, 96, 109–111, 112, 115, 117, 121; success, as a factor in, 34, 101, 109, 120; teacher salary discrepancies, 142, 143; women and, 192, 218. *See also* college

The Education-Jobs Gap (Livingstone), 134

employment. *See* occupations

endogamy, 66–69

entrepreneurs and entrepreneurialism: American respect for, 18, 153, 154, 174; education vs., 103, 104–105; entrepreneurial capitalists, 157, 158; entrepreneurial traits, 171, 173; franchisees not considered as entrepreneurs, 155; irregular economy, participation in, 156; luck as part of success, 18, 149; random-walk hypothesis, 172; social capital, use of, 79, 85; upward mobility, aiming for, 104, 216. *See also* self-employment

Etcoff, Nancy, 209–210

ethics. *See* moral character

Forbes magazine income listings, 25–26, 55–56, 195

franchises, 155, 170

free-market economy, 8–9, 154

The Frontier in American History (Turner), 9

frontier influence in America, 9, 103, 154

functional theory of inequality, 10

gambling, 146, 147, 148, 156

Gates, Bill, 70, 145, 153, 172–173, 235

Gendall, Murray, 220

Gilded Age, 57, 69, 235

Gini coefficient, 53–54

Gladwell, Malcolm, 35, 138

glass ceiling, 81, 159, 196, 200
government programs: education funding, 117, 226, 228; health care, 227, 228; highway subsidies and suburb development, 12, 142; home ownership, encouraging, 167, 232; land giveaways, 154; the poor as targets of, 128, 184, 229; proposed asset-building policies, 232–233; "thousand points of light" as alternative, 234; transfer payment, 52
Granovetter, Mark, 79–80
Great Depression, 69, 167, 237
Great Recession: African Americans affected by, 168, 232; age discrimination during, 206; class issues resulting from, 237; debt and bankruptcies, rise of, 221; factors leading to, 167–168; home ownership during, 167, 168; mortgage debt as contributor, 12; retirement delays caused by, 220; self-employment increase, 154; white-collar crime leading to, 37

Hamermesh, Daniel S., 208, 210
hard work: beauty achieved through, 210; capitalism, associated with, 5, 6; consumption as reward, 6; as determinant of inequality, 11; increased work hours as a coping strategy, 219–220; modest effects of, 16; self-made men and, 103; as a success factor, 2, 31, 34, 35, 45, 215
health: health care plans, 15, 61, 132, 132–133, 174, 227; older workers, 220; wealth affecting, 16, 58, 61–62, 71, 223
Herrnstein, Richard, 24, 25
hierarchy-of-needs theory, 30, 228
higher education. *See* college
hiring practices, 38–43, 89, 119
Hispanics, 159, 168, 182, 187, 189, 190
Hochschild, Jennifer, 2
hockey player success, 138
Home Advantage (Lareau), 87
home ownership, 11–12, 167, 168, 188–190
homosexuality and discriminatory practices, 201–203, 217
human capital, 38, 107, 108, 125, 133, 228

IBM, 172–173
immigrants, 4, 24, 142, 156, 168, 244n1
individualism: as culturally dominant, 10; democracy, expressed through, 6, 7–8; as greatly valued, 153, 171; immigrants and, 4; as part of the entrepreneurial personality, 171; pioneer spirit reinforcing, 9; through self-employment, 216; self-help books promoting, 32
inequalities: charitable giving as a means of reducing, 234–235; conflict and functional theories of, 10–11; economic inequalities, 1, 24, 32, 55, 71, 217, 223, 237; educational system and, 17, 101–102, 106–107, 109, 111, 112, 114, 117, 121; gender inequality, 200–201; government spending as a factor, 226, 229; ideologies of, 3–4; labor unions working to reduce, 236; matrix of domination, 211; residential inequalities, 188, 189; taxes and, 224–225, 234; in wages and income, 53, 137, 139, 168, 182, 194–195; in wealth, 19, 35, 51–54, 57, 71, 168, 187, 222, 232
inheritance: advantages of wealth inheritance, 16, 57–64, 71; attitudes towards, 1, 65; baby boomers and, 56–57, 63; conflict theories, within, 11; cultural capital and, 86, 93–94, 96; domestic partnerships and, 202; estate and inheritance taxes, 224, 225; of estates, 54, 71; *Forbes* magazine, heirs listed in, 55–56; inequalities, perpetuating, 10, 106, 232; luck and, 18; as a natural right, 225; nepotism and, 83–85; as a nonmerit factor, 215–216, 224, 234, 235, 237, 238, 239, 240; old money and, 64–65; parental motivation, 51, 216; primogeniture, 105; relay race, compared to, 16, 49–50, 71, 215; wealth distribution through, 232; women and inheritance of wealth, 195
In Praise of Nepotism: A Natural History (Bellow), 83–85
An Inquiry into the Nature and Causes of the Wealth of Nations (Smith), 8

integrity, 31, 36
inter vivo transfers, 59–60, 224, 232
investments, economic, 5, 8, 34, 38, 53, 54,
    57, 63, 148, 217, 224–225, 226, 232
IQ and IQ tests, 23–24, 25, 44, 108, 145,
    243n3
irregular economy, 142, 156–157, 160, 174

Jencks, Christopher, 113, 144
jobs. *See* occupations
Jones, Janelle, 132–133

Kildall, Gary, 172–173
Kozol, Jonathan, 112

labor unions, 70, 194, 235–237
Lareau, Annette, 87–88
Lears, Jackson, 147
Lewis, Oscar, 29–30
Livingstone, David W., 134, 136
lookism, 18, 208, 209, 210, 211, 217
lottery, 14, 18, 146, 149
lower class. *See* working class
luck: denial of, 147, 148; with gambling,
    148; getting ahead, as a factor in, 1,
    216, 239–240; lottery and, 146; as a
    nonmerit factor, 216; as part of
    capitalism, 147; in striking it rich, 18,
    149; wealth attainment and, 18,
    144–145, 149

marriage: career interruptions due to, 194;
    marrying into money, 1, 68; the poor
    and, 29, 68–69; sexual discrimination
    and, 201–202, 232; trailing partners and
    hiring practices, 41; upper class and,
    32, 63, 65, 66–67, 68
Marx, Karl, 157
Maslow, Abraham, 30, 228
Massey, Douglas S., 185, 187
Matthew effect, 138
matrix of domination, 211
Medicare, 15, 225
mentors, 40, 78, 81, 183, 196–197
meritocracy: affirmative action and, 230;
    American promotion of merit, 1, 2, 2–3,
    4, 8, 238; coping strategies, 19, 222;
    credentials, lack of as a barrier, 136; as
    a desired outcome, 223; discrimination

as the antithesis of merit, 18–19,
    179–180, 183, 191, 192, 196, 198–199,
    211, 216–217, 229, 231; education as a
    merit filter, 17, 101, 108, 109, 114, 115,
    117, 120, 186, 187, 216; employment
    opportunities, 127, 142, 183;
    entrepreneurial success, 172; fairness of
    the system, 38, 55, 215, 217, 238;
    folklore of, 36; government spending
    and, 227–228; in the hiring process,
    39–43, 45; human capital factors, 38,
    107, 125; income based on merit, 195;
    inheritance as a nonmerit factor, 16,
    49–50, 51, 54, 63–64, 68, 215–216,
    224, 234, 235, 237, 238, 239–240;
    intergenerational wealth transfers, 232;
    legacy preferences as nonmerit based,
    115–116, 231; luck as a nonmerit
    factor, 144, 146, 148, 216, 239–240;
    market trends, 137–138; meritocratic
    aristocracy, 106–107; nepotism as
    nonmeritorious, 83–85; the new elite as
    extra-meritorious, 31; noblesse oblige
    increasing potential for, 235; nonmerit
    factors suppressing merit, 11, 138, 140,
    215, 231; Barack Obama as example of,
    95, 96; the past, reverence for, 65;
    physical attractiveness as a nonmerit
    factor, 208, 210; pure merit system,
    238–239; reform movements and, 236,
    237; self-employment as an expression
    of, 216; social and cultural capital as
    nonmerit factors, 17, 59, 77, 78, 81–82,
    86, 89, 92–93, 94, 97, 216; structural
    mobility and, 60–61; talents and
    abilities of the merit formula, 16, 25,
    27, 28, 38, 45; taxes and nonmerit
    advantages, 223
Mexican Americans and Mexican
    immigrants, 29, 156, 180, 188
Microsoft, 172–173
middle class: America as not middle class,
    71; asset building, 233; cultural capital,
    87–88; deferment of gratification, 30;
    education and, 60, 101, 114; Great
    Recession affecting, 237; home
    ownership, 189; inner cities, flight
    from, 81, 142; Barack Obama,
    background of, 95; old class vs. new,

157–158; precarious status of, 222; sports choices of, 26; upper-middle class, 66, 68

The Millionaire Mind (Stanley), 31

millionaires, 31, 70, 85

minority groups: affirmative action, 230–231, 231–232; asset accumulation, 232–233; core employment, underrepresentation in, 183; disadvantages of, 96; discrimination experiences, 18, 180–181, 183, 184–186, 188, 190, 196, 201, 206, 207; education issues, 186–188; as inner city dwellers, 142; opportunities expanding, 11, 82, 113; self-employment and, 159; social capital, lack of, 81, 83, 192

moral character, 36–37, 45

Mormons, 207

Murray, Charles, 24, 25, 31–32

Muslims, 207

National College Athletic Association (NCAA), 27

nepotism, 83–85, 182

net worth: affirmative action and, 232; defined, 52; by income group, 52; of minority groups, 182; of Barack Obama family, 96; of one percenters, 16, 64, 71; of Walton heirs, 55–56; wealth scale, 53

new elite, 31, 32

noblesse oblige, 233–235

Obama, Barack, 95–96, 181, 184, 200

Obama, Michelle, 96

occupations: attitude as a factor, 16, 33; blue-collar jobs, 127, 128, 129, 174, 193; CEO salaries, 53, 129; changes in opportunities, 126–127, 126; cultural capital and, 89–90, 94; the disabled and employment difficulties, 203; discrimination, 180, 181, 182–183, 188, 191, 200, 203; downsizing, 128, 129, 140, 148, 171, 206; education linked to, 17, 101–102, 106, 108, 111, 112–113, 118–119, 120, 132–134, 137, 138, 148–149, 188, 227–228; fastest growing jobs, 129–132, 130–131; health hazards, 62; nepotism and, 84,

85; occupational mobility, 51–52, 60; occupational segregation, 193, 194–195; outsourcing, 128, 135, 148, 156, 160, 222; physical attraction and occupational success, 208; self-employment and, 155; self-made men, 102–103; social capital and occupational opportunities, 77, 79, 81; wages, 128, 129, 134, 136–137, 139–140, 141, 144; white-collar jobs, 103, 104, 120, 135, 142, 193

Occupy Wall Street (OWS), 237

old boy networks, 81, 183, 196–197

old money, 64–65, 89–90

Outliers: The Story of Success (Gladwell), 35, 138

outsourcing, 128, 135, 148, 156, 160, 222

ownership class, 16, 53, 57, 71

Paterson, Tim, 173

Peale, Norman Vincent, 32–33

pensions, 14–15, 52, 132, 202, 205, 220

pink-collar ghetto, 193–194

poverty: children affected by, 58, 61; culture-of-poverty theory, 29–30, 33; full-time work below poverty level, 134; as a matter of attitude, 32; meritocracy and, 49, 50; minority rates of, 182, 188; poverty threshold, 132; regional variations in poverty rates, 141; senior citizens and poverty rates, 15; U.S. poverty rates, 53

The Power of Positive Thinking (Peale), 32–33

Protestants and the Protestant ethic, 4–6, 32, 36, 64, 147

Puritan values, 5–6

racism and racial issues: affirmative action, 229–232; athletes and, 26; crime and the legal system, 184–186; disabilities, disproportionate experience of, 203; discrimination and, 18, 140–141, 180–181, 189, 190–191, 211, 217, 238; in education, 186–188; employment, affecting, 183; Great Recession worsening racial equality, 232; home ownership, 189; ideologies of inequality, as part of, 3; income gaps,

182; language skills and, 191; Obama, election of, 96, 181; scientific racism, 23–24; segregation, 180, 188–190, 201; social capital and, 81, 83, 88, 192; white flight, 12, 142

random-walk hypothesis, 172

recession. *See* Great Recession

references, 42, 78, 82

retirement: as part of the American Dream, 14, 205; delayment as a coping strategy, 217, 220–221, 222; home ownership and funding of, 189; as jeopardized, 11, 15–16; proposed supplementation, 233; self-employment and, 158, 160, 174

right attitude, 16, 29, 30, 33, 45, 215

The Rise of Meritocracy, 1870–2033: An Essay on Education and Equality (Young), 2, 240

Rivera, Lauren, 89

Rosenau, Pauline Vaillancourt, 44

Schmitt, John, 132–133

schools. *See* education

segregation: educational, 181, 186; occupational, 182, 183, 193, 194–195; racial, 180, 187, 188, 189, 201; residential, 66, 184, 188–191; of the wealthy, 66–67; white flight, 12. *See also* discrimination

self-employment: American Dream, as exemplifying, 153; franchises, 155; freelancing, 156, 159; income, 160–161; irregular economy and, 156–157, 160, 174; petty bourgeoisie and, 157; psychological characteristics, 159; rates of, diminished, 14, 18, 126, 154–155, 171, 173–174, 216, 216; risk, 156, 159, 161, 174; subcontractors, 156; taxes, 156, 160; women and minorities, 158–159

self-help books, 32, 36

self-made individuals, 18, 31, 83, 102–103, 145, 173

sexual harassment, 199–200

Shapiro, Thomas, 187, 232–233

slaves and slavery, 3, 7, 9, 153, 180, 233

small businesses, 120, 142, 156, 158, 161, 166, 170–171, 174, 216

Smith, Adam, 8

social capital: benefits of, 78–79, 216; defined, 17, 59, 77; discrimination and, 180, 192; economic opportunities, having access to, 142, 147, 230; education and, 77, 79, 85, 109, 110, 112, 115, 117, 121; mentorship as a form of, 196; nepotism and, 83–85, 182; racism and lack of, 81, 83, 88, 192; restricted access, effects of, 81–82, 83; social climbing, 17, 77, 90–94, 97; of U.S. presidents, 94–96; weak ties, 79–80

social climbing, 17, 77, 90–94, 97

social clubs, 65, 68, 89–90

social mobility: athletic and artistic abilities, associated with, 25, 26–27, 28; cultural capital as a factor in, 77; education link, 17, 102, 120; hard work as a factor, 34; individual merit, 92; integrity hindering, 36; marrying for money, 68; reduction of opportunities, 171, 223; during Republican administrations, 129; role of government, 228, 229; social climbing, 90–91; status attainment, 107; through self-employment, 159

social reform movements, 235–237

Social Register, 65

social reproduction theory, 109, 117

Social Security, 14–15, 52, 205, 220, 225

Something for Nothing: Luck in America (Lears), 147–148

the South, 128, 140–141, 142, 180, 181

Stanley, Thomas, 31

status-attainment theory, 107–108

Stevens, Mitchell, 116

stock market, 57, 147, 167, 216

student loans, 13, 116–117

success: athletic success, 26, 27–28; attitudes associated with, 29, 31, 33; birth timing and, 138, 140; cultural capital, 87, 90, 96, 109; discrimination, achieving success through, 18; education, as a factor in, 34, 101, 109, 120, 188; entrepreneurial success, 153, 172, 173; God's grace, success as sign of, 3, 5; hard work and, 2, 31, 34, 35, 45; human capital factors, 38; individualism as key to, 7; intelligence as a determinant, 24; luck as important, 148; meritocracy myth and, 240; mind-power ethic as success formula, 32–33; moral character and, 2, 16, 36, 37; parental involvement, 51, 110, 113; the right stuff, being made of as key, 16, 23, 45, 215; small businesses and, 161; social capital increasing likelihood of, 79, 85; suburban living as marker of, 12; 10,000 hour rule, 35; women and, 198, 200

supply side, 17, 38, 125, 128, 133, 224–225

Survival of the Prettiest (Etcoff), 209–210

Swift, Adam, 239

talent and abilities: American aristocracy, 2; American Dream, leading to, 1; of athletes and celebrities, 27; education enhancing, 17, 101, 106–107; functional theory of inequality, 11; jobs matched to talent, 134; success achieved through, 3, 4, 16, 28, 95, 215; talent-use gap, 134; upward mobility and, 24, 25–26, 26–27

taxes: capital gains, 225–226; estate taxes, 60, 70, 223–225; government policies linked with, 226, 229; incentives and credits, 232–233; income taxes, lowered by Republicans, 128; irregular economy, avoiding, 156; progressive taxation, 223, 225, 229, 234; property taxes and school funding, 112; self-employment and, 156, 160; Social Security affected by, 15, 225; the South and lower taxes, 141; tax breaks for the wealthy, 52, 184, 187, 224–225; of urban areas, 12, 142

Thurow, Lester, 53, 145

Tocqueville, Alexis de, 7–8, 148

tracking, 109, 111–112, 183, 187

Turner, Frederick Jackson, 9

Unequal Childhoods (Lareau), 88

upper class: charitable giving and, 234; cultural capital, holders of, 58, 85, 90, 94, 96; deferred gratification, capability of, 30; distinctive lifestyle, 69, 71; education, 101, 114; endogamy,

tendency towards, 66–69; as exclusive, 64–65, 71; as isolated, 66; one percenters as members, 53; Plymouth Puritans as wellspring, 5; political power, 70; social clubs, frequenting, 89–90; virtues found in, 32; WASP background of, 64; women of, 64, 68, 194

upward mobility: attitudes as affecting, 30; barriers to, 24; through college education, 104; credentialism and, 119; downward mobility, vs., 60; through entrepreneurialism, 216; glass ceiling as limiting, 196; integrity as suppressing, 36; irregular economy, as avenue, 157; marriage as a means of, 67–68; Michelle Obama as example, 96; slowing rates of, 217. *See also* social climbing; social mobility

Vedder, Richard, 117, 133

virtue, 2, 3, 4, 32, 36, 37, 153

Walmart, 170

Walton, Sam, 55, 69, 153

wealth: accumulation gaps, 182, 188, 232; advantages of wealth inheritance, 16, 57–64; capital investments, 148; charitable giving and the wealthy, 234, 235; culture of, 31, 33; discrimination and, 179, 191; distribution as skewed, 24–25; *Forbes* magazine listings, 25–26; gambling, attainment through, 147; government intervention, 232–233, 238; Great Recession affecting, 221; guilt feelings, 65; hard work as negligible, 34; inequalities of, 19, 35, 51–54, 57, 71, 168, 187, 222, 232; lottery, wealth attainment through, 146; luck as a factor, 18, 144–145, 149; marriage rates, affecting, 32; nepotism aiding in transference of, 84; old money, 64–65, 89–90; one percenters, 16, 53, 64, 71, 237; ostentatious displays of, 69; political power, 70; property ownership producing, 34, 188; pursuit of as a moral issue, 36, 37; race affecting, 189; social and cultural capital, converted to, 17, 97; the

superwealthy, 57, 63, 66; tax breaks for the wealthy, 184; taxes on, 223–225; transfers of, 55–57, 56, 232; women and, 195. *See also* inheritance; self-employment
Weber, Max, 5
welfare, 52, 81, 128, 184, 223, 225, 229
white Anglo-Saxon Protestants (WASPs), 4–5, 64
white-collar crime, 36–37, 185
Wilson, William Julius, 69, 95
Winfrey, Oprah, 25–26
Wisconsin school, 107–108
women: attractiveness as a success factor, 208, 209, 209–210; discrimination against, 9, 18, 180, 183, 191–192, 194–195, 196, 197–198, 199–200, 217; economic disparities, 27, 81, 194–195; educational attainment, 192, 218; family concerns, 197–198, 198–199, 218–219; glass ceiling, experiencing, 81, 159, 196, 200; inferiority, feelings of, 3–4; labor force participation, increasing, 217–218, 220; mentorships, access to, 81, 196–197; occupational disparities, 68, 183, 192–194, 194–195, 198–199; political underrepresentation, 200–201; self-employment and, 158–159; as trailing partners, 41; of the upper class, 64, 68, 194
working class: American Dream and, 129; cultural capital, lack of, 87–88, 109; economic instability, 68–69; education issues, 101, 109, 114; hard work and, 34; health risks, 62; home ownership, 189; lower class value stretch, 30; nepotism, effect of, 84; the new lower class, 32; women and incomes, 194
work. *See* hard work; occupations

Young, Michael, 2, 240

About the Authors

Stephen J. McNamee is interim dean of the College of Arts and Sciences and professor of sociology at the University of North Carolina Wilmington. He is the recipient of the University of North Carolina Wilmington Distinguished Faculty Scholar Award, the University of North Carolina Wilmington Distinguished Teaching Professorship Award, and the University of North Carolina System Board of Governors Award for Excellence in Teaching.

Robert K. Miller Jr. is professor emeritus of sociology at the University of North Carolina Wilmington. He has published widely on the topic of social and economic inequality and is coeditor with Stephen J. McNamee of *Inheritance and Wealth in America*.